## Newport and Southeastern Connecticut 131
**In Three Days**
**Don't Miss** ✦ The Breakers ✦ Newport beaches
✦ The Astors' Beechwood
**At Your Leisure** 10 more places to explore
**Where to...** Stay ✦ Eat and Drink ✦ Shop ✦ Be Entertained

## Coastal Maine to the White Mountains 149
**In Six Days**
**Don't Miss** ✦ Portsmouth and Strawbery Banke ✦ Kennebunk and
Kennebunkport ✦ Acadia National Park ✦ The White Mountains
**At Your Leisure** 7 more places to explore
**Where to...** Stay ✦ Eat and Drink ✦ Shop ✦ Be Entertained

## Walks and Tours 173
1 Boston's Beacon Hill and Back Bay
2 Old King's Highway
3 Southern Vermont
4 Newport's Cliff Walk

## Practicalities 187
✦ Before You Go ✦ When to Go ✦ When You Are There

## Index 193
## Atlas 197

Written by John Rosenthal

Where to sections by Kathy Arnold and Paul Wade

Copy edited by Donna Dailey, Janet Tabinski
Page layout by Nautilus Design (UK) Limited
Illustrations by Raymond Turvey Illustrations
Verified by Colin Follett
Indexed by Marie Lorimer

Edited, designed and produced by AA Publishing
© Automobile Association Developments Limited 2000
Maps © Automobile Association Developments Limited 2000

Published in the United States by AAA Publishing,
1000 AAA Drive,
Heathrow, Florida 32746
Published in the United Kingdom by AA Publishing

ISBN 1-56251-336-2

Color separation by Leo Reprographics
Printed and bound in China by Leo Paper Products

10 9 8 7 6 5 4 3 2 1

# SPIRAL GUIDES

*Travel with Someone You Trust*®

# BOSTON & NEW ENGLAND

# Contents

## *the magazine* 5
✦ Birthplace of a Nation ✦ Seasons to Remember
✦ Darn Sox ✦ The New England Lobster
✦ The Life of a New England Innkeeper ✦ L.L. Bean
✦ The Best of New England ✦ Literary Greats

## Finding Your Feet 31
✦ First Two Hours
✦ Getting Around
✦ Accommodations
✦ Food and Drink
✦ Shopping
✦ Entertainment

## Boston 39
**In Three Days**
**Don't Miss** ✦ The Freedom Trail ✦ Museum of Fine Arts
✦ Museum of Science ✦ Harvard
**At Your Leisure** ✦ 12 more places to explore
**Where to...** Stay ✦ Eat and Drink ✦ Shop ✦ Be Entertained

## Cape Cod and the Islands 73
**In Four Days**
**Don't Miss** ✦ Cape Cod National Seashore ✦ Provincetown
✦ Nantucket
**At Your Leisure** 6 more places to explore
**Where to...** Stay ✦ Eat and Drink ✦ Shop ✦ Be Entertained

## The Berkshires 95
**In Two Days**
**Don't Miss** ✦ Tanglewood ✦ The Appalachian Trail ✦ Jacob's Pillow
Dance Festival
**At Your Leisure** 4 more places to explore
**Where to...** Stay ✦ Eat and Drink ✦ Shop ✦ Be Entertained

## Vermont 109
**In Four Days**
**Don't Miss** ✦ Hildene ✦ Fishing around Manchester
✦ Marsh-Billings-Rockefeller National Historical Park
**At Your Leisure** 6 more places to explore
**Where to...** Stay ✦ Eat and Drink ✦ Shop ✦ Be Entertained

# Birthplace
## *of a Nation*

**N**EW ENGLAND IS WHERE IT ALL STARTED. THE SEEDS OF AMERICA'S 200-YEAR-LONG EXPERIMENT IN DEMOCRACY WERE SOWN HERE, AND REMINDERS OF THOSE DAYS STAND PROUDLY IN THIS NORTHEAST CORNER OF THE UNITED STATES.

Name a landmark event in colonial American history, and it almost assuredly happened somewhere in New England. The Pilgrims' landing at Plymouth Rock, the Salem Witch Trials, the Boston Massacre, the Boston Tea Party, Paul Revere's ride, the first shot of the

**The first Pilgrims landed at Plymouth in 1620, an event commemorated each year**

**The *Mayflower* (left) landed at Provincetown, before continuing to Plymouth (abo**

American Revolution, the Battle of Bunker Hill – they all happened here. You could easily spend a month touring the historic sites in Boston alone, not to mention those found elsewhere in the region.

The best historic sites are linked by the Freedom Trail (► 44–47), a red line on the Boston sidewalk that seems never to run out of historically important attractions.

A new chapter of history began in 1620, with the Pilgrims' landing. Originally intent on Virginia, they landed first at Provincetown rather than brave a difficult storm, but found no source of fresh water, and so continued on to Plymouth. A rock – who can say for sure whether it is *the* rock – marks their disembarkation spot in Plymouth (► 64). A stone tower memorializes their landing at Provincetown (► 81–82).

Almost half of the 102 Pilgrims who came over on the *Mayflower* died within the first year, falling victim to pneumonia, influenza, malnutrition and scurvy. The others survived, but only with the help of the friendly Wampanoag Indians, who taught the new arrivals how to live off the land. They planted corn and other native vegetables, and when the first harvest came around in the fall of 1621, the Pilgrims and the Indians celebrated the first Thanksgiving.

In 1692, New England experienced another first: the first bout of religious intolerance. The Puritan ethic, so valuable for building communities, was not as successful in abiding those who did not share the same views. Quakers, Baptists and other dissidents were persecuted and sometimes prosecuted. Religious hysteria reached its most fevered pitch in Salem, where 19 men and women were put to death for allegedly practicing witchcraft (➤ 62).

The infamous Salem witch trials of 1692 resulted in 19 executions

**Being an Account of the**

# TRYAL

OF

## Several Witches,

Lately Excuted in

## NEW

**In 17th-century Salem, Puritans who fled England to escape religious persecution turned just as intolerant in the New World**

The 17th century was New England's "first" period. The first settlers arrived in Salem in 1626; Boston became the first capital of Massachusetts in 1632; Boston Latin opened its doors in 1635, becoming the first public school; Harvard College was founded a year later, making it the first institution of higher learning in the United States; in 1638, colonists built their first printing press in Cambridge; and in 1639, Richard Fairbank opened the country's first post office.

The 18th century brought many more settlers to the western edge of the Atlantic, and fundamental changes to the colonial way of life. In their quest for more space, the colonists' once-symbiotic relationship with the Native American tribes turned hostile. At the same time, many residents also began to feel

**During the Boston Tea Party, colonists threw tea into the harbor in protest at the high taxes levied on it**

## YANKEE DOODLE DANDIES

........................

On Patriots' Day (the third Monday in April), the events of April 19, 1775, are commemorated. Early that morning, Paul Revere rode west from Boston, warning the colonists that the British were coming. Later that day, minutemen (patriots who were ready to fight at a minute's notice) and redcoats skirmished in Lexington and Concord, and the "shot heard 'round the world" set off the American Revolution.

Patriots' Day is a public

the strain of ties to Britain. In an effort to pay off the debt amassed during the Seven Years' War (the French and Indian War), King George III attempted to levy taxes on colonial sugar (1764), stamps (1765) and tea (1767) and other British imports. Each new tariff provoked greater outrage among the free-trade-minded colonists, who adopted the revolutionary slogan of "No taxation without representation." The King sent British troops to quell the unrest in 1770, but ended up fanning the flames of independence when the redcoats killed five colonists outside

*The British are coming!*

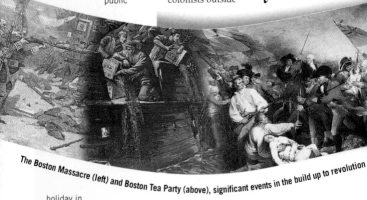

The Boston Massacre (left) and Boston Tea Party (above), significant events in the build up to revolution

holiday in Massachusetts and Maine, and a myriad of activities take place around Boston. In Lexington and Concord, Revolutionary War aficionados in full period costume reenact the battle at Concord's Old North Bridge, to the delight of onlookers. The Boston Marathon courses its way from Hopkinton to downtown Boston, and the Red Sox play a home game at Fenway Park beginning at 11 a.m., an unusually early starting time.

the Old State House (▶ 45).

In 1773, patriots disguised as American Indians snuck aboard a British merchant ship and dumped the tea into Boston Harbor as a protest against the tax on tea (▶ 57). Parliament responded in 1774 by imposing the Boston Port Act, which closed the port, and the Coercive Acts, which quartered soldiers in colonists' homes. A year later, a full-scale revolution was brewing, beginning with the "shot heard 'round the world" (▶ panel, left).

On July 4, 1776, the colonies declared their

independence from Britain – the document was read to the citizens of Boston from the balcony of the Old State House 14 days later – but the Revolution raged on for six more years. However, most of the important battles were fought outside of Boston. One of those battles took place in Bennington, Vermont. In August, 1777, a colonial militia confronted British troops seeking to seize arms and munitions stored at Bennington, and thoroughly routed the redcoats.

After the last British troops

Faneuil Hall in Boston, called the Cradle of Liberty for the fiery speeches that went on here in Revolutionary days, is now a centerpiece of the bustling Quincy Market complex of stores and restaurants. The 1970s Hancock Tower reflects the fine 1870s Trinity Church

**Modern-day minutemen re-enact the events at Concord's Old North Bridge each year**

*Boston combines its historic and modern faces: Trinity Church reflected in the John Hancock Tower*

*"the shot heard 'round the world"*

left America in 1783 and the United States officially became independent, New England's historical importance began to wane. The new nation set up its capital farther south, first in New York, then Philadelphia, and finally Washington, D.C. But New England enjoyed a cultural renaissance in the late 19th century, when Nathaniel Hawthorne, Herman Melville, Bronson and Louisa May Alcott, Henry Wadsworth Longfellow, Ralph Waldo Emerson and Henry David Thoreau among other authors made it the center of the Transcendentalist movement.

Today, New England embraces its history while integrating it into modern life.

across the skyline, rather than condemning it to the shadows of a giant skyscraper. And homes where George Washington, John Adams and other Founding Fathers once slept are now museums or even bed-and-breakfasts.

## REVOLUTIONARY READING

Bernard Bailyn's Pulitzer Prize winning *Ideological Origins of the American Revolution* is an excellent, if heady, examination of the colonists' war for independence. *Johnny Tremain*, an historical novel by Esther Forbes, presents the same events in a style accessible to everyone.

# SEASONS
## *to Remember*

**A**NYONE WANTING TO FIND THE PERFECT IMAGE TO ILLUSTRATE THE FOUR SEASONS WOULD DO WELL TO STUDY NEW ENGLAND, A REGION WHICH GLORIES IN A VARIETY OF SEASONAL BEAUTY.

Spring (April and May) is bright and green, with buds on the trees, new grass taking root on lawns too long over-whelmed by ice and snow, and students shedding sweaters for shirtsleeves long before sane people dare to venture outdoors without an overcoat. Spring is preciously short, and usually

## SPRING FLINGS

• The Nantucket Daffodil Festival, held in late April, and the Lilac Festival at Vermont's Shelburne Museum, which takes place a month later, remind you that warmer days are on the way.
• If you're in Boston on the third Monday of April, don't miss the Patriots' Day events (➤ 8).

In New England, spring is encroached upon by cold winters and hot summers

encroached upon by cold winters and hot summers.

Summer (June, July and August) is idyllic, with long sunny days, punctuated only occasionally by thunder-storms. The color of New England summer is blue – blue skies and blue waters ripe for fishing, swimming, boating, sailing or simply for cooling your toes. Areas close to shore become hot and humid in July and August, making a dip in the Atlantic Ocean the perfect antidote. In the mountains of New Hampshire, Vermont and Maine, days are warm, and nights are often cool enough to warrant a jacket or sweater for outdoor dining. Maine in summer may be the finest place on Earth. Maine residents will tell you that their state has two seasons – winter and August – but that the glory of that month makes it worth muddling through the rest of the year.

At Walden Pond, near Concord, visitors can experience the solitude that inspired author Henry David Thoreau

Fall (September, October and November) marks New England's finest hour. From late September, the deciduous trees distinguish themselves from their Hampshire, Connecticut and even Rhode Island. These wanderers come to collect the season's last corn and first

The area's multitude of beaches provide the perfect escape from oppressive city summers

evergreen cousins by donning fabulously gaudy coats of red, yellow and orange. The metamorphosis begins in the northern reaches of Maine and, week by week, descends upon the more southerly states, drawing thousands of "leaf-peepers" from the urban enclaves of Boston and New York to rural Vermont, New

pumpkins, and to hike, bicycle, stroll, ride horseback or drive through the regions beautiful ochre-colored forests.

Winter (December, January and February) is the harshest season, bringing subfreezing temperatures to most of the region, and attendant snow and ice to roadways. New Englanders make the best of it, though, with skis,

A long summer day: Race Point Beach, on Cape Cod

## ENDLESS SUMMER

Everywhere in New England is best in summer, but Cape Cod and the islands of Martha's Vineyard and Nantucket hold a special place in many people's hearts. Plan to spend as long as you can here.

Fall in New England is beautiful, with only a hint of the cold winter to come

snowboards, skates or sleds. Cross-country touring centers lace the area, as do long stretches of wilderness where those with their own skis can make their way through ungroomed, and often unvisited, forests. As for downhill skiing, though some New England resorts have a reputation for being crowded and expensive, don't let that deter you: there are still a few places, particularly in Maine, where you can find an affordable weekend of skiing without having to spend half your time waiting in a lift line.

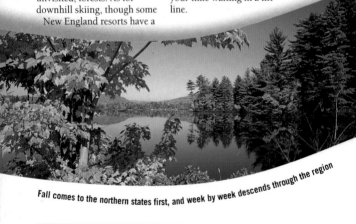

Fall comes to the northern states first, and week by week descends through the region

## FALL DOWN

The Head of the Charles Regatta, a rowing race on Boston's Charles River, is held on the third Sunday in October and draws preppies from all over New England. Boats race against the clock, so it is difficult to tell who is winning. One thing is guaranteed though: you will probably never see so many button-down Oxford shirts in one place again.

New England also has a unique fifth season known as mud season, which occurs unofficially at the end of March and the beginning of April. While the rest of the United States is in the throes of spring fever, New England takes a little longer to wade past the vernal equinox. The snow and ice that cover the ground each winter don't evaporate all at once. Rather, they melt under the warm spring sun during the day, transforming the ground into a muddy, sloshy ragout that solidifies at night when temperatures drop back below freezing. A late April snow-

## WINTER WONDERLANDS

The best ski resorts in New England are Killington (tel: 802/773-4181) and Stowe (tel: 802/253-3000) in Vermont, and Sunday River (Bethel, tel: 800/543-2754) in Maine. The altitudes here may not rival the Rockies or the Alps, but if you've just got to strap on skis or a snowboard, they offer a variety of terrain to keep you entertained for a weekend.

mud season no matter how much money you save, because barring a late snowfall or an unusually long

*Freezing temperatures and heavy snowfalls characterize winter in New England*

storm is never out of the question in New England: in Vermont, New Hampshire and Maine, the big piles of snow that grow taller each time snow is cleared from the driveways often don't disappear until the middle of May.

Mud season is when most New England innkeepers go on their own vacations. Occasionally, you can find a bargain price at this time, but quite often lodgings simply close down entirely for renovations and other yearly maintenance that can be performed only when the house is empty. You would probably regret taking a trip to the northern states during

stretch of warm nights, there is not much to do: it is too cold and muddy to go walking or out on a bicycle, and too slushy to be able to count on skiing. But if your idea of a vacation is days spent hunting for antiques or reading in front of a fire, and nights dining in a country tavern, then mud season just might be the perfect time for you.

*Winter is the cruelest season*

# DARN
## *Sox*

**T**HERE IS PERHAPS NO BETTER METAPHOR FOR THE NEW ENGLAND SPIRIT THAN THE BOSTON RED SOX, THE BASEBALL TEAM THAT CAPTURES THE HEARTS OF NEW ENGLANDERS FROM CONNECTICUT TO MAINE EACH SPRING, THEN MERCILESSLY BREAKS THEM EACH OCTOBER WITH ITS FAILURE TO WIN THE WORLD SERIES.

Pedro Martinez hopes to hurl the Red Sox to a World Series championship

The Red Sox's misadventures can be traced back to 1918, the last time the team captured the world championship. Two years later, owner Harry Frazee sold star pitcher and slugger Babe Ruth to the dreaded rival New York Yankees for $125,000 (plus a $300,000 loan so he could finance a production of *No No Nanette*). Ruth, of course, went on to become baseball's greatest player, leading the Yankees to four World Series championships in his career, and swatting a total of 714 home runs. The Red Sox went on to see victory within their grasp four times, only to have it elude them, each letdown crueler than the last.

The Red Sox have made it to four World Series since

1918, and, usually because of some bizarre twist of fate, have lost in the deciding seventh game each time. True Sox fans will explain this not as a heartbreaking series of coincidences, but rather "the curse of the Bambino," a divine punishment for trading away baseball's greatest player that has supposedly doomed the Red Sox to a lifetime of losing. They'll tell you how shortstop "Johnny Pesky held the ball" in 1946, how in 1975 manager Darrell Johnson "pulled pitcher Jim Willoughby too soon," and how pitcher Bob Stanley threw away the tying run and first baseman Bill Buckner let the winning run go between his legs in 1986. In 1999, in

*"Johnny Pesky held the ball"*

Every seat in tiny Fenway Park, the Sox's home ground, is right on top of the field

an act of sheer desperation, the management brought the Babe's daughter to a playoff game against the Sox's arch rivals, the New York Yankees, in an effort to exorcize the curse, but to no avail: the dreaded New Yorkers dispatched the team in five games and went on to win their 25th World Series.

## "What might have been"

The Red Sox's seasons parallel those of New England. The team may be unusually hot in April and cool in August, but for the most part, the Sox's fortunes adhere to a rough script whose ending is firmly immutable.

**Don't miss the opportunity to see a Red Sox game while you are in Boston**

### GETTING IN

For tickets to Red Sox games call the ticket office at (617) 267-1700. It can be hard to get into games on Opening Day (usually around April 1), any time the Yankees are in town, and any time the team is playing really well. Tickets for the game on Patriots' Day sell out long before the season starts: it's very unlikely you will be able to get in. For Celtics' and Bruins' games call Ticketmaster on (617) 931-2222), but be aware that there's a hefty service charge for the convenience of buying tickets over the phone. Seats are scarcest when the opponents are strongest.

for the chance to play in a big-league game, some of whom will blossom into stars of the future. Others will falter early and wither, like tulips felled by a killing frost.

Midsummer evening games at Fenway Park are shirtsleeve warm, the perfect weather for sitting outside, drinking a cold beer, eating peanuts out of the shell and enjoying the langorous pace of a baseball game. If the Sox are playing well, you can feel the excitement with each pitch. If they're playing poorly, well, it

Opening day in Red Sox country, like everywhere else in the country, is full of hope. Every team in the American League starts with the same record on April 1, and (theoretically, anyway) the same chance of winning the pennant. The heroes of the previous season return to their accustomed positions, steeling themselves for another chance at glory. They are joined by raw young newcomers, straining at the leash just

Right: Ted Williams, a legend amongst Red Sox faithful

## THE GREATEST RED SOX PLAYER EVER

Ted Williams. Despite giving up three years of his playing days to fight in World War II and two more during the Korean War (he was a naval aviator), "Teddy Ballgame" hit 521 home runs in his career, just 193 fewer than Babe Ruth. His eyesight was so good he could read the commissioner's name on the baseball as it was hurtling toward him at speeds exceeding 90 miles an hour. But perhaps his finest hour was in 1941, when he went into the final day of the season with a batting average of .3996. If Williams had taken the day off, he would have been credited with an even .400 once his numbers were rounded off, a phenomenal accomplishment in a sport where .300 is considered excellent. But the Splendid Splinter wouldn't rest on those laurels. He played both games of a doubleheader, got six hits in eight at-bats, and finished the season with a .406 average, a mark that has never been equaled since.

## A ROOKIE'S GUIDE

• Never wear a New York Yankees cap in Fenway Park. Somebody will snatch it off your head and you could have a hard time getting it back.

• The Cask and Flagon, a sports bar just outside the entrance to Fenway Park, is packed with Red Sox fans before and after games. Feel free to join in the festivities, but be prepared for a raucous crowd.

was still a nice evening out.

Fall is appropriately named in Red Sox country, as it heralds the inevitable. About once every decade, though, the team makes a valiant run at the impossible, and tests the fates. In such a season, the Red

Sox may even survive into the World Series, and play a winner-takes-all seven-game series against the champion of the National League in the last week of October.

Though as surely as the leaves must descend from the branches, no matter how spectacular their performance, so too must

the Red Sox fall from their lofty perch. For as soon as the region collectively articulates the thought "This just might be the year," some minor miscue will occur, causing the entire house of cards to collapse. At this point, the last leaf falls from the last tree, leaving the forests a bleak shade of gray, freezing cold weather settles in for an extended visit, and some other city proclaims itself "home of the world champions" for the next six months.

By December, the pain of the past season has faded. The owner might even go out and sign a highly prized player as his personal Christmas present to New England. Meanwhile, Boston's notoriously rabid sports fans turn to the city's other teams for their entertainment. The resurgent Patriots (the Pats) of the National Football League play their home games in Foxboro, an hour south of the city, but millions follow the team's fortunes on TV or radio and in the papers. Closer to home, the once proud but now woeful Celtics of the National Basketball Association and the Bruins of the National Hockey League both play at the Fleet Center, a 1995 replacement for the storied but dilapidated Boston Garden.

Come February, unless the Celtics or Bruins are exceptionally good, even the most devoted sports nut starts thinking about where to take the kids skiing this weekend, or where to escape to during the darkest days of winter. And by March, fans may even permit themselves to stop wondering what might have been and start thinking "Wait until next time."

# THE NEW
## *England Lobster*

**T**HE LOBSTER.
OH, THE LOBSTER.
IT MAY NOT LOOK LIKE MUCH AT
FIRST, AND IT CERTAINLY DOES
NOT LOOK LIKE FOOD. YOU MAY
WONDER HOW HUNGRY THE FIRST
PERSON TO EAT LOBSTER MUST
HAVE BEEN TO BOTHER DIGGING
AROUND THE INSIDES OF THE
HARD-SHELLED CRUSTACEANS.

In fact, the lobster started out
as poor folks' food. For years,
fishermen thought of

markets sold the best quality
fish to the wealthy, and they
pawned the lobsters off on
those who couldn't afford
anything else. Lobster was so
reviled in those days that pris-
oners in Maine penitentiaries
rioted when forced to eat it for
days on end.

My, how things have
changed. Today, hundreds
of restaurants with
names like

**Many of the region's lobster restaurants are informal and moderately priced**

lobsters as the junk that came
up with the daily catch. Fish

the
Lobster Box,
the Lobster Shack or
Larry's Lobsters make a whole
year's worth of profits just by
serving lobster dinners for four

## CLAM CHOWDER

New England's other seafood specialty is clam chowder, the
kind made with milk and potatoes, not the red liquidy stuff
served in Manhattan. Real New England clam chowder is thick
enough to stand a spoon upright and rich enough to accommodate a heaped helping of pepper. Oyster crackers don't so
much float in the bowl as hover over the top, waiting for a
spoon to submerge them in the creamy depths. The arguments
over who makes the best clam chowder in New England are
endless – Boston holds a contest every year – but you can do
your own taste test; it is on the menu just about everywhere.

# How To Eat a Lobster

◁ A whole lobster

Grab the lobster with one hand on the tail ▷
and another on the torso, then twist the
tail off the body and allow any water from
inside to drip onto your plate.

◁ Bend the tail backwards, squeeze it
like a handlebar, or crack it open with a
nutcracker to release the meat inside.

Remove each claw from the body at the ▷
shoulder joint. Break off the claw and separate the smaller pincer from the big one.

◁ Crack open the big pincer with the nutcracker; there is a big piece of meat in there.
Use the nutcracker, the little fork or your
fingers to extricate the meat in the smaller
joints of the claw.

Break off the eight thin claws, snap them ▷
at the joints and suck the meat out. You
can use the little fork if you prefer.

◁ Adventurous diners can remove the shell
from the torso and poke around inside. The
liver – the green stuff that looks like
Japanese mustard – is called tomalley; some
people like it, others hate it.

months in the summertime. Most of these restaurants are in Maine, but you can find them along the coasts of New Hampshire, Massachusetts (especially on Cape Cod) and Rhode Island. While they will serve steak, you go there for their specialty.

You look at the prices on the menu and think no over-grown shrimp can be worth that much money. You see countless other diners struggling to crack open the hard claws with nutcrackers and you think no food can be worth this much work. Your waiter ties a bib around your neck and you think no meal can be worth looking this silly.

But then your meal arrives on a plate as large as a hubcap, adorned with corn on the cob and boiled new potatoes. The smell of the melted butter alone may make you realize

what all the fuss has been about. Some say the claws are the tastiest part of the lobster, other camps claim nothing can compare to the tail. Attack whichever end you like first and come to your own conclusion, but don't worry about getting messy; everybody else is doing it too.

And finally, you dunk the much-hyped morsel into the butter and deliver it into your mouth. Could it possibly be as good as everybody says it is? No. It's even better! Sweet and chewy, with a hint of salt, and a taste that can only be found in food that was alive minutes before it hit your plate.

Dessert complements the meal perfectly. Though its decadence is equal, its sweetness is of another kind entirely. Blueberry pie is the traditional accompaniment, à la mode for the bold.

Lobsters are celebrated throughout the region. The best come from Maine, but they are almost as good anywhere along the New England coast

# THE LIFE
## *of a New England Innkeeper*

**H**AVE YOU EVER BEEN ON VACATION AT A SMALL INN OR BED-AND-BREAKFAST AND THOUGHT, "GEE, I COULD DO THIS, COULDN'T I? I COULD BUY A BIG OLD HOUSE, FILL IT UP WITH ANTIQUES, AND DO NOTHING ALL DAY BUT MAKE BREAKFAST AND CHAT WITH MY GUESTS."

with his wife Pam, says a typical day for him begins with seating guests for breakfast at around 7 in the morning, and might not end until the last dinner check is cashed out sometime around midnight. In between, he and Pam share out

*A few rooms and a deft hand at breakfast doesn't make you an innkeeper*

Well, welcome to the club. Being an innkeeper is one of the most popular career fantasies there is, right behind professional athlete and movie star, but talk to those who do it for a living, and you realize it's not all coffee and muffins. The job is so demanding, in fact, that many people drop out within about two years.

Gorty Baldwin, who owns the Four Columns Inn in Newfane, Vermont, along

the day's errands: picking up forms from the printer, making up the bills, helping departing guests with reservations up the road, tending bar before dinner, and performing any of a hundred other chores.

"It sounds like a very scheduled day," says Baldwin, "but what happens most of the time is that you end up putting out fires. Little things, like a towel rack fell down. In a big hotel, you call somebody and it's

*"We had a major crisis once a week"*

## "We took a real leap in the dark"

fixed. But in an inn, a little thing going wrong can ruin your schedule. When we first got here, we had a minor crisis three times a day, and a major crisis once a week". But now, after four years of running the inn, "we have a minor crisis only about twice a week."

"For me, the hardest part is getting up in the morning," says Peggy Houdek, co-owner (with her husband, Dick) of Walker House, an inn in Lenox, Massachusetts. "But I like serving breakfast because it's the only chance I

sometimes feels "like Cinderella, watching all my guests go out for the evening while I stay in."

Max and Merrily Comins, owners of the picturesque Kedron Valley Inn in South Woodstock, Vermont, had no idea what they were getting into when they opened their inn in 1985. They had no experience running a hotel or a restaurant, only Max's lifelong desire to be an innkeeper. "We took a real leap in the dark," says Merrily. "We had to do a lot of on-the-job learning." Fourteen years later, the Cominses are more

Thousands of historic New England homes have been converted into inns

have all day to meet my guests and talk to everybody."

Walker House does not serve dinner, so Houdek's day isn't as long as a typical innkeeper's day but it is still packed with activity. "I'm in the public areas of the inn all day, answering questions, being here if people want to know where to eat dinner or how to get Tanglewood tickets. It's hard work having to be on all the time." She adds that she

accomplished. "There are still a couple of days a year when we wish we weren't doing this," Merrily admits, "but everybody has bad-hair days."

Running an inn is no cheap undertaking either. "Almost everybody sinks their entire savings, however much that may be, into the place they buy," says Merrily Comins. Most innkeepers then proceed to lose money for at least the

**Right: The challenge for an innkeeper is to create an environment where people can relax**

first five years. "The only thing that kept us in business the first four years was our tax advisors," Comins says.

Then, after about 10 years, according to Gorty Baldwin, "you have to reevaluate your inn and decide whether you want to make another major capital outlay, take another trip back to the bank, and live through another renovation." Add

If I someday come in and I'm yelling at inn guests, just kindly lead me out the back door and tell me it's time to retire or to do something else."

For the meantime, however, the Baldwins are doing things right: their inn is turning a profit a year ahead of schedule, and they're going back to the bank to "try to lose some more money," as Gorty puts it.

Transforming an historic house into a successful bed-and-breakfast takes real commitment

to this the fact that an especially hot summer, rainy spring, or snowless winter can play havoc with annual budgets and you might wonder why anybody would ever become an innkeeper.

"A lot of people think they're going to make a lot of money and not have to work very hard, and that's just not the way it is," says Peggy Houdek. "You're never going to show much of a profit in this business, but that's not really the reason to do it."

The reason to do it, says Baldwin, is "to see if you can create an environment where people can relax – and if they're not relaxing, to see if you can turn things around for them.

"We've still got rooms to renovate."

Merrily Comins says what keeps her and Max going is the fact that "there is hardly anything like a typical day. Our work involves an enormous amount of variety. We both love covering different bases and wearing a lot of hats." For her, the rewards of being an innkeeper are not monetary, they are personal. "What other business could you be in where people come up to you and thank you for doing your job? They even send you thank-you notes for doing your job, and bring you presents. In traditional business environments, that just doesn't happen."

"There is hardly anything like a typical day"

# Bean

**L.L. BEAN** RETURNED FROM A HUNTING TRIP IN 1912 WITH COLD, DAMP FEET. HIS SUBSEQUENT ATTEMPT TO CREATE A WATERPROOF HUNTING SHOE HAS GROWN INTO ONE OF THE GREATEST SUCCESS STORIES IN RETAIL HISTORY.

**Leon Leonwood Bean, inventor of the Maine Hunting Shoe**

But he went back to the drawing board, perfected the process, and sent out brochures about the boots to anybody with a Maine hunting license.

Leon Leonwood Bean hired a local shoemaker to attach leather uppers to

By 1917, L.L. had become successful enough

Hunters and fishermen were the first to take to Bean's waterproof boots

rubber boots, and thus was born the Maine Hunting Shoe. Today, the Bean name is known around the world, and the boots are worn not just by hunters, but by millions of preppies, housewives, business people and anybody else looking for warm, dry feet.

Bean's success, however, was not overnight. In fact, the first run of boots proved a disaster: the uppers separated from the rubber bottoms, forcing L.L. to give refunds to 90 of his first 100 customers.

to move out of his brother's basement and open his own retail store on Main Street in Freeport. In 1927, he expanded his product line from one to several dozen, adding equipment for camping and fishing. By 1934, the three-page flier had expanded to a 52-page catalog. And still the growth continued. L.L. Bean topped $1 million in sales in 1937, supplying customers as diverse as baseball legend Babe Ruth, author Ernest Hemingway and Eleanor Roosevelt.

## L.L. FACTS

L.L. Bean sales topped $1 billion in 1998, almost all of it from catalog sales. More than 3.5 million people visit the Freeport store every year, spending a total of more than $140 million.

By 1951, legions of hunters and fishermen were knocking on the door of Bean's Freeport store in the wee hours of the morning to purchase equipment before setting out on a hunting or fishing trip. So he did what any smart businessman would do: he opened the store 24 hours a day, 365 days a year. "We have thrown away the keys to the place," he proudly announced. These days, the people shopping at odd hours are more likely to be vacationers sifting through shelves of sweaters and piles of polos than hunters, but it is still a sight that would make old Leon Leonwood proud.

L.L. died in 1967, drawing more than 50,000 letters of condolence from customers past and present. His grandson Leon A. Gorman took over the company, using the same operating principle his grandfather had espoused: "Sell good merchandise at a reasonable profit, treat customers like human beings, and they will always come back for more."

Over the years, the one catalog gave way to dozens of different ones, each aimed at a specific sort of customer, be it kids, hunters, serious campers, or men and women simply looking for well-made casual clothing. But no matter which catalog you buy from, and there are now 50 from which to choose, the quality is the same, and the customers have kept coming back.

The L.L. Bean catalogs now sell a wide variety of goods

## L.L. TRAFFIC

Once a small coastal village, Freeport now resembles an outdoor mall of factory outlet and other stores peddling everything from candies to candles. L.L. Bean's success has drawn literally hundreds of smaller stores here, filling every nook and cranny along Main Street. Gap, J. Crew, Calvin Klein, Polo, Jockey, Patagonia, Reebok, Timberland, Dexter and Nine West are just a few of the most recognizable names. All of this outlet shopping brings with it maddening traffic, especially when rain spoils a summer day that might otherwise have been spent exploring the Maine wilderness. Bring your wallet and your patience, and, most important of all, park your car and walk around town – nothing is very far from anything else.

# THE BEST
## *of New England*

### Best New England experiences

• **Eating lobster** Chances are, if you have one lobster dinner in New England, you are likely to have another one soon thereafter. Once you get a taste for

lobster, you just have to have it again. Maine is where the best-tasting lobsters are, but they're not too shabby in coastal Massachusetts, New Hampshire and Rhode Island either (▶ 18–20).

• **Biking** The flat topography in New England's beach towns makes them ideal for exploration on two wheels. Cape Cod, Nantucket, Martha's Vineyard, Newport and the Maine coast are full of places that rent bikes, and you should take advantage of them. You will also save yourself traffic headaches.

• **Leaf-peeping** The annual arrival of autumnal colors draws foliage fans from all over the world. They clog Vermont's roads to a virtual stand-still, but

why hurry? If you want to get somewhere fast, take the highway. The driving tour on pages 181–183 is an attractive route between two of the state's top resort destinations, but an equally good way to see the scenery is to find your way onto some dirt roads and try to get lost.

• **Eating ice cream** New Englanders are forever arguing (and holding contests) to determine who makes the best ice cream. They're so crazy for the stuff that they continue their research long into winter when temperatures outside are colder than the cones they're holding. You can get Ben & Jerry's in most grocery and convenience stores, but there is no substitute for getting it freshly scooped at a local ice-cream parlor. Or take a drive up to Waterbury, Vermont, and tour the main factory where Chunky Monkey and Cherry Garcia are packed.

### Best place to buy antiques

• **Sheffield,** in the Berkshire Hills of western Massachusetts, is home to more antique dealers than you could possibly see in a day. Go with something specific in mind, otherwise the endless possibilities of places to peruse could be dizzying.

## Best sporting event

• Boston's Fenway Park is old and tiny, making it a cherished reminder of the days when the uniforms were wool and games were all played during the daytime. The **Red Sox** are pretty good these days, so get tickets in advance; they can sell out quickly (➤ 14–17 and 60).

## Best thing to do at 2 a.m.

• If you are anywhere near Maine with nothing to do late at night, head up to Freeport and the **L.L. Bean store** (➤ 24–25) – it never closes. The town may be quiet as a church mouse at this hour, but at Bean, you'll find a surprising number of fellow shoppers, as well as extremely helpful salespeople.

## Most romantic place to watch the sunset

• **Maddaket Beach,** Nantucket (➤ 84). On North America's eastern coast, there are precious few places where you can watch the sun melt into the ocean. Trees, hills or buildings usually mar the view, but Maddaket is west-facing, with 30 miles of open sea between it and the next landfall. Bring a bottle of wine and a blanket to complete the experience; it can get cool once the sun sinks.

## Best place to watch the sunrise

• The top of **Cadillac Mountain,** in Maine's Acadia National Park (➤ 158–160), is the first place in the U.S. to greet the sun each day. You have to get up pretty early and drive up to the top of the mountain in the dark, but if you like sunrises, it's worth it.

## Best view point

• **Top of the Hub,** Prudential Center, Boston (➤ 58). The food here isn't as good as the view, but you'll not soon forget the experience of sipping a drink while getting a glimpse of all New England.

## IF YOU ONLY GO TO ONE . . .

### Restaurant

**Legal Sea Foods** (➤ 68) is the quintessential New England restaurant, with outlets all over Boston (and gradually expanding outside New England, too). The seafood is always of the best quality, and the atmosphere is warm yet sophisticated.

### Store

**Filene's Basement** (➤ 71), where you can see ordinary men and women turn into crazed bargain hunters. The four-times-a-year bridal sale is a spectacle.

### Museum

The obvious choice is Boston's **Museum of Fine Arts** (➤ 48–51), with one of the greatest and most varied collections in the world.

### Historic Home

The **Astors' Beechwood** (➤ 139–140) is not the most luxurious Newport mansion, but the tour, delivered by actors in period costume who never break character, makes a visit particularly entertaining.

# LITERARY
## *Greats*

Thoreau and several other prominent New Englanders gathered periodically to discuss philosophy, religion and literature. From 1840 to 1844, they published their writings on these subjects in a journal called *The Dial.* They also helped to found Brook Farm, near Boston, an experimental cooperative community (1841–47) in which each of the 24 members participated in both the day's labor and the

**Ralph Waldo Emerson, father of Transcendentalism**

**Henry David Thoreau, Emerson's most prominent disciple**

**T**ranscendentalism, the philosophical belief that God is present in both man and nature, grew out of a series of meetings by a group of friends in Boston and Concord during the mid-19th century. Ralph Waldo Emerson, Henry David

evening's intellectual discourse. In the end, they proved better thinkers than farmers. The sandy soil of West Roxbury doomed their agricultural endeavors, but the ideas exchanged at Brook Farm paved the way for John Dewey's progressive education movement, and sowed the seeds of the abolitionist movement.

The preeminent spokesman of the Transcendentalist movement in America was Emerson (1803–82). His 1836 essay entitled "Nature" was the first to espouse the principles of the movement. His belief in the mystical unity of nature originally drew scorn from those who thought he was repudiating Christianity (he was prohibited from speaking at Harvard, his alma mater, for nearly 30 years). But it attracted the attention of intellectuals up and down the East Coast, many of whom came to Concord to share their thoughts.

Thoreau (1817–62) was Emerson's most prominent protégé. At the age of 24, he went to live in Emerson's house, serving as handyman, assistant, editor, and later as author of several pieces of poetry and prose for *The Dial*. Thoreau's most lasting contribution to the movement,

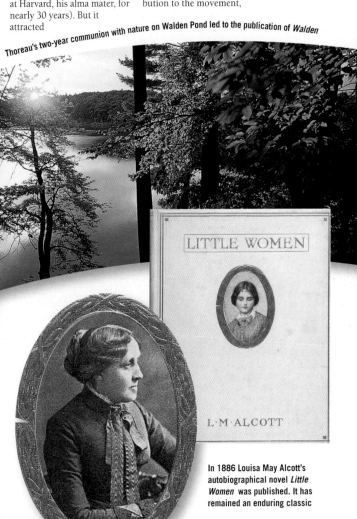

Thoreau's two-year communion with nature on Walden Pond led to the publication of *Walden*

LITTLE WOMEN

L·M·ALCOTT

In 1886 Louisa May Alcott's autobiographical novel *Little Women* was published. It has remained an enduring classic

## HAWTHORNE AND MELVILLE

Though they wrote at the same time as the Transcendentalists, Nathaniel Hawthorne (1804–64) and Herman Melville (1819–91) distanced themselves from the movement because they did not share its optimism (some might say idealism). Nevertheless, they are often mistakenly considered to be Transcendentalists because they moved so freely among them. Hawthorne's wife, Sophie Peabody, was a follower of the movement, and they lived for three years in the Concord house where Emerson wrote "Nature." That house, The Old Manse, is today open for tours. It stands right next to the Old North Bridge.

Nathaniel Hawthorne (above) and Herman Melville (left), though commonly associated with the movement, were not part of it

however, came in 1845, when he eschewed all material possessions and went to live in a small cabin he built for himself on the shore of Concord's Walden Pond. For more than two years, he led a largely introspective life, reading, observing nature and writing his thoughts in a detailed journal, which he published in 1854 as *Walden*.

The career of Amos Bronson Alcott (1799–1888) is often overshadowed by his more famous daughter Louisa May Alcott, author of *Little Women* (1868). But the younger Alcott's accounts of the experiment in progressive education would not have been possible without her father's tireless advocacy of social and educational reform. His Temple School, which stressed the importance of children's mental, physical and spiritual development, was ultimately a failure, though it was imitated with much greater success in England (Alcott House).

Louisa May Alcott (1832–88) is not usually considered to be one of the Transcendentalists, but her account of growing up in the progressive Alcott household has conveyed the same spirit to young girls ever since. Just about every American girl over the age of six has read and loved *Little Women*, Alcott's autobiographical novel about four sisters growing up in an unconventional home in New England. A highly moralistic account of daily domestic life, it nonetheless became a best-seller and made Louisa the most highly paid author of her day. The trials and triumphs of Meg, Jo, Beth and Amy have since been chronicled in three separate Hollywood adaptations of *Little Women* (the latest, in 1994, featured Winona Ryder as Jo, the tomboyish writer based on Alcott herself). Orchard House, the Alcott home in Concord, was often visited by the giants of the Transcendentalist movement. Today, the home is still full of family mementos, though the visitors tend to be tourists, rather than world-class authors (▶ 61).

# Finding
# Your Feet

# First Two Hours

## Arriving By Air: Boston

- Most travelers begin their New England vacations at **Boston's Logan International Airport**, and all international carriers arrive at Terminal E. Northwest Airlines also arrives at Terminal E; American at Terminal B, United and Delta at Terminal C, and Continental at Terminal A.
- There's a currency exchange (open until 10 p.m.) as soon as you clear customs in Terminal E, as well as ATMs, a visitor information booth, and desks for most car rental agencies.

### Cabs

- You'll find taxi stands at all the airport terminals. Rates are **metered** and a ride from the airport to most hotels costs about $20, plus approximately $4 in tolls depending on the route you take. Though relatively expensive, cabs are convenient if you have a lot of luggage. Up to **four people** are permitted in each taxi.

### Public Transportation

- This is a faster way to get into Boston when airport traffic is heavy (usually between 3 and 7 p.m.) but involves at least one transfer and often two.
- To get to Airport subway stop, take the free **Massport Shuttle Bus.** Bus 22 stops at Terminals A and B and Bus 33 at Terminals C, D, and E. The service is frequent, but because of congestion can be slow. Both the "T" and the shuttles shut down from 1–5:30 a.m.
- Follow signs for the **Blue Line Train Inbound** to get to central Boston. For details on major intersections ➤ 33.
- **Travelers with disabilities** should call for the free van, which serves all airport locations. There are courtesy phones near baggage claim at every terminal, or call (617) 561-1770.

## Arriving By Air: Outside Boston

- Several airlines operate services to **Providence,** Rhode Island and **Manchester,** New Hampshire. These two smaller New England airports are each about an hour and a half outside Boston, but the low prices and efficient service make it an alternative worth considering.
  Visitors to Vermont or the Berkshires might consider flying into **Burlington,** Vermont; **Albany,** New York; or **Bradley International Airport,** 15 miles north of Hartford, Connecticut.

## Arriving By Rail

- Intercity **Amtrak** trains from New York, Philadelphia, Chicago, Washington and other points arrive at South Station; many trains stop at Back Bay Station as well. For information on fares and schedules, call Amtrak at (tel: 1-800/872-7245; web: www.amtrak.com).
- From South Station, it is about a $10-$15 cab ride to most downtown hotels. The Red Line also stops at South Station.

## Arriving By Bus

- **Greyhound** (tel: 1-800-231-2222; web: www.greyhound.com) provides a nationwide bus service, and can give you the names of several smaller regional carriers that offer services between Boston and other points in New England.Buses arrive at the South Station bus terminal, adjacent to the train station.

# Getting Around

## Boston

Boston is extremely compact. Most of its attractions are within easy walking distance of each other, and those that aren't are linked by a simple, efficient subway system (the "T").

### The "T"

- The "T" has four different lines, each radiating out from the city's center. The four major downtown stops are **Park Street** (the unofficial center of the system, where the Red and Green lines intersect), **Government Center** (where the Green and Blue lines intersect), **State** (where the Blue and Orange lines intersect), and **Downtown Crossing** (a pedestrian mall, where the Orange and Red lines meet).
- The system uses the terminology **"inbound"** and **"outbound."** Inbound always means toward Park Street, the center of the system, and outbound means away from Park Street. If you don't know which direction you need to take, just ask. It's not an uncommon question, and most people will be happy to help you.
- Note that many of the stops on the Green Line are so close together that it's almost faster to walk between them.
- The **fare** for most trips on the "T" is 85 cents and you can buy tokens from vending machines or from ticket offices at any subway station.
- A **visitor's pass** gives unlimited rides for a flat fee. It costs $5 for one day, $9 for three days, and $18 for seven days and is available at the Airport, South Station, North Station, Back Bay Station, Government Center, and Harvard T stops, as well as at some hotels and tourist information kiosks. Contact MBTA on (617) 222-3200 or visit their website www.mbta.com for more information.

### Cabs

- The "T" stops running after about 1 a.m., but cabs can usually be found (or called) at most places frequented by tourists. You can try to hail a cab almost anywhere: you will usually have better luck at cab stands (in front of most hotels, popular restaurants and tourist attractions).
- Taxis are **metered** and they are not cheap, but no cab ride within the city limits should cost more than $15.
- The initial fare is $1.50, and you pay 25 cents for each additional eighth of a mile. Tip drivers 15 percent of the fare.
- If you can't find a cab, try calling **Checker Taxi** (tel: 617/536-7500), **ITOA** (tel: 617/426-8700), **Town Taxi** (tel: 617/536-5000) or **Boston Cab** (tel: 617/536-5010).

### Driving

- Don't even attempt to drive in Boston. The traffic is blood-boiling, the one-way streets will drive you insane, and legal parking spaces are an endangered species. Parking ticket stories are legendary, including the (true) one about the man who got a summons while dying of a heart attack in a no-standing zone.
- If you have a car, park it in a garage when you arrive and leave it there until you leave. If the prices at your hotel's garage seem too high, try the large parking lots under **Boston Common** (tel: 617/954-2096) or under **Prudential Center** (tel: 617/267-1002).

# Outside Boston

To see the rest of New England, you'll have to have a car. Train and bus services (➤ 32) to the rest of New England are spotty and you'll find it next to impossible to get around the woods of Vermont, the beaches of Cape Cod or the small towns of the Berkshires without wheels of your own.

## Driving

- If you're planning to do a lot of driving around New England, invest in a good map.
- The multibillion dollar construction project in Boston known as the Big Dig (which aims to bury the John F. Fitzgerald Expressway running along the city's eastern edge) will be changing traffic patterns on an almost daily basis until 2004. If you are leaving the city by car, be prepared for things on the ground to look different from the map.
- Reserve your rental car at least a few days in advance and pick it up on the day you leave Boston.
- Most major car rental agencies have locations at the airport, as well as locations in town. For more information contact the companies direct:

**Alamo** (tel: 800/327-9633)  **Enterprise** (tel: 800/566-9249)
**Avis** (tel: 800/831-2847)  **Hertz** (tel: 800/654-3131)
**Budget** (tel: 800/527-0700)  **National** (tel: 800/227-7368)
**Dollar** (tel: 800/800-4000)  **Thrifty** (tel: 807/367-2277)

- To rent a car, you usually need to be **aged 25** or above and hold a major credit card in your name.
- An overseas driver's license is valid on all U.S. roads, though it is helpful to have an international driving permit. Bring your passport, too.
- Check to see if your automobile insurance at home covers you for rentals. Otherwise, you'll have to pay the **hefty per-day surcharges** that all the rental companies impose for liability insurance.
- Call your credit card company to see if they will assume the **Collision Damage Waiver (CDW)**, another per-day surcharge that absolves you of responsibility for damage to the vehicle in an accident. Most gold cards offer collision coverage to their customers, but do not cover liability.

## Getting Out of Town

- **The Berkshires** Take the Massachusetts Turnpike (U.S. 90) west to Stockbridge.
- **Cape Cod and the Islands** Take the Fitzgerald Expressway (U.S. 93) south to Route 3 south. Cross the Cape Cod Canal onto Route 6. For ferries to Nantucket and Martha's Vineyard, take Route 132 south at Barnstable and follow the signs to Hyannis and the ferry docks.
- **Maine** Take the Fitzgerald Expressway (U.S. 93) north to U.S. 95 north.
- **New Hampshire** Take the Fitzgerald Expressway (U.S. 93) north
- **Rhode Island and coastal Connecticut** Take the Fitzgerald Expressway (U.S. 93) south, then U.S. 95 south.
- **Vermont** Take the Massachusetts Turnpike (U.S. 90) west to U.S. 95. Exit at Route 2 west, toward Concord. Stay on Route 2 to U.S. 91 north.

## Admission Charges

The cost of admission for museums and places of interest mentioned in the text is indicated by price categories

**Inexpensive** – up to $5 **Moderate** – $6–10 **Expensive** – over $10

# Accommodations

New England in general, and Boston in particular, has some of the most luxurious hotels in the United States, as well as 19th-century inns, with plenty of character and antiques to match.

## Hotels and Inns

- Though hotels in Boston and New England's other major cities tend to be expensive, they often offer attractive discounts for weekend visitors.
- Victorian or colonial-style **country inns**, found throughout the region, offer guests a real New England experience. Inns vary in character and price: Some are inexpensive homely family places, others set out to re-create the grandeur of yesteryear, with prices to match.

## Resorts

- New England's mountains and beaches were the nation's first summer playgrounds. Today, many resorts are as grand as ever, offering a wide range of activities, from golf and swimming to spas and *haute cuisine*.

## When To Go

- Peak or **high season varies** from town to town. During this time expect elevated prices, with minimum stays required of two to four nights.
- **Ski resorts** in the mountains of Vermont and New Hampshire are crowded on the major holiday weekends in winter. Bargains to be had in March.
- Peak season in **Cape Cod** and the **Berkshire Hills** is in July and August.
- With its plethora of colleges, **Boston** is busy at graduation time in May/June, and crowded in September at the start of the academic year.
- Increased numbers of visitors during the **fall foliage season** make hotel rooms everywhere hard to come by. The Columbus Day weekend and the second weekend in October are particularly busy. In Vermont, where millions of "leaf-peepers" pour into the state, some Chambers of Commerce co-ordinate lodgings in private homes to take the strain.

## Diamond Ratings

- AAA tourism editors evaluate and rate lodging establishments based on the overall quality and services. AAA's diamond rating criteria reflect the design and service standards set by the lodging industry, combined with the expectations of our members
- Our one (◆) or two (◆◆) diamond rating represents a clean and well-maintained property offering comfortable rooms, with the two diamond property showing enhancements in decor and furnishings. A three (◆◆◆) diamond property shows marked upgrades in physical attributes, services and comfort and may offer additional amenities. A four (◆◆◆◆) diamond rating signifies a property offering a high level of service and hospitality and a wide variety of amenities and upscale facilities. A five (◆◆◆◆◆) diamond rating represents a world-class facility, offering the highest level of luxurious accommodations and personalized guest services.

## Taxes

Lodging and meal taxes vary from state to state. Taxes are not usually included in quoted prices.

| | | | |
|---|---|---|---|
| **VT** | 9 percent | **ME** | 7 percent |
| **NH** | 8 percent | **CT** | 12 percent |
| **MA** | 9.7 percent (average) | **RI** | 5 percent |

# Food and Drink

Dining out has changed dramatically in New England in the past decade, and you can find sophisticated restaurants in smaller towns and villages, as well as in Boston and the other major cities. Many country inns serve evening meals, and though you can expect to pay similar prices to those in an independent restaurant, it could be the highlight of your vacation.

## Traditional New England Cuisine

■ **Lobster,** which is still abundant and affordable, is the best-known New England specialty, though clams, oysters, and Atlantic and freshwater fish are widely available.

■ The best place to eat lobster in New England is at a simple **lobster shack.** Plain boiled lobsters are served with a tub of melted butter and diners wear paper bibs to catch the drips. Although Maine is most famous for lobster or clam shacks, you can find them in towns and villages up and down the New England coastline. They are open for lunch and early dinner in summer, but close in winter.

■ Lobster shacks serve other seafood **specialties,** including milky oyster stew and thick clam chowder. Menus may feature steamers, quahogs (pronounced ko-hogs), cherrystones and littlenecks: these are all clams.

■ For real baked beans, which were invented in Boston, brown bread (made with molasses) and Indian pudding (a dessert made from cornmeal and molasses), try **Durgin-Park** in Boston (➤ 67).

## Modern American/New England Cuisine

■ Modern New England cooking focuses on **locally produced ingredients:** coastal seafood, firm Atlantic fish and trout from mountain streams. Maine produces blueberries, New Hampshire grows apples and Massachusetts crops tons of cranberries. Organically grown vegetables and salads are readily available. Vermont maple syrup and dairy products, especially cheeses and ice cream, are renowned. In the fall, game is plentiful, as are pumpkins and squash.

■ Immigration has influenced cooking styles in the region. Boston's North End is the city's Little Italy, while Chinatown, although compact, is home to a large number of Asian eateries. Out on Cape Cod, descendants of Portuguese origin still bake Portuguese breads.

## Practical Tips

■ Eating hours are early by European standards. **Lunch** is usually served from 11:30 or noon to 2 or 2:30 p.m. and **dinner** from 5–9:30 or 10 p.m.

■ Some top-class restaurants offer **special menus** for those dining early. Lunch menus are always less expensive than dinner.

■ Expect to leave a **tip** of 15–20 percent at the best restaurants.

■ When eating out in New England, the dress code is rarely more formal than **smart-casual**.

## Diamond Ratings

As with the hotel ratings (➤ 35), AAA tourism editors evaluate restaurants on the overall quality of food, service, decor and ambiance – with extra emphasis given to food and service. Ratings range from one diamond (◆) indicating a simple, family-oriented establishment to five diamonds (◆◆◆◆◆) indicating an establishment offering superb culinary skills and ultimate adult dining experience.

# Shopping

New England offers some of the most varied and best-value shopping in the United States. In addition to upmarket malls, Boston boasts chic avenues such as Newbury Street. Although the region is known for its fine antiques and crafts shops, its numerous discount outlets make it popular with those in search of a bargain.

## Specialty Shopping

■ Boston's **Faneuil Hall Marketplace** redevelopment (➤ 71) is the place to go for unusual gifts.

## Farm Stands and Country Stores

■ Throughout the six states, country lanes are studded with **stalls selling local produce**, from organic vegetables to jars of honey and maple syrup, even goat's cheeses.
■ For pure nostalgia, nothing beats the traditional Vermont **country store** (➤ 129), which once supplied farmers and their families with everything that they needed. Today, customers can once again buy long cotton night-shirts, patent medicines and SnoreLess pillows.

## Antiques and Crafts

■ New England is known for its antiques shops and collectibles. **The Old King's Highway** (Route 6A) on Cape Cod (➤ 94), is a fertile hunting ground, as is **Route 7**, running through Vermont, Western Massachusetts and into Connecticut.
■ The region also has a thriving **contemporary crafts** industry, with potters, jewelers, weavers and furniture-makers producing top-quality goods. The best craftsmen are registered with state craft associations.

## Factory Outlets

■ In the past decade, factory outlets have become hugely popular. They sell everything from jewelry and books to designer-label clothes, shoes and bags, all at knockdown prices. **Freeport,** Maine is one of the best known destinations, though Kittery (➤ 171) is also popular.
■ Since New Hampshire has no sales tax, canny shoppers regularly hop across the state line for bargains. The hikers and skiers who flock to the White Mountains usually leave time to stock up at the outdoors shops in **North Conway**, as well as seeking out more glamorous designer label clothing. In southern Vermont, the outlet shops in **Manchester Center** (➤ 129) boast big names such as Burberry's, Calvin Klein and Armani.
■ Not to be outdone, Massachusetts has a whole mall of outlet stores, west of Boston at **Worcester Common Fashion Outlets.**

## Opening times

■ In towns, stores are usually open from 9 or 10 a.m. to 6 or 7 p.m. Malls usually stay open later, especially during the peak season.

## Sales Tax

■ In New England, a small sales tax is added to the price of the goods that you buy (though it is already included in the price of petrol, tobacco and alcohol). Taxes vary from state to state. For clothing, expect to pay an additional 5 percent, except in Rhode Island and Connecticut, where the rate for clothing is zero.

# Entertainment

New England has an impressive literary, artistic and theatrical heritage. There is world-class music in the cities and countryside. There are also well-organised festivals. Check with the tourist board for details.

## January
**Stowe,** VT: the Winter Carnival is fun even when it's freezing.
**Connecticut:** Warm up to Winter celebrations feature Early American Hearth Tours across the state.

## February
**Newport,** RI: the 10-day Winter Festival offers everything from snow sculpture to hot air ballooning.

## March
**Boston,** MA: New England Spring Flower Show.
**New Hampshire:** on Maple Syrup Weekend, sugar houses show you how the sticky treat is made.
**Boston,** MA: goes green for St. Patrick's Day (17th)

## April
**Concord,** MA: Patriot's Day celebrations, re-enactments.
**Vermont:** the statewide Maple Festival celebrates food, fiddle players and fun.
**Hartford,** CT: Hubbard Park is ablaze with daffodils, fireworks and fun.
**Bristol,** RI: Daffodil Days, one of New England's biggest displays of the golden flower.

## May
**Providence,** RI: Waterfire lights up the Providence River (through October)
**Moose Mainea,** ME: an excuse to go moose-mad for a month; moose everything from safaris to mountain bike races.
**New Hampshire:** the Lilac Festival also features parades, rides and fireworks.

## June
**Farmington,** CT: the state's biggest antiques fair, with 600 stalls.

**Providence,** RI: during the Festival of Historic Houses, mansions open their gardens and host candlelight tours.
**Boothbay Harbor,** ME: tall ships gather for the annual Windjammer Days Festival.
**Portland,** ME: the city parties at the Old Port Festival.
**Mount Washington,** NH: enthusiasts run up the 6,288-foot peak in the world's toughest foot race.
**Burlington,** VT: the Lake Champlain Festival features hot air balloons and crafts.

## July
**Stowe,** VT: the Stoweflake hot air balloon festival

## August
**Newport,** RI: the world's greatest artists at the famous Jazz Festival.
**Rockland,** ME: the world's biggest lobster festival.

## September
**Gloucester,** MA: Schooner Festival with 100 windjammers.
**Hampton,** NH: the Seafood Festival marks the end of summer.

## October
**Northeast Kingdom,** VT: the Fall Foliage Festival celebrates the autumn colour.
**Mystic,** CT: try New England's special dish at Chowderfest.

## November
**New Haven,** CT: Pick up a gift at the Celebration of American Crafts event.

## December
**Portsmouth,** NH: the Candlelight Stroll wanders through the old town.
**Everywhere:** celebrations for First Night (31st), the last and best party of the year.

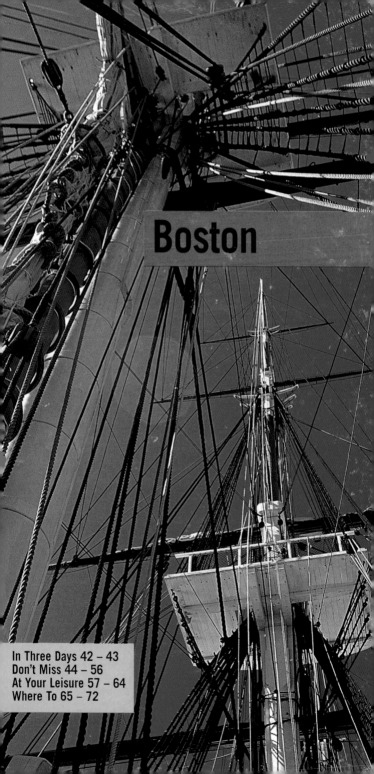

# Boston

In Three Days 42 – 43
Don't Miss 44 – 56
At Your Leisure 57 – 64
Where To 65 – 72

# Getting Your Bearings

Some people find Boston a hard city to love. The streets are all one-way in the wrong direction, the weather is brutally cold in winter and often muggy in summer, and the bars close at midnight.

Yet when you talk to people who live in Boston, you'd think there was no place else to live and that the world revolves around their city.

It doesn't, of course, but Boston blends historic city and modern metropolis so successfully that it's easy to forget that. As one friend put it, "when you see candidates for Governor holding a debate at Faneuil Hall [where John Adams and Thomas Jefferson sowed the seeds of liberty], it makes you proud to live here."

The city has other charms, too. Boston is a college town of the highest order. Harvard, the Massachusetts Institute of Technology (MIT), Boston College, Wellesley and Boston University are just a few of the

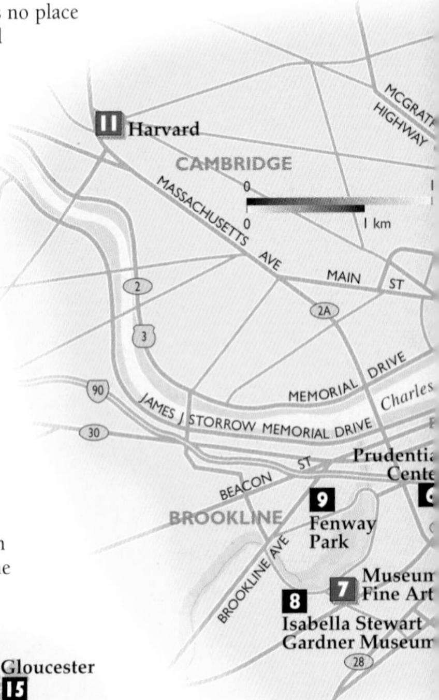

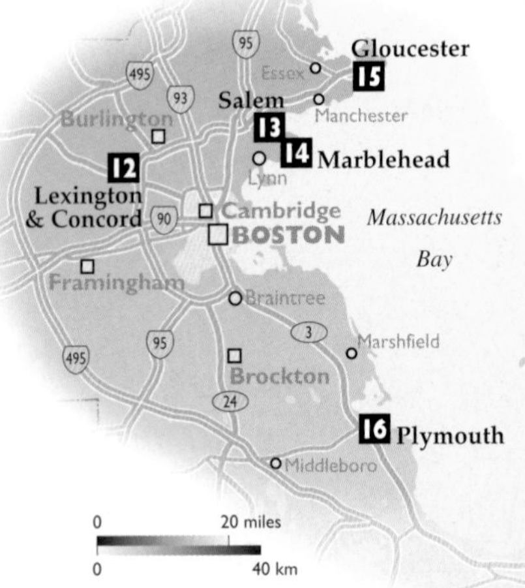

**11** Harvard
CAMBRIDGE
MCGRATH HIGHWAY
MASSACHUSETTS AVE
MAIN ST
2
2A
3
90
JAMES J STORROW MEMORIAL DRIVE
30
MEMORIAL DRIVE
Charles
BEACON ST
Prudential Center
BROOKLINE
**9** Fenway Park
BROOKLINE AVE
**8**  **7** Museum of Fine Art
Isabella Stewart Gardner Museum
28
0      1 km

95
495
93
Essex
Burlington
Salem
**13**
Manchester
**12**
Lexington & Concord
90
Lynn
Cambridge **14** Marblehead
BOSTON
Framingham
Braintree
Massachusetts Bay
95
495
3
Marshfield
Brockton
24
**16** Plymouth
Middleboro
**15** Gloucester

0      20 miles
0      40 km

Previous page: USS *Constitution*, at the end of the Freedom Trail

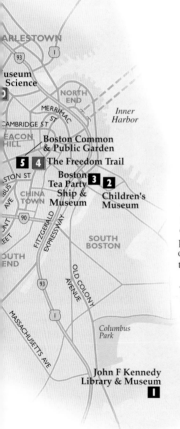

## ★ Don't Miss

**4** **The Freedom Trail**
➤ 44

**7** **Museum of Fine Arts**
➤ 48

**10** **Museum of Science**
➤ 52

**11** **Harvard** ➤ 54

## At Your Leisure

**1** John F. Kennedy Library
and Museum ➤ 57

**2** Children's Museum
➤ 57

**3** Boston Tea Party Ship
and Museum ➤ 57

**5** Boston Common and the
Public Garden ➤ 58

**6** Prudential Center ➤ 58

**8** Isabella Stewart Gardner
Museum ➤ 59

**9** Fenway Park ➤ 60

## Farther Afield

**12** Lexington and Concord
➤ 61

**13** Salem ➤ 62

**14** Marblehead ➤ 62

**15** Gloucester ➤ 63

**16** Plymouth ➤ 64

scores of colleges and universities that call the area home. That means the city is full of thousands of undergraduates seeking enlightenment and entertainment. But it is also full of professors, graduate students and other professional people who give the city a sophisticated air.

Most of the city's attractions are within easy walking distance, and the most significant Revolutionary sites are all linked by a red line on the sidewalk (the Freedom Trail). The historical flavor doesn't stop at the city limits, either. Plymouth, where the Pilgrims first landed, is less than an hour to the south. Within commuting distance to the west of the city are Lexington and Concord, where the first shots of the American Revolution were fired and where the Transcendentalist movement began a century later. To the north are Salem, infamous for its 17th-century witch trials, and the idyllic coastal towns of Gloucester and Marblehead.

Sample the city's historic sites, cheer the
Red Sox with the home crowd at Fenway Park, enjoy
some of Boston's finest museums, meander through Harvard
University's storied quadrangles and soak up the laid-back
atmosphere at Harvard Square.

# Boston in Three Days

## Day One

### Morning

Beginning from Boston Common Visitor
Center, follow the **Freedom Trail** (➤ 44–47)
as far as Faneuil Hall Marketplace, soaking
up some of the city's historic sights (including the New State House, right) en route.

### Afternoon

Wander around **Faneuil Hall**,
Boston's old public meeting
hall, and the surrounding
shops of **Quincy Market** (left),
stopping for lunch at Ye Olde
Union Oyster House, a city
institution since 1826, or Durgin-Park (➤ 67). Complete the Freedom Trail,
then take the water shuttle back to the city.

### Evening

Make your way to **Fenway Park**, last of a dying breed of old-time ballparks, for
a Boston Red Sox home game (➤ 60). If the Sox aren't in town, check out
the shops and restaurants along Newbury Street. Fans of good, old-fashioned
steaks should head for Capital Grille (➤ 67).

# Day Two

### Morning
Take a leisurely stroll in the **Public Garden** (➤ 58) or go for a ride on one of the park's famous swan boats. If the weather won't cooperate, check out **Filene's Basement** (➤ 71), an attraction all its own, regardless of whether you're looking for a bargain.

### Afternoon
Have lunch at Pho Pasteur (➤ 69), an inexpensive Vietnamese restaurant in Chinatown, then spend the afternoon at the **Museum of Fine Arts** (➤ 48–51). Afterward, if you have got the energy, go to the **Isabella Stewart Gardner Museum** (➤ 59) two blocks away.

### Evening
See the sun set over the city from the 50th-floor Skywalk (above) at the **Prudential Center** (➤ 58), then head to Top of the Hub (➤ 69) for a drink, followed by some of Boston's best seafood at Legal Sea Foods (➤ 68).

# Day Three

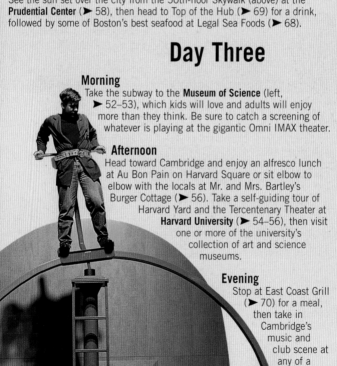

### Morning
Take the subway to the **Museum of Science** (left, ➤ 52–53), which kids will love and adults will enjoy more than they think. Be sure to catch a screening of whatever is playing at the gigantic Omni IMAX theater.

### Afternoon
Head toward Cambridge and enjoy an alfresco lunch at Au Bon Pain on Harvard Square or sit elbow to elbow with the locals at Mr. and Mrs. Bartley's Burger Cottage (➤ 56). Take a self-guiding tour of Harvard Yard and the Tercentenary Theater at **Harvard University** (➤ 54–56), then visit one or more of the university's collection of art and science museums.

### Evening
Stop at East Coast Grill (➤ 70) for a meal, then take in Cambridge's music and club scene at any of a handful of local joints.

# The Freedom Trail

If you have time for only one Boston attraction, make it the Freedom Trail. This 3-mile walking tour not only takes you past several of the best Revolutionary War historic sites, but also gives a good orientation to the city as a whole. You will wander through the cemetery where patriots like Samuel Adams and John Hancock are buried, and navigate the narrow one-way streets they once walked. You'll see Faneuil Hall, named for Peter Faneuil, where the seeds of the American Revolution were sown, and the adjoining Quincy Market, a shopping complex that revitalized downtown Boston in the early 1980s. You can also tour the house where Paul Revere lived and stop for a bite to eat at one of the bustling Italian restaurants that have sprung up in that neighborhood.

Faneuil Hall (above) and the Granary Burying Ground (right), two of the top stops on the Freedom Trail

Most people begin at the visitor center on Boston Common. If you want a guided tour, head for the National Park Visitor Center at 15 State Street, across from the Old State House. Tours are limited to 30 people on a first-come, first-serve basis. You can also get a map at the visitor center, but the red-brick line in the sidewalk links all 16 sites, so it's just about impossible to get lost. The walk takes about 3 hours depending on how many sites you stop at and how long you spend lingering.

**Boston Common** is the first attraction. Its 48 acres, set aside as parkland in 1634, are an oasis of greenery within the otherwise relentlessly urban center of downtown Boston. On fine summer days, you will find people relaxing on the lawns or just soaking up the sun.

Walk up the hill to the gold-domed **Massachusetts State House**. Built by architect Charles Bulfinch in 1798 – Samuel Adams himself laid the cornerstone – it's new only in comparison to the Old State House, erected some 85 years earlier. The Massachusetts legislature meets here, and if that tempts you to linger long here, remember that there are still 14 historic attractions to go.

At the corner of Park and Tremont streets is **Park Street Church**. The church was known as "Brimstone Corner" not so much for the fiery sermons delivered within (although abolitionist William Lloyd Garrison did give his first antislavery speech here in 1829), but because gunpowder was stored here during the War of 1812.

Next door is the **Granary Burying Ground**, the first (and best) of the small city cemeteries on the tour. The list of people buried here reads like a *Who's Who* of American history: John Hancock, Paul Revere, Samuel Adams, Peter Faneuil and the victims of the Boston Massacre are among the scores of early Americans memorialized by gravestones that over the years have sunk halfway into the ground. The giant obelisk in the center marks the burial plot of the parents of statesman and scientist Benjamin Franklin. The bodies of the people buried here don't actually lie beneath their own headstones – the stones have been moved into rows that can

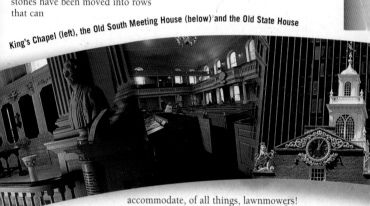

King's Chapel (left), the Old South Meeting House (below) and the Old State House

accommodate, of all things, lawnmowers!

Cross Tremont Street to the **King's Chapel and Burying Ground**. This was the site of the first Anglican Congregation in Boston, and the adjacent burying ground is Boston's oldest.

Down **School Street** is the site of the country's first public school and Boston's old City Hall. The school's alumni include Samuel Adams, John Hancock, Benjamin Franklin, Puritan minister Cotton Mather and poet Ralph Waldo Emerson. The old City Hall is now a private office building, thanks to an ambitious 1973 preservation job that saved it from the wrecking ball.

At the end of School Street is the **Old Corner Book Store**. Once the center of literary Boston (Emerson, Nathaniel Hawthorne and Henry Wadsworth Longfellow held forth here), it's now just a store selling *Boston Globe* T-shirts and other paraphernalia.

Half a block up and across Washington Street is the **Old South Meeting House**, best known for the meeting on December 16, 1773, when 5,000 colonists congregated here to protest against the tax on tea, an uprising that resulted in the Boston Tea Party.

At Washington and Court streets stands the **Old State House**, built in 1713; the Declaration of Independence was first read to the citizens of Boston from the balcony. Although the New State House long ago replaced this building as the seat of government, the Declaration is still read aloud here every Fourth of July. In front of the State House, a ring of stones marks the site of the 1770 Boston Massacre, when British soldiers shot five colonists here, one of the fateful events in the buildup to the American Revolution.

Follow Congress Street downhill to **Quincy Market** and **Faneuil Hall** (pronounced "FAN yull"). On your left, you'll pass architect Louis Kahn's brutally ultramodernist City Hall. Faneuil Hall itself is the public meeting hall nicknamed "the Cradle of Liberty" in honor of all the incendiary rhetoric that went on here in colonial times; Quincy Market is the collection of stores and restaurants around the site to entertain hungry visitors. The entire complex is known as the Faneuil Hall Marketplace, the first, and still the best, of the Rouse Co. projects turning abandoned waterfronts into successful visitor attractions (Baltimore's Inner Harbor and New York's South Street Seaport are other examples).

Past Faneuil Hall, the trail crosses a sprawling highway construction site, known locally as the Big Dig, and into the North End, Boston's thriving Italian-American neighborhood, with dozens of restaurants lining the main drag, Hanover Street. **Paul Revere House**, at 19 North Square, is a highlight of the tour. For a nominal admission fee you can see the only

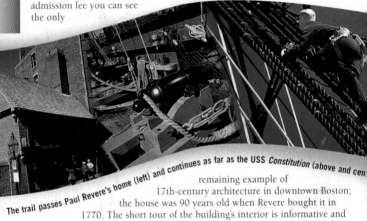

The trail passes Paul Revere's home (left) and continues as far as the USS *Constitution* (above and cen

remaining example of 17th-century architecture in downtown Boston; the house was 90 years old when Revere bought it in 1770. The short tour of the building's interior is informative and entertaining, and if the historic interest doesn't persuade you to stop here, the fact that the house is air-conditioned might.

The next stop is **Old North Church**, best known for the two lanterns that shone here on April 18, 1775, to indicate that the British were coming by water. A "Behind the Scenes" tour leaves every hour, but you can just poke your head inside to see the closed pews encircled by 4-foot-high walls.

Up Hull Street on your right is **Copp's Hill Burying Ground**, which is notable not so much for who is interred here, as for its splendid view of Boston Harbor.

Faced with the prospect of a long walk across the bridge to Charlestown, tired legs often return to Hanover Street for a plate of biscotti and a glass of chianti. But those intent on finishing the tour should cross the bridge and follow the red-brick road to the **USS Constitution**. "Old Ironsides" earned its nickname not during the American Revolution, but rather in the War of 1812, when British cannonballs bounced off the ship's oak hull.

Try to get to the ship before 4 p.m., which is when the last guided tour leaves, led by U.S. Navy officers in full period costumes. After that, you can take a self-guiding tour of only the top deck until sunset. The film in the nearby museum "walks" you through the ship's lower decks.

From the *Constitution*, you can see the top of the **Bunker Hill Monument**, commemorating the first battle of the Revolution. If you still have the energy, you can walk the last quarter mile to the obelisk and climb all 294 steps to the top, or you can just walk to the end of the pier behind the Constitution Museum and take the water shuttle back to Long Wharf, near the Aquarium. The ferry journey is faster than walking back, cheaper than a cab (if you can find one), and prettier than a bus ride.

## TAKING A BREAK

Faneuil Hall Marketplace is a good place to stop for lunch, a snack or just a cool drink on a hot day, though you will seldom see an actual Bostonian here. **Durgin Park** (► 67), known for its gigantic portions of prime rib and its short-tempered waitresses, is part of the traditional Boston experience.

🚩 198 C2 Begin at the Information Center on Boston Common, 15 State Street

### New State House
🚩 198 C2 ⊠ Beacon and Bowdoin streets ☎ (617) 727-3676 🕓 Mon.–Fri. 10–4 🚇 Green Line or Red Line to Park Street 🎫 Free

### Park Street Church
🚩 198 C2 ⊠ Park and Tremont streets ☎ (617) 523-3383 🕓 Tue.–Sat. 9:30–3:30, Jul.–Aug.; winter by appointment 🚇 Green Line or Red Line to Park Street 🎫 Free

### Granary Burying Ground
🚩 199 D2 ⊠ Park and Tremont streets 🕓 Daily 8 a.m.–sunset 🚇 Green Line or Red Line to Park Street 🎫 Free

### Old State House
🚩 199 D3 ⊠ 206 Washington Street ☎ (617) 720-3290 🕓 Daily 9–5 🚇 Blue Line or Orange Line to State 🎫 Inexpensive

### Paul Revere House
🚩 199 E4 ⊠ 19 North Square ☎ (617) 523-2338 🕓 Daily 9:30–5, Apr. 15–Oct., 9:30–4:15, Nov.–Apr. 14 🚇 Green Line or Orange Line to Haymarket, Blue Line to Aquarium 🎫 Inexpensive

### Old North Church
🚩 199 E4 ⊠ 19 North Square ☎ (617) 523-6676 🕓 Daily 9–6 (also Thu.–Fri., 6–8 p.m.)

🚇 Green Line or Orange Line to Haymarket, Blue Line to Aquarium 🎫 Donations requested. Tours: moderate

### USS *Constitution*
🚩 199 D5 ⊠ Charlestown Navy Yard ☎ (617) 242-5670 🕓 Tours: daily 9:30–5:30 🚇 Green Line or Orange Line to North Station 🎫 Free

### Bunker Hill Monument
🚩 Off map 199 D5 ⊠ Monument Square ☎ (617) 242-5644 🕓 Daily 9–5 (last entry 4:30) 🚇 Green Line to North Station, Orange Line to Community College 🎫 Free

USS Constitution, nicknamed Old Ironsides

## THE FREEDOM TRAIL: INSIDE INFO

**Top tip** Many people poop out before the last two stops of the tour, especially on steamy hot or blustery cold days. If you have your heart set on visiting "Old Ironsides," take a cab or bus No. 92 to Charlestown and start at the USS *Constitution*, then follow the trail backward into Boston.

**One to miss** Don't bother paying the admission to view the interior of the Old South Meeting House. It's not worth the money, and you still have eight more stops to go on the trail.

# Museum of Fine Arts

The Museum of Fine Arts (MFA) is the kind of museum that can keep you absorbed for hours on end. Its collection encompasses the entire globe and ranges across the entire span of human existence. The quantity of its Asian and African art and artifacts is matched only by the quality of its European and American paintings. The holdings here are so vast and varied that you'll wish you had a week to visit, not just a mere afternoon.

Compounding the problem of insufficient time is the fact that the MFA has no must-see work of art. There are plenty of internationally recognizable paintings and sculptures, but nothing as closely identified with it as, say, the *Mona Lisa* is with the Louvre in Paris. The MFA's strength is in its overall breadth and depth, not the brightness of its individual constellations.

**The museum's collection of Asian and Buddhist temple art is one of its strengths**

The MFA's galleries are least crowded on weekdays during the winter

Some say this lack of star power makes it second-best to New York's Metropolitan Museum of Art. But the MFA outstrips its competitor to the south in its curatorship. Attention has been given not only to acquiring and displaying the art, but also to making it accessible to the least practiced museum-goer.

Each collection is neatly segregated into its own portion of the museum, conveniently color-coded on the map. Helpful signs and plaques explain individual paintings and sculptures, as well as the origins and importance of entire artistic movements. For example, **European painters** such as Titian, Tintoretto, El Greco, Rubens, Poussin and

*The Market at Pontoise* by Pissarro, part of the museum's popular Impressionist collection

Velasquez are arranged together in a single gallery (designed in the style of a European palace) by period, rather than by country, because their influences crossed national, rather than chronological, boundaries. This collection of European paintings, called the Koch Gallery, is on the second floor of the Evans Wing.

If the MFA has one area of particular strength, it is the second-floor **Asian collection,** especially Buddhist temple art. In the late 19th century, Bostonians Ernest Fenollosa and William Sturgis Bigelow and their Japanese colleague Okakura Kakuzo "rescued" thousands of pieces dating from the 12th century from Japanese and Chinese temples that had become impoverished through lack of local government support. They brought entire temples, piece by piece, to the United States and re-created them for American audiences.

An entire second-floor gallery is devoted to animals in Japanese art, which includes two hand-scroll paintings by Onishi Chimen (both entitled *One Hundred Turtles*) showing these reptiles walking, talking, dancing, singing, smoking and doing 95 other things.

By far the most popular portion of the museum, however, is the second-floor gallery devoted to the **Impressionist painters** of the 19th century: Renoir, Cezanne, Degas, Monet and Pissarro. Postimpressionists like Van Gogh and Gauguin make an appearance, too. Students from any of a dozen nearby colleges congregate in front of Renoir's *Dance at Bougival* as part of their introduction to modern art. They compete for space with out-of-towners and folks from the neighborhood who can come by anytime.

This wouldn't be Boston without a serious collection of 18th-century **American art,** and the MFA's Evans Wing gallery is prodigious. Of particular note are Gilbert Stuart's

1796 portraits of George Washington and Martha Washington. Similar portraits (commissioned at the same time) hang in the National Gallery in Washington, D.C. The single most recognizable painting is probably John Singleton Copley's portrait of Paul Revere (1768). It was unique in colonial American painting in that it shows Revere, in plain white shirt and open waistcoat, as a craftsman at work, rather than in a formal portrait pose. Later artists are represented as well, including John Singer Sargent (notably *The Daughters of Edward Darley Boit*, 1882), Georgia O'Keeffe, Winslow Homer (his 1874 *Boys in a Pasture* hangs here) and Childe Hassam (whose 1885–86 *Boston Common at Twilight* is a favorite).

Kids may be bored in most of the museum, but they might like the scale models of 6th-century Egyptian pyramids and the exhibit on Egyptian funerary arts, better known as mummies. This gallery is on the first floor near the Huntington Avenue entrance.

Throughout the museum are chairs or benches marked "Please Be Seated." Far from ignoring tired tourists, the museum encourages visitors to sit on these art/furniture combinations. Some of the seats are in keeping with the style of the surrounding art, some are simply interesting to look at, and some are just a comfortable place to take a load off.

The museum's growing collection necessitated an expansion of its quarters in 1981. I.M. Pei answered the call, designing the 80,000-square-foot granite and glass West Wing, which contains the main entrance, the gift shop and an auditorium. In 1999, the museum commissioned English architect Sir Norman Foster to oversee yet another renovation and expansion. A site plan is anticipated for early 2000, and construction is expected to last several years.

### TAKING A BREAK

The dining options within the museum are all good and priced to any budget. Least expensive is the serve-yourself **Courtyard Café**, which has a good salad bar and views of the sculpture in the Calderwood Courtyard. The **Fine Arts Restaurant** is the most elegant and costly.

**⊞** 200 C1 **✉** 465 Huntington Avenue **☎** (617) 267-9300; web: www.mfa.org **🕐** Mon.–Tue. 10–4:45, Wed. 10–9:45, Thu.–Fri. 10–5 (also West Wing only, Thu.–Fri. 5–9:45), Sat.–Sun. 10–5:45 **🚇** Green Line E train to Museum (of Fine Arts), or Orange Line to Ruggles **🚌** 39 stops in front of museum **💲** Expensive. Reduced-price entry for senior citizens and students. Children moderate on schooldays up to 3 p.m., otherwise free for children under 18. After 4 p.m. Wed, donations

Renoir's *Dance at Bougival* may be the single most recognized painting in the museum

---

## MUSEUM OF FINE ARTS: INSIDE INFO

**Top tips** Admission is reduced after 5 p.m. on Thursdays and Fridays, when only the West Wing, home to most of the museum's traveling exhibitions, is open. None of the collections highlighted above are in the West Wing.
• The Huntington Avenue entrance is almost always less crowded than the main entrance. Start your visit there, and you won't wait so long in line.

**Ones not to miss** Don't leave the museum without seeing Renoir's *Dance at Bougival* (on the second floor, in the Impressionism Gallery), John Singleton Copley's portrait of Paul Revere (on the first floor in the colonial portrait gallery), or Childe Hassam's *Boston Common at Twilight* (on the first floor of the Evans Wing).

# Museum of Science

This top-flight museum makes science not only palatable but fun for kids, science-phobes and even jaded adults. There are so many interactive displays that require you to pull, push, press, open, close, shift, slide, buzz, bang, hit or climb, it's practically a theme park.

You can crawl into a replica of an Apollo command module and pretend you're blasting off to the moon. You can compare the size of a 100-foot-long blue whale with the relatively puny 12-foot-tall African elephant, mark the passage of time by counting the rings on a 2,000-year-old giant sequoia stump or watch a visible music exhibit translate popular songs into intricate light patterns. Or you can simply see proof of the earth's rotation in the form of a Foucault pendulum, which seems to rotate imperceptibly but actually swings in an unchanging direction as the earth rotates.

The museum is divided into three wings, the Red, the Green and the Blue. The museum is small enough for it not to matter which one you choose first; you can always go back and do the other two wings later. Just follow your nose to what interests you. Or better yet, follow an enthusiastic child.

The most curious, and popular, exhibit is the Archimedean Excogitation, a 10-foot-high Rube Goldberg device that carries billiard balls up, down, in and around wire cages, over a stepped xylophone, through windmills, and back up again. The effect is mesmerizing, especially to young eyes.

**Below: The Archimedean Excogitation captivates young visitors**

Youngsters will also like the natural history dioramas and realistic taxidermy animals in the Green Wing, while older brothers and sisters will gravitate toward a series of exhibits called "The Observatory" that show how your eyes can deceive your other senses.

At some point during your visit, make sure to catch a showing at the oversized Mugar Omni IMAX Theater. The features here are shown on a concave planetarium-size screen that puts you right into the middle of the action, be it a climb up Mount Everest, a voyage under the sea or a trip through New York City. Features change periodically, but with two different films shown each day, there's usually something exciting for everybody.

**Below: The museum's exhibits explain science in an accessible way**

Even the projection booth for the Omni theater is worth a look. It is encased within glass, rather than tucked away at the back of the theater, so you can see each frame peel away from the gigantic (3-foot-diameter) reels. When you leave the theater, you descend the curious Soundstair, which uses photo-electric sensors to play a different note each time a person steps on each stair. It can produce up to four sounds simultaneously, quite simply making music out of motion.

➕ 198 B4
✉ Science Park
☎ (617) 723-2500; web: www.mos.org
🕐 Museum: daily 9–7 (also Fri. 7–9 p.m.), Ju.l 5–Labor Day; 9–5 (also Fri. 5–9), day after Labor Day.–Jul. 4. Omni Theater and Planetarium: usually open until 9 or 10 most nights
🚇 Green Line to Science Park
🎟 Museum: moderate. Omni Theater, the Planetarium and the Laser Light Show: moderate. Combination tickets that let you enter the museum and one or more shows are sold at a discount

### TAKING A BREAK

Worth a visit just for the stunning view of the Charles River and Boston's skyline, the **museum's café** (tel: 617/732-2500) is convenient and well priced.

## MUSEUM OF SCIENCE: INSIDE INFO

**Top tip** Omni Theater shows often sell out, so make sure you ask for admission to the museum and a show (or two, if you have time) when you enter. Show up at the theater at least 20 minutes before show time to get the best seats.

**Hidden gem** On Tuesday and Wednesday nights the Omni offers special discounts. Come on either of those two nights for a feature that starts at 7 p.m. or later (the last showing can be as late as 9 p.m.) and get reduced-price admission. The museum is closed at this time, but if all you want to see is the show, these are the nights to do it. Omni Theater tickets are also available any time by calling 333-FILM, though there is a surcharge for the service.

# Harvard

Just across the Charles River from Boston is the city of Cambridge, home to Harvard University. Founded in 1636, it is the nation's oldest institution of higher education, and, if you ask a Harvard graduate, also its finest.

## Harvard University

Start your visit in Harvard Yard by the **statue of John Harvard**, in front of University Hall. Known as the "Statue of Three Lies," it wrongly lists 1638 as the date of the university's founding. It also incorrectly identifies John Harvard as the college's founder (he was merely a major benefactor), and although the statue purports to be John Harvard, no record of his likeness existed when it was commissioned in 1884, and undergraduate Samuel Leverett won a contest to model for the statue. Rubbing John Harvard's left foot will supposedly bring good luck – notice how it's a lot more polished than the right one.

Above: Touching the left foot of John Harvard's statue is thought to bring good luck

Below: Harvard University's Widener Memorial Library

Follow John Harvard's gaze across the Yard and you'll see **Massachusetts Hall**, the oldest building at the university, dating to 1720. During the Revolutionary War, it housed colonial soldiers. Today it is home to the offices of the university's president.

The remaining buildings on this quadrangle, all in keeping with Mass Hall's red-brick Georgian style, are dormitories housing most of Harvard's freshmen during their first year here. The general public is not allowed inside any of the buildings in the Yard, but if you visit during the school year, you can sometimes peer into first-floor windows and see what a freshman dorm room looks like. In all, five U.S. Presidents received their graduate educations here: the two Adamses, the two Roosevelts and John F. Kennedy.

**Harvard is in Cambridge, just across the Charles River from Boston**

Behind University Hall is a second quadrangle, known as **Tercentenary Theater** because that's where Harvard held its 300th anniversary celebration in 1936. Every June, the university's several thousand graduating students, their parents and all the graduate schools crowd into this space for Harvard's annual commencement ceremonies.

The imposing building with the commanding stairway in front is **Widener Memorial Library**, named for Harry Elkins Widener, a 1907 graduate who perished when the SS *Titanic* sank because he was unable to swim 300 feet in freezing water to a waiting lifeboat. According to undergraduate legend, as a condition of Widener's mother's bequest, she insisted that Harvard require every student to pass a swimming test before graduation.

Outside the confines of Harvard Yard, the architecture becomes more diverse, and visitors are free to have a look around inside as well as out. Some say José Lluis Sert's Science Center, across Cambridge Street at the north end of the Yard is designed to look like a Polaroid camera. The Carpenter Center for the Visual Arts, west of the Yard across Quincy Street, is the only building in North America designed by the French architect Le Corbusier (Charles-Edouard Jeanneret).

Harvard also has several museums worth investigating. The **Fogg Art Museum** (32 Quincy Street) focuses on paintings and sculptures of Europe from the 17th, 18th and 19th centuries. The adjacent **Busch-Reisinger Museum** has one of the best collections of works by artists of the early 20th-century German Expressionist school, including Vasili Kandinsky and Paul Klee. The **Botanical Museum** (within the Harvard Museum of Natural History, 26 Oxford Street) is home to the renowned Glass Flowers exhibit, a collection of more than 3,000 replicas of some 800 different species of plants. They actually look like flowers, and you'd never know they were breakable.

## Harvard Square

No visit to Cambridge would be complete without an hour or two spent wandering through Harvard's namesake neighborhood. Harvard Square is not just a crossroads for undergraduates. Everybody comes here, whether it's the guys playing speed chess for money in front of Au Bon Pain, the street performers in front of the Coop, the skateboarders who do tricks on the stairs in front of Out of Town News, or the young professionals in town for dinner and a movie at the art house theater. The

Challenge the master: speed chess at Au Bon Pain

square teems with life at all times of day and, in good weather, all through the night as well. Recently, chain stores have elbowed out many of the family-run establishments that give Harvard Square its character but the vibrant pulse that comes with 6,000 bright, idealistic undergraduates remains.

### TAKING A BREAK

**Mr. and Mrs. Bartley's Burger Cottage** (1360 Massachusetts Avenue, tel: 617/354-6559), noisy, fun and full of students, is a classic among burger joints. At **Herrell's Ice Cream** (15 Dunster Street, tel: 617/497-2179), just around the corner from the Harvard T-stop, the ice cream is made on the spot, whether it's caramel almond swirl or plain vanilla.

### Events and Information Center
✚ 200 B4 ✉ Harvard Square, Cambridge, MA 02138 ☎ (617) 495-1573 (events and information); web: www.harvard.edu 🚇 Red Line to Harvard Square

### Harvard University Art Museums (includes the Fogg, Busch-Reisinger and Arthur M. Sackler museums)
✚ 200 C5 ☎ (610) 495-9400; web: www.artmuseums.harvard.edu 🕐 Mon.–Sat. 10–5, Sun. 1–5 💲 Inexpensive (ticket is valid for all three museums)

### Botanical Museum
✚ 200 C5 ✉ 26 Oxford Street ☎ (617) 495-3045; web: www.hmnh.harvard.edu. 🕐 Mon.–Sat. 9–5, Sun. 1–5 💲 Inexpensive. Free on Sat mornings

---

## HARVARD: INSIDE INFO

**Top tip** The Harvard art museums offer **free admission** on Saturdays from 10 to noon. The Botanical Museum is free from 9 to noon on Saturday.

**One to miss** Free student-led tours leave periodically from Holyoke Center (tel: 617/495-1573), but they won't tell you a lot more than any guidebook. Instead, pick up a map and a self-guiding walking tour at the Harvard Events and Information Center and go at your own pace.

# At Your Leisure

## 1 John F. Kennedy Library and Museum

I.M. Pei, who masterminded the controversial glass pyramid outside the Louvre in Paris, designed this glass and concrete structure, and J.F.K. himself narrates the moving film that serves as the introduction to the short tenure of America's 35th President. Exhibits cover Kennedy's entire life, from the sailboat he navigated as a boy to the programs he initiated when in office.

The end of the self-guiding tour brings you to a dark room where news reports of Kennedy's assassination play in an unending loop, and to a glass pavilion, housing simply a bench, an American flag and quotes from John F. Kennedy.

🕇 Off map 199 D1
✉ Columbia Point, Dorchester
☎ (617) 929-4523; web:
www.cs.umb.edu/jfklibrary/main.html
🕐 Daily 9–5 (also Wed. 5–8 in summer) 🚇 Red Line to JFK/UMass, then the free shuttle (every 20 minutes)
💵 Moderate. Discounts for seniors, students and children 13–17; children under 13 free

## 2 Children's Museum

The giant 40-foot-high milk bottle out front lets you know that this museum is kids-oriented in every way, with touching encouraged (if not required). Joining in the fun is an inevitable part of every visit.

Children can play on the Giant's Desktop, peer Under the Dock at sea creatures living in Boston's waters, climb the oversize two-story-high maze, try on old clothes from Grandparents' House, race golf balls along curving tracks, or just wander around the Hall of Toys. The most popular exhibit is TV & Me, where kids (and adults who aren't too sheepish) can see themselves on television. There are also exhibits replicating life in a Native American kitchen, a Japanese train and a Latin American market.

🕇 199 F1 ✉ 300 Congress Street
☎ (617) 426-8855; web:
www.bostonkids.org 🕐 Sat.–Thu. 10–5 (also Fri. 5–9) 💵 Moderate. Reduced price admission Fri. 5–9 🚇 Red Line to South Station

## 3 Boston Tea Party Ship and Museum

Here you can revisit the events of December 16, 1773, when a band of patriots protesting against King George III's tax on tea, snuck on board a merchant ship disguised as American Indians and dumped all the tea into Boston Harbor. The event, known as the Boston Tea Party, marked a watershed in the settlers' relations with England. The brig *Beaver II* is a full-size working replica of one of those merchant ships, and anyone can come aboard and dump a bale of tea into the harbor. Afterward, you can tour the restored galley, captain's quarters and cargo hold.

🕇 199 E1 ✉ Congress Street Bridge
☎ (617) 338-1773; web: www.
historictours.com/boston/teaparty.htm
🕐 Tours: daily 9–6, Jun.–Aug.; 9–5, Mar.–May and Sep.–Nov. 🚇 Red Line to South Station 💵 Moderate. Half price for children aged 4 to 12; children under 4 free

**Boston Tea Party Ship & Museum**
3 2
**Children's Museum**

SOUTH BOSTON

OLD COLONY AVENUE

*Columbus Park*

**John F Kennedy Library & Museum**
1

# ⑤ Boston Common and the Public Garden

On a warm summer day, a crisp fall morning or even a bright but cool

The ever-popular swan boats in the Public Garden, an unmistakable sign of spring

winter afternoon, there is no better place to walk than Boston Common: Bostonians from John Adams to John Kennedy have strolled this oasis of city-center greenery. There are scores of places for picnicking, sunbathing or daydreaming. There was a time when Boston's upper crust succeeded in closing the Common to the public, creating a private playground for the wealthy. But today it is inviting to all. Kids will love to splash in the Frog Pond in summer, or ice skate on it in winter.

The adjacent Public Garden, across Charles Street, may be even prettier than the Common. The season to be here is late spring, when the beautifully manicured gardens start to bloom and the famous swan boat rides begin operating. The boats, which really look like swans and move at the same sedate pace, are incredibly popular and you may have to wait in line around 30 minutes for a ride.

🚇 198 C2 ✉ Bounded by Charles, Beacon, Boylston, Tremont and Park streets. (Public Garden bounded by Charles, Beacon, Boylston and Arlington streets) ⊙ Swan boats: daily 10–5, Jun. 21–Labor Day; 10–4, Apr. 1–Jun. 20; Mon.–Fri. noon–4, Sat.–Sun. 10–4,

Labor Day to mid-Sep. 🚇 Red Line to Park Street or Green Line to Park Street, Boylston or Arlington. The Arlington stop is closest to the swan boats 💵 Inexpensive

# ⑥ Prudential Center

Until the Sears Building in Chicago was built, Boston's Prudential Center laid claim to being the tallest building in the continental United States (the taller Empire State Building being on Manhattan Island technically isn't part of the continental U.S. and wasn't counted).

The top of the Prudential Center is one of the best places from which to see the city

Although the Pru's boast about its size is mostly hot air, the 360-degree view from the 50th-floor Skywalk is nothing to sneeze at. On a clear day, you can get a bird's-eye view of the entire city, not to mention Cape Cod and southern New Hampshire. For the best views, arrive about an hour before dusk, visit Skywalk for about half an hour, then go upstairs for a drink at Top of the Hub (▶ 69).

In the Pru's ground floor there is an upscale shopping mall, with a Saks Fifth Avenue, Lord and Taylor, and many other stores.

🚇 201 E2 ✉ 800 Boylston Street ☎ (617) 236-3318;

web: www.prudentialcenter.com 🌐
Skywalk: 10–10. Stores: Mon.–Sat.
10–8, Sun. 11–6. Restaurants stay open
later than the shops 🚇 Green Line B,
C or D train to Hynes/ICA or Green
Line E train to Prudential
🎟 Skywalk: inexpensive

Whistler and John Singer Sargent
(whose portrait of Gardner hangs
here), as well as
Impressionists
like Degas, Manet and
Matisse.

As you walk through the
museum, you realize that this was a
private home, and that one person
amassed these rare treasures and
actually lived amid them. The
arrangement of the art remains as it
was when Mrs. Gardner lived here
(her will forbids changing anything).
Sometimes it is hard to say which is
more astounding, the house itself or
the collection within it. The manicured formal garden in the central
courtyard is itself a work of art. On
winter days, this bounty of flora is a
reminder of lazier summer days gone

### 8 Isabella Stewart Gardner Museum

This museum owes its appeal almost
entirely to its namesake, Isabella
Stewart Gardner (1840–1924). She
designed her home in the style of a
Venetian palazzo, then filled it with
2,500 European and American paintings and sculptures. Her taste ran to
Rembrandt, Titian (*The Rape of
Europa*), Botticelli (*Madonna and
Child of the Eucharist*), Raphael (he
merits an entire room) and Giotto.
She also displayed the work of
personal friends like James McNeil

**The plant-filled central courtyard at the
Isabella Stewart Gardner Museum**

### For Kids

Children can quickly get bored at
museums, but Boston has two that
will appeal. The **Museum of Science**
(▶ 52–53) and the **Children's
Museum** (above, ▶ 57) have
interactive exhibits that practically
beg to be touched, pushed, pulled or
climbed on.

A **swan boat** ride through the
lagoon in the Public Garden
(▶ 58) makes a welcome break from
sightseeing and will appeal to kids of
all ages.

CAMBRIDGE ST
BEACON HILL
Charles River
BEACON ST
BACK BAY
BOYLSTON ST
COLUMBUS AVE
CHINA TOWN
Prudential Center
BROOKLINE
BROOKLINE AVE
Fenway Park
Museum of Fine Arts
Isabella Stewart Gardner Museum
Boston Common & Public Garden
**5** **4** The Freedom Trail
**3** **2**
**9**
**6**
**7**
**8**

## Neighborhoods Tailor-Made for Strolling

- The red-brick and black-shuttered colonial town houses of **Beacon Hill** are quintessentially blue-blood Boston (➤ 174–177).
- **Newbury Street** is Boston's most fashionable shopping street. Its boutiques, stores, galleries and trendy restaurants are teeming with beautiful people and yuppies at all times, but especially on sunny Saturdays.
- **The South End** is the hippest area in town. You can see interior renovations going on from the windows along Tremont Street, which is now lined with bistros specializing in brunch and late suppers.
- Wander along some of the quieter backstreets of the **North End**, Boston's Italian-American district, around sunset and scout out the perfect restaurant for dinner.

by. On weekends from September to April, the museum hosts concerts.

✚ 200 B1 ✉ 280 The Fenway
☎ (617) 566-1401; concert tickets (617) 734-1359; web: www.boston. com. gardner ⏰ Tue.–Sun. 11–5 🚇 Green Line E train to Museum or Orange Line to Ruggles 🚌 39 💳 Moderate. Children under 18 free. Concert tickets $15 (reduced rates for seniors and children), includes admission.

### 9 Fenway Park

Built in 1912, Fenway Park is the oldest baseball field in the major

**Characteristic Back Bay brownstones on Commonwealth Avenue**

leagues and one of only a few neighborhood ballparks remaining. It was carved into a square city block and, due to space limitations, the distance from home plate to the left field wall was too short for a legitimate home run. So a 37-foot wall, known locally as the Green Monster, was added to make roundtrippers more difficult.

The Red Sox play home games here between April and September and tickets are hard to get only when the team is playing particularly well. Fenway's tiny capacity means that there are no bad seats. Every seat is right on top of the field.

Fenway will probably go the way of 25-cent haircuts some time in the not too distant future. There are plans to build a new ballpark a few blocks away, though the proposed site is still occupied by thriving stores and private residences. No date has been set for ground breaking, but it will probably happen before the end of the next decade.

✚ 200 B2 ✉ Lansdowne Street and Yawkey Way ☎ Ticket office: (617) 267-1700. Tours: (617) 236-6666
🚇 Green Line to Kenmore 💳 Moderate for standing room, expensive for the best seats. To purchase tickets by mail, write to Boston Red Sox Ticket Office, 4 Yawkey Way, Boston, MA. 02215-3496. To order tickets by phone, call (617) 482-4SOX. On the Internet, go to www.Redsox.com

# Farther Afield

## 12 Lexington and Concord

Both Lexington and Concord claim to be the birthplace of the American Revolution, but it was in Concord that the first shot was fired. On April 19, 1775, American militiamen massed at the Old North Bridge and launched a volley into British troops who had been sent to destroy a cache of weapons in the town of Concord. On that day, the resistance officially became a revolution.

Today, both Lexington and Concord are prosperous Boston suburbs, with pockets of history sprinkled amid the modern drugstores, restaurants and other signs of

Concord's historic Old North Bridge, where the first shots of the Revolution were fired

21st-century life. You can walk between most of the major attractions, especially in Concord. The Battle of Lexington and Concord is reenacted each year on Patriots' Day (April 19), but you can visit Old North Bridge any time.

The best place to soak up the colonial flavor is at the well-maintained **Minute Man National Historical Park**. The 900-acre park ranges over Lexington, Concord and the neighboring town of Lincoln. Begin your visit at the **North Bridge Visitor Center**, which will give you

an overview of the events of that fateful day. From there, you can walk across the Old North Bridge and follow the Battle Road Trail by foot or bicycle, all the way to Lexington, so retracing 5.5 miles of the route taken by the defeated British troops back to Boston.

Concord's second heyday came nearly 100 years later, when authors Henry David Thoreau, Ralph Waldo Emerson, Nathaniel Hawthorne and Bronson Alcott made it the center of their Transcendentalist movement. Houses belonging to each of them are open for touring. The most popular with any girl over the age of eight is **Orchard House**, where Louisa May Alcott grew up and upon which she based her best-selling novel *Little Women*.

South of Concord lies **Walden Pond**, where Thoreau went in 1845 in search of serenity. There is still natural beauty here (the park, the hiking trails and Thoreau's cabin have all been preserved), but the kind of solitude Thoreau experienced is a thing of the past. Get here early on sunny summer or fall days, as the place fills up quickly.

**North Bridge Visitor Center**
✠ 205 D1 ✉ 174 Liberty Street, Concord ☎ (978) 369-6993; web: www.nps.govmima ⓘ Daily 9–4

**Orchard House**
✠ 205 D1 ✉ 399 Lexington Road
☎ (978) 369-4118 ⓘ Mon.–Sat.10–4:30, Sun. 1–4:30, Apr.–Oct.; Mon.–Fri. 11–3, Sat. 10–4:30, Sun. 1–4:30, Nov.–Mar; closed Jan. 1–Jan. 15

**Walden Pond**
✠ 205 D1 ✉ on Route 126
☎ (978) 369-3254

## 🔞 Salem

Salem, less than 20 miles from Boston, is considered a day trip, but you might be tempted to spend the night because there is so much to do.

Salem's deep harbor made it a major colonial port and shipping center but it was the events of 1692 that gave Salem its place in American history: the infamous Salem witch trials resulted in the execution of 19 men and women.

Today, the city makes the most of its intolerant past, with several attractions revisiting some aspect of 17th-century life in Salem.

The best of the bunch is the **Salem Witch Museum.** The life-size audio-visual display gives a comprehensive account of the hysteria that engulfed the town during the late 17th century, including a re-creation of a man being stoned to death.

For a more interactive experience, be sure to catch a performance of **Cry Innocent,** a live reenactment of the witch trial of Bridget Bishop, in which you play the grand jury.

As Salem was an important colonial port, it boasts a museum with a much grander collection than you would expect from a city of this size. The **Peabody Essex Museum** grew out of a society of sea captains who

pledged to bring back items of interest – some might say loot – from their voyages around Cape Horn and the Cape of Good Hope. Today, the museum's holdings number more than a million treasures from around the world, and its Phillips Library houses the original court papers from the witch trials.

Finally, there is the **House of the Seven Gables,** which Salem native Nathaniel Hawthorne made famous in his book of the same name. It still has all seven gables, and is open for tours year round. The author's birthplace, originally on Union Street, has been moved here so that fans can do all their sightseeing in one place.

The best place to begin a visit to Salem is the **National Park Service Visitor Center** at 2 New Liberty Street, or call the Salem Office of Tourism (tel: 978/744-3663).

### Salem Witch Museum
➕ 205 E1 ✉ 19 ½ Washington Square
☎ (978) 744-1692; web: www.salemwitchmuseum.com 🕙 daily 10–5 (also 5–7 p.m., Jul.–Aug.)

### Cry Innocent
➕ 205 E1 ✉ Old Town Hall, Derby Square
☎ (978) 927-2300 ext. 4747 🕙 Fri.–Tue. 11:30, 1:30 and 3:30 seasonal

### Peabody Essex Museum
➕ 205 E1
✉ East India Square
☎ (800) 745-4054; web: www.pem.org
🕙 Mon.–Sat. 10–5, Sun. noon–5

### House of the Seven Gables
➕ 205 E1
✉ 54 Turner Street
☎ (978)744-0991; web: www.7gables.org
🕙 daily 10–5:30

## 🔢 Marblehead

The self-proclaimed Yachting Capital of America, Marblehead attracts sailing enthusiasts from around the world, especially in July for Race Week. But the town offers much more than its famed harbor. Visitors can wander around the old town and see its 17th- and 18th-century houses (each of which has a plaque

**The House of the Seven Gables was made famous by author Nathaniel Hawthorne**

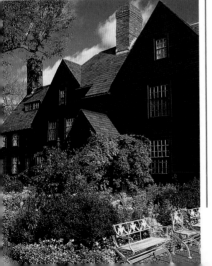

Gloucester was America's first seaport and fishing is still vital to the town's prosperity

identifying the original owner, builder and date of construction), shop in the quirky stores and dine in restaurants overlooking the water.

The best spots for a picnic (whether or not there's a sailboat race going on) are Fort Sewall, at the far eastern end of Front Street, and Crocker Park, at the western end. A walk from one to the other, even if you stop at every store along the way, won't take more than an hour. Note that most of Marblehead closes up shop shortly after the summer tourists stop coming in September.

**Marblehead Chamber of Commerce**
➕ 205 E1
✉ 62 Pleasant Street
☎ (781) 631-2868

### 🔟 Gloucester

Gloucester was America's first seaport, and the big "Man at the Wheel" fisherman statue in the middle of Stacy Boulevard should tip you off that the sea is still vital to the town's importance. Besides having a thriving fishing industry and a good number of excellent seafood restaurants, Gloucester is home to the bustling **Rocky Neck Art Colony,** which claims to be the oldest ongoing art colony in America. Winslow Homer, Fitz Hugh Lane and Milton Avery are just a few who found inspiration here in the past; more than two dozen artists have studios here today, many of which open their doors to the visiting public.

Gloucester is the central town on the Cape Ann peninsula, and it has the best beaches. When Bostonians go to the beach for the day, they often go here. **Wingaersheek Beach,** on the north side of town, is popular with families because of its gentle bayside waves. **Good Harbor Beach,** on the eastern side of town, fronts the Atlantic. **Cape Ann Chamber of Commerce** has information about all the towns on the peninsula.

**Gloucester Tourism Commission**
➕ 205 E1
✉ Stage Fort Park, where Routes 127 and 133 intersect
☎ (800) 649-6839

**Cape Ann Chamber of Commerce**
➕ 205 E1
✉ 33 Commercial Street, Gloucester
☎ (800) 321-0133; web: www.capeann.com/cacc

The "Man at the Wheel" statue in Gloucester honors those who lost their lives at sea

THEY THAT GO
DOWN TO THE SEA
IN SHIPS
1623 — 1923

## 16 Plymouth

On December 21, 1620, a group of 102 pilgrims landed here, becoming the first permanent settlers in what was to become the 13 colonies. It wasn't their intended destination, nor was it their first landing (a lack of fresh water uprooted them from Provincetown, where they had stopped for about five weeks), and although the conditions at Plymouth proved less than hospitable, enough Pilgrims survived, with the help of the friendly Wampanoag Indians, to celebrate the first Thanksgiving.

The logical place to start a visit is **Plymouth Rock** itself, on the beach at Water Street. The columned granite shelter that surrounds the rock was designed by the architectural firm of McKim, Mead and White in 1920. At first sight it may not look like much, but there are some good historical displays here.

To see how the earliest settlers lived, visit **Plimoth Plantation,** a re-creation of the village as it was in 1627, right down to the dirt roads. Actors play the roles of 17th-century villagers, baking bread, planting

**Right:** At Plimoth Plantation, the life of the early settlers is re-created

**Below:** *Mayflower II*, a replica of the ship used by the first Pilgrims, was built in England and retraced the original voyage

corn, mending fences, splitting wood and shearing sheep, but never breaking character. Even Governor William Bradford is on hand. A Wampanoag Indian homesite is also on the premises.

The Plantation also runs the *Mayflower II*, a full-size replica of the ship that carried the Pilgrims across the Atlantic. Located at State Pier, about a block away from Plymouth Rock, it is shockingly small – just over 100 feet long, or approximately one foot of length for each passenger. Like the Plantation, it is staffed by

costumed guides. *Mayflower II* sailed from England on April 20, 1957, re-creating the Pilgrims' voyage. The journey shaved nearly two weeks off the 66 days it took the original *Mayflower* to make the crossing.

### Plimoth Plantation
✛ 206 D2 ⊠ Exit 4 on Route 3
☎ (508) 746-1622; web: www.plimoth.org
🕐 Daily 9–5, Apr.–Nov.

### Mayflower II
✛ 206 D2
⊠ Plimoth Plantation, MA 02362
☎ (508) 746-1622; web: www.plimoth.org
🕐 Daily 9–5, Apr.–Nov.
🎫 Combined admission to ship and Plimoth Plantation: expensive

# Where to... Stay

## Prices
Expect to pay for two people sharing a double room, excluding taxes
$ under $150  $$ $150–250  $$$ over $250

### ◆◆◆ Boston Harbor Hotel $$$

The principal attraction of this large modern hotel (part of the 1980s Rowes Wharf redevelopment) is its harborside location. The interior is opulent: The lobby gleams with brass and polished wood, and the spacious bedrooms are furnished with reproduction antiques. The service here is impeccable. It might be expensive but it is well worth it. The Logan Airport water shuttle docks here.

✚ 199 F2  ⊠ 70 Rowes Wharf,
Boston, MA 02110  ☎ (617) 439-7000
or (800) 752-7077; fax: (617) 330 9450;
web: www.bhh.com  Ⓣ Aquarium

### ◆◆◆ Boston Marriott Long Wharf Hotel $$$

This enormous red-brick hotel juts out into the water next to the New England Aquarium. Most rooms are large and comfortable; all have angled views of the water. The vaulted lobby, noted for its Rufus Porter fresco, is much used for informal business meetings. At the weekends, the atmosphere changes as families take advantage of the attractive rates. Facilities include a swimming pool and spa.

✚ 199 E3  ⊠ 296 State Street,
Boston, MA 02109  ☎ (617) 227-0800,
(800) 228-9290; fax: (617) 221-2867;
web: www.marriott.com  Ⓣ Aquarium

### Copley Inn $

In a residential neighborhood near bustling Copley Square, with the T stop, tourist trolley and restaurants just minutes away, this four-story town house offers great value for money. The large, attractive rooms are traditionally furnished and are equipped with mini-kitchens and a dining table, so you don't have to eat out for every meal. Children under 12 stay free. Rooms are nonsmoking.

✚ 201 F2  ⊠ 19 Garrison Street,
Boston, MA 02116  ☎ (617) 236-0300
or (800) 232-0306; fax: (617) 536-0816; web: www.copleyinn.com
Ⓣ Prudential

### ◆◆ Copley Square Hotel $$

Budget-minded visitors are happy to put up with the old-fashioned atmosphere in this century-old hotel in exchange for paying a little less in a prime location. Bedrooms are comfortable, with useful touches such as ironing boards and coffeepots. Café Budapest is known

as one of the city's most romantic restaurants.

✚ 201 F3  ⊠ 47 Huntington Avenue,
Boston, MA 02116  ☎ (617) 536-9000
or (800) 225-7062; fax: (617) 236-0351;
web: www.copleysquarehotel.com
Ⓣ Copley, Back Bay

### ◆◆◆ Fairmont Copley Plaza $$–$$$

One of Boston's architectural landmarks, the Fairmont Copley Plaza epitomizes the grandiose style of the early 1900s. The lobby glitters with gold, and huge crystal chandeliers hang from its ceilings. Over the years, presidents, high society and newlyweds have stayed here. Right on Copley Square, it is within easy reach of the main sights. The Oak Room is regularly voted one of the best steak houses in town, and the Oak Bar is famous for its martinis.

✚ 201 F3  ⊠ 138 St. James Avenue,
Boston, MA 02116  ☎ (617) 267-5300
or (800) 527-4727; fax: (617) 247-6681; web: www.fairmont.com
Ⓣ Copley, Back Bay

### ♦♦♦ Newbury Guest House $

It's a delight to find such good value in the heart of the trendy Back Bay area. In this 19th-century town house, rooms are attractive and practical, rather than chic. Prints from the nearby Museum of Fine Arts brighten the walls. A Continental buffet breakfast is served and guests can sit out on the patio in summer. Two rooms are suitable for guests with disabilities.

✚ **201 E3** ⊠ **261 Newbury Street, Boston, MA 02116** ☎ **(617) 437-7666 or (800) 437-7668; fax: (617) 262-4243; web: www.hagopianhotels.com** Ⓜ **Hynes/ICA, Copley**

### Omni Parker House $$

The Omni boasts of being America's oldest hotel and the one-time employer of Malcolm X and Ho Chi Minh, both of whom worked as waiters. The huge hotel in the heart of downtown underwent an expensive renovation in 1998, but the restored splendor of the lobby is not matched by the rather small

rooms. It's historic, well-known and handy for the business district, but be prepared for a somewhat proper atmosphere.

✚ **199 D2** ⊠ **60 School Street, Boston, MA 02108** ☎ **(617) 227-8600 or (800) 843-6664; fax: (617) 742-5729; web: www.omnihotels.com** Ⓜ **Park Street, Government Center**

### ♦♦♦ Ritz-Carlton $$$

Since it opened in 1927, the Ritz-Carlton, overlooking the Public Gardens, has been one of Boston's most famous hotels. Discretion and luxury are bywords here. Though some rooms are quite small, all are very comfortable. Prices are high, but this is a special occasion place: nowhere is more formal than the dining room or exclusive than the Ritz Bar, and nothing more romantic than the summer dinner-dances at the Ritz Roof restaurant.

✚ **198 A2** ⊠ **15 Arlington Street, Boston, MA 02117** ☎ **(617) 536-5700 or (800) 241-3333; fax: (617) 536-9340; web: www.ritzcarlton.com** Ⓜ **Arlington**

### ♦♦♦ Seaport Hotel $-$$

Across from the World Trade Center, this large hotel is just a 4-minute ride from the Logan Airport. Rooms are modern and comfortable without being glamorous, and have practical extras such as umbrellas, plus the usual high-tech gadgetry. There is an attractive "no tipping" policy. The Aura restaurant impresses with modern New England dishes.

✚ **Off map 199 F1** ⊠ **1 Seaport Lane, Boston, MA 02210** ☎ **(617) 385-4000 or (877) SEAPORT; fax: (617) 385-4001; web: www.seaporthotel.com** Ⓜ **South Station (free shuttle Mon.–Fri.)**

## CAMBRIDGE

### ♦♦♦ A Cambridge House Bed and Breakfast $-$$

If you want somewhere small and intimate to stay, this could be the place. In the main house, bedrooms are romantic, with Japanese prints, four-poster beds and lacy bolsters.

In the Carriage House next door are four more rooms, all with fireplaces. Breakfast is an event, with specialty breads, Italian sausage and strawberry waffles.

✚ **Off map 200 C5** ⊠ **2218 Massachusetts Avenue, Cambridge, MA 02140** ☎ **(617) 491-6300 or (800) 232-9989; fax: (617) 868-2848; web: www.acambridgehouse.com** Ⓜ **Davis Square**

### ♦♦♦ Charles Hotel in Harvard Square $$-$$$

The attractive rooms in this modern luxury hotel, a 5-minute walk from Harvard University, are decorated in Shaker style with plain furniture and bold patchwork quilts. Guests can use the fitness club, listen to jazz in the Regattabar, or try the Rialto restaurant, one of Boston's best. Recommended for business guests as well as families.

✚ **Off map 200 C5** ⊠ **1 Bennett Street, Cambridge, MA 02138** ☎ **(617) 864-1200; fax: (617) 864-5715; web: www.charleshotel.com** Ⓜ **Harvard**

# Where to...
## Eat and Drink

**Prices**
Expect to pay per person for a three-course meal, excluding drinks and service
**$** under $15   **$$** $15–30   **$$$** over $30

### Antico Forno $$

Fans of this simple trattoria in the Italian North End come for the uncomplicated home-style dishes. Try *ribollita*, a traditional Tuscan bread soup, or *arrosto di agnello*, a sandwich of roast lamb with onions and peppers. Pizzas are cooked in the wood-fired brick oven, as is the more unusual *sarta di riso*, Neapolitan rice with meatballs and peas. The decor is rustic, with wooden tables and a tiled floor.

➕ 199 E4 ✉ 93 Salem Street
☎ (617) 723-6733 🕐 Daily 11:30–10 (also Fri.–Sat. 10–10:30 p.m.) 🚇 Haymarket

### Barking Crab $

Near the Children's Museum, this informal restaurant is part tent, part clam shack. Expect plastic cups and paper plates on tables, and lobster pots and nets for decoration. The specialty is seafood – a board advertises the daily menus, plus a fish of the day and specials featuring scallops, clams or mussels. Try the lobster salad or the fish and chips, with cod and thick-cut French fries. In summer, get a table overlooking the water.

➕ 199 F1 ✉ 88 Sleeper Street
☎ (617) 426-2722 🕐 Daily 11:30–10 (till 9 p.m. in winter) 🚇 South Station

### ◆◆ Capital Grille $$$

This is a paradise for meat eaters: a sober, plush steak house, with dark paneling and comfortable banquettes, where you can enjoy excellent steaks. Although grilled fish such as tuna and salmon are first-class, don't buck the trend. Act like a millionaire, sip a lethal martini, order dry-aged porterhouse steak and the best wine you can afford. If you still have room, try the delicious flourless chocolate torte for dessert.

➕ 201 E3 ✉ 359 Newbury Street
☎ (617) 262-8900 🕐 Daily 5–10 (also Thu.–Sat. 10–11 p.m.). Lunch noon–2 p.m., Dec. only 🚇 Hynes/ICA

### ◆◆◆ Clio $$$

In the Eliot Suite Hotel, chef Ken Oringer creates dishes that would make New York foodies gasp. Take a starter such as roasted *foie gras* steak, which comes with spiced pineapple and a sweet-and-sour glaze. Entrees can be as simple as roast cod with figs, herb-rubbed roast chicken or rack of lamb with a curry carrot broth. Allow plenty of time to enjoy one of the city's hot spots, where prices are steep but service is attentive.

➕ 201 D3 ✉ 370A Commonwealth Avenue ☎ (617) 536-7200
🕐 Daily 5:30–10 (also Fri.–Sun. 10–10:30 p.m.) 🚇 Hynes/ICA

### ◆ Durgin-Park $$

Still Boston's most famous restaurant after an astonishing 150 years in the business, these "market dining rooms" serve traditional New England home-style cooking, with filling dishes such as molasses-rich Boston brown bread, thick chowders, pot roasts, Boston baked beans, plainly cooked seafood such as scrod, and Indian pudding. Diners share long wooden tables, which are all part of the fun.

➕ 199 D3 ✉ 340 Faneuil Hall Marketplace ☎ (617) 227-2038
🕐 Mon.–Sat. 11:30–10 (also Fri.–Sat. 10–10:30 p.m.), Sun. 11:30–9 🚇 Government Center

## Franklin Café $$

This tiny restaurant in the gentrified South End has been a hit since it opened in 1996. The no reservations rule means diners wait in line to enter the dimly lit room, where walls, tables, bench seats and carpet are all black. Chef-owner Dave Du Bois was inspired by the "little places around the corner" in Europe, but he cooks with modern American flair. A signature dish is the turkey meat loaf with a spiced fig gravy. No desserts are served. Open late, this is where chefs come after hours to unwind.

🚶 Off map 198 C1 🗺 278 Shawmut Avenue ☎ (617) 350-0010 🕓 Daily 5–2 a.m. (kitchen open 5:30–1:30 a.m.). Closed Dec. 25 🚇 Back Bay

## ◆◆ Grill 23 and Bar $$$

This establishment is best known as an upscale steak house for gray suits clinching deals. The bar is equally impressive, with bartenders shaking and stirring classic cocktails with panache. While

munching on homemade potato chips, you can sit at the bar, sipping your way through an ever-changing selection of wines by the glass.

🚶 198 A1 🗺 161 Berkeley Street ☎ (617) 542-2255 🕓 Mon.–Sat. 5:30–10:30 (also Fri. and Sat. 10:30–11 p.m.), Sun. 5:30–10 🚇 Arlington

## ◆◆ Hamersley's Bistro $$$

The food at Hamersley's Bistro is what Boston's cooking revolution is all about. Chef Gordon Hamersley may be inspired by Europe, but the menu is pure New England, using the freshest seasonal and regional ingredients. Try the clam chowder prepared with smoked bacon, vegetables, wine and cream, or the toasted carrot cake with Bourbon sauce. The ambience is less formal than a restaurant, more plush than a bistro.

🚶 Off map 201 F1 🗺 553 Tremont Street (at Clarendon Street) ☎ (617) 423-2700 🕓 Mon.–Fri. 6–10 p.m. (also Fri. 10–10:30 p.m.), Sat. 5:30–11, Sun. 5:30–9:30 🚇 Back Bay

## Hungry I $$$

It's easy to miss the steps down to the basement entrance of this popular Beacon Hill restaurant, one of the city's most romantic spots. Tables are set for two, with fresh flowers and crisp table linens. Chef-owner Peter Ballarin prepares complex dishes, and portions are generous. Desserts are unctuous; the favorite, walnut pie, is never taken off the menu.

🚶 198 B3 🗺 71½ Charles Street ☎ (617) 227-3524 🕓 Lunch: Tue.–Fri. noon–2, Sun. 11–2; dinner: daily 5:30–9 (also Fri.–Sat. 9–10 p.m.) 🚇 Charles/MGH

## ◆◆ Icarus $$$

The decor in this basement restaurant is eccentric, with huge mirrors and a circle of blue neon. The atmosphere is rather formal, prices rather expensive. During the week, executives discuss business over dinner; at weekends, couples come in from the suburbs. There is live jazz on Friday nights. The seasonal

menu uses New England ingredients. Everything is made in house, from the focaccia bread to desserts.

🚶 201 F2 🗺 3 Appleton Street ☎ (617) 426-1790 🕓 Mon.–Fri. 6–9:30 p.m. (also Fri. 9:30–10 p.m.), Sat. 5:30–10:30, Sun. 5:30–9:30 🚇 Back Bay

## ◆ Legal Sea Foods Restaurant $$

One of 19 nationwide in the Boston chain whose boast is: "If it isn't fresh, it isn't legal." The simple 30-year-old formula still works. The sawdust and bare tables of old have given way to sophisticated dining, and Cajun and Asian dishes sit alongside the New England clam chowder (served at Presidential inaugurations), casseroled seafood, bluefish with mustard sauce and Boston cream pie. Reservations are recommended.

🚶 201 F3 🗺 100 Huntington Avenue ☎ (617) 266-7775 🕓 Mon.–Sat. 11–10 (also Sat. 10–10:30 p.m.), Sun. noon–9 🚇 Copley

## Maria's Pastry Shop $

Everyone wants to try authentic Italian pastries in the North End, and they don't come more genuine than at Maria's. Choose from a vast range of cookies, traditionally eaten at *merenda* (teatime). Buy *osse di morte* at Halloween, panettone at Christmas, or Maria's own nougat-like *torrone*. Her cannoli (pastry horns) are regularly voted "Best of Boston." Only the coffee is American. There are just a few tables in this plain room, decorated with a mural of palm trees, sand and red parrots.

⊞ 199 E3 ⊠ 46 Cross Street
☏ (617) 523-1196 ⊙ Mon.–Sat. 7–6, Sun. 7–noon 🚇 Haymarket

## Pho Pasteur $

One of the popular chain of restaurants bearing the word Pho in their name that has sprung up across Boston, Pho Pasteur is a typical example of Vietnamese entrepreneur Duyen Le's simple recipe for success: good food at low prices in a no-frills setting. Close to Chinatown, you can feast here on shrimp with lemon grass, grilled pork and egg rolls, all at remarkably low prices.

⊞ 198 C1 ⊠ 682 Washington Street
☏ (617) 482-7467 ⊙ Daily 9 a.m.–10 p.m. 🚇 Chinatown

## Terramia $$$

The cooler and more elegant sister of Antico Forno (▶ 67) is run by Italian chef Mario Nocera, who according to his Italian-American wife has a voice almost as good as Pavarotti's. This is one of a handful of restaurants that draw food-lovers to the Italian North End. No desserts are served, but waiters direct you to Biscotti's Pasticceria Italiana right across the street, one of several local pastry shops that also serve coffee to complete your evening out.

⊞ 199 E4 ⊠ 98 Salem Street
☏ (617) 523-3112 ⊙ Mon.–Thu. 5–10, Fri. 5–10.30, Sat. 4–10.30, Sun. 1–10 🚇 Haymarket

## ◆◆◆Top of the Hub $$$

Fifty-two floors up, at the top of the soaring Prudential Tower, this is a dramatic and romantic place to eat. Chef Dean Moore creates innovative New England/Asian cuisine. His imagination hops from prawns and shrimp with sugarcane and soma noodles to beef tenderloin and egg rolls stuffed with potatoes and lobster. Desserts range from pineapple ice, made with fresh and dried fruit, to warm chocolate cake. Sunday brunch is particularly popular; reservations essential.

⊞ 201 E2 ⊠ 800 Boylston Street
☏ (617) 536-1775 ⊙ Mon.–Fri. 11:30–2, 5.30–10 (also Fri. 10–11 p.m.), Sat. 11:30–2, 5–11, Sun. 11–2.30, 5–10 🚇 Prudential

## Bars

## Boston Beer Works $

Just a fast pitch away from Fenway Park, this brewpub is filled with jubilation when the erratic Red Sox are winning. When the team loses, be ready to join fans crying into their Fenway Pale Ale and Boston Red. Other home brews include Belgian-style flavored beers such as Blueberry and Lucky Seven (flavored with raspberries). Food is traditional burger fare.

⊞ 200 B2 ⊠ 61 Brookline Avenue
☏ (617) 536-BEER ⊙ Daily 11:30 a.m.–1 a.m. 🚇 Fenway

## The Commonwealth Fish and Beer Co. $

Handy for the FleetCenter, home of the Boston Bruins (ice hockey) and the Celtics (basketball), this cavernous brewpub is packed before and after games. It offers the widest range of cask-conditioned ales in New England, including the award-winning Special Old Ale. It's family friendly with good seafood and a well-priced children's menu.

⊞ 199 D4 ⊠ 138 Portland Street
☏ (617) 523-8383 ⊙ Mon.–Sat. 11:30 a.m.–midnight (also Fri.–Sat. midnight–1 a.m.); Sun. noon–9. 🚇 North Station

## Irish Embassy $

Irish pubs in Boston can be a cliché, but this is the real thing, with live Irish bands playing during the week. Come on Saturday for a traditional fried breakfast, and watch live soccer from the U.K. on TV surrounded by expatriates.

🚇 199 D4 ⊠ 234 Friend Street ☎ (617) 742-6618 🕒 Daily 11:30 a.m.–2 a.m. 🚇 North Station

## Sevens Ale House $

This genuine local tavern with booths and a dartboard has been a fixture in the neighborhood for nearly 70 years. Regular customers come for the conviviality as much as the well-filled pitchers of ale. It is just around the corner from the now touristy Bull & Finch pub, on which the "Cheers" TV program was, theoretically, based. Beer and wine and plain food are served.

🚇 198 B3 ⊠ 77 Charles Street ☎ (617) 523-9074 🕒 Mon.–Fri. 11:30 a.m.–1 a.m., Sat.–Sun. noon–1 a.m. 🚇 Charles/MGH

## CAMBRIDGE

## East Coast Grill $$$

Chef Chris Schlesinger's successful cookbook *The Thrill of the Grill* confirmed the popularity of this restaurant. His attitude is simple: take the freshest seafood and finest meat, use an open-pit, wood-fired grill and some imagination. Classics include Grilled Big Black-and-Blue Steak for Two, a 2-inch thick steak, seared on the outside but rare in the middle. His travels have introduced Caribbean and Asian spicing to his cooking. Try the excellent Sunday brunch.

🚇 205 D1 ⊠ 1271 Cambridge Street ☎ (617) 491-6568 🕒 Mon.–Sat. 5:30–10 (also Fri.–Sat. 10–10:30 p.m.), Sun. 11–2:30, 5:30–10 🚇 Central

## House of Blues $$

Part of the organization that gave you the Hard Rock Café, this was the first of the chain of blues-oriented clubs. The décor is Southern sugar shack, with plenty of blues memorabilia. Fun and friendly, this is the place to slurp beer and chew ribs as you listen to live music. The Sunday morning Gospel brunch is a highlight.

🚇 205 D1 ⊠ 96 Winthrop Street ☎ (617) 491-2583 🕒 Mon.–Sat. 11:30 a.m.–1 a.m., Sun. 10 a.m.–1 a.m. (kitchen closes at 11 p.m.) 🚇 Harvard

## Up Stairs at the Pudding $$$

Climb the stairs of the 19th-century building that houses Harvard's Hasty Pudding drama club to reach this comfortable, cheerful restaurant. Chef Deborah Hughes' menus reflect the seasons. In fall, you could find braised chicken with harvest vegetables and apple pie served with burnt-sugar ice cream. Windows open onto a small terrace for outdoor dining.

🚇 205 D1 ⊠ 10 Holyoke Street ☎ (617) 864-1933 🕒 Mon.–Sat. 11:30–2:30, 5:30–9:30 (also Fri.–Sat. 9:30–10:30 p.m.), Sun. 11–2, 5:30–9:30 🚇 Harvard

## Casablanca $–$$

One of the most sophisticated bar-restaurants in town, just off Harvard Square, this has been the preferred watering hole of Harvard's literati for decades. Take a table, or stand at the wraparound bar and admire the bold mural depicting Rick's Café America in the movie "Casablanca."

🚇 205 D1 ⊠ 40 Brattle Street ☎ (617) 876-0999 🕒 Daily 11:30 a.m.–1 a.m. (also Thu.–Sat. 1–2 a.m.). Kitchen closes at midnight 🚇 Harvard

## Club Passim $

The cramped room at Club Passim has echoed to Muddy Waters, Tom Rush, Arlo Guthrie and Bob Dylan. "Financially affordable fresh folk food," such as kabobs, soups and salads is on offer.

🚇 205 D1 ⊠ 47 Palmer Street ☎ (617) 492-7679 🕒 Daily 11–11 🚇 Harvard

# Where to... Shop

From essentials to luxury goods, Boston has it all. No wonder folk from New England have long flocked to the city, for window-shopping or to give their credit cards a workout.

**Downtown** Downtown has two useful department stores: **Macy's East** (450 Washington Street, tel: 617/357-3000) and **Filene's** (426 Washington Street, tel: 617/357-2100). Filene's Basement has long had a reputation for rock-bottom prices, though in recent years it has been overtaken by the outlet malls, where bargains are sold in more attractive surroundings.

At **Faneuil Hall Marketplace** locals rub shoulders with visitors in three buildings crammed with things to buy. As well as the inevitable T-shirts and souvenirs, there are more upscale shops. Try the **Boston Pewter Company** (South Market Building, tel: 617/523-1776) for pewter and New England specialties such as scrimshaw, cranberry glass and weathervanes. For handmade sweaters, try **Kristina's Accents** (South Market Building, tel: 617/723-8114). For gifts with a cultural flavor, there is the **Museum of Fine Arts gift shop** (South Market Building, tel: 617/720-1266).

**Back Bay** Serious shoppers head for Back Bay. At the glamorous **Copley Place** indoor development (on Huntington Avenue, between Dartmouth and Exeter streets), internationally recognized names such as **Tiffany & Co.** (tel: 617/353-0222), **Neiman Marcus** (tel: 617/536-3660), **Louis Vuitton** (tel: 617/437-6519) and **Gucci** (tel: 617/247-3000) are among the 100 stores under the huge atrium. From here, you can take the glassed-in skybridge above the cars to the **Shops at Prudential Center**. The two heavyweights here are department stores **Saks Fifth Avenue** (tel: 617/262-8500) and **Lord & Taylor** (tel: 617/262-6000), but you will also find a bookstore, clothing for men, women and children, and sporting specialists.

**Newbury Street** For a real Boston experience, take a stroll down Newbury Street. Lined with specialty shops, cafés and art galleries, it runs from Boston Common to Massachusetts Avenue. In addition to famous names such as **Burberry's** (2 Newbury Street, tel: 617/236-1000), there are the boutiques: **Bijoux** (141 Newbury Street, tel: 617/424-8877) stocks evening dresses, leather accessories and costume jewelry. **Brooks Brothers** (46 Newbury Street, tel: 617/267-2600), **Cole Haan** (109 Newbury Street, tel: 617/536-7826) and **Allen-Edmonds** (36 Newbury Street, tel: 617/247-3363) rival one another for high-quality men's shoes and clothing, and **Cigar Masters** (176 Newbury Street, tel: 617/266-4400) caters to the current fashion for fine tobacco.

Among the art galleries are **Vose Galleries of Boston** (238 Newbury Street, tel: 617/536-6176), established in 1841. They often have fine examples of American Impressionist and Hudson River School paintings. By contrast, **Judi Rotenberg** (130 Newbury Street, tel: 617/437-1518) represents contemporary American artists.

**Cambridge** The **Harvard Coop** (1400 Massachusetts Avenue, tel: 617/499-2000) sells everything from books to clothes, as well as popular souvenirs, including crimson sweatshirts. Wander down **Brattle Street**, lined with small shops, but don't miss the **Cambridge Artists Cooperative** (59A Church Street, tel: 617/868-4434), which sells crafts and paintings by local artists.

# Where to...
# Be Entertained

Boston has a thriving entertainment scene. Choose from dance, theater, movies, and concerts of classical and contemporary music. There are listings of what's on in monthly magazines such as *Boston* and *Where*, but for the most authoritative and up-to-the-minute information, see the Calendar section of the *Boston Globe* newspaper on Thursdays. All are available at newsstands.

**Dance** The **Boston Ballet** (tel: 617/695-6950), which often performs at the **Wang Center for the Performing Arts** (270 Tremont Street, tel: 617/482-9393), is one of America's leading companies. Its annual *Nutcracker* is part of the city's Christmas tradition.

**Theater** The city has a rich theater tradition, from world-class musicals to experimental drama, and is often used to try out future Broadway productions. Old-style theaters include the **Colonial** (106 Boylston Street, tel: 617/426-9366), the **Wang Center for the Performing Arts** (270 Tremont Street, tel: 617/482-9393), the **Shubert** (265 Tremont Street, tel: 617/426-4520) and the **Huntington** (264 Huntington Avenue, tel: 617/266-0800). In Cambridge, head for the **American Repertory Theatre** (Loeb Drama Center, 64 Brattle Street, tel: 617/547-8300).

Hit shows sell out early, so try to plan in advance. Call the theater direct, or contact **Ticketmaster** (tel: 617/931-2000). For half-price tickets on the day, contact **Bostix** (tel: 617/482-BTIX). Tickets go on sale at 11 a.m. at booths in Copley Square and Faneuil Hall.

**Music** Boston is particularly strong on classical music. The **Boston Symphony Orchestra** plays in the beautiful Symphony Hall (301 Massachusetts Avenue, tel: 617/266-1492), but you can hear the stars of the future at the **New England Conservatory** (Jordan Hall, 290 Huntington Avenue, tel: 617/536-2412), **Berklee College of Music** (Berklee Performance Center, 136 Massachusetts Avenue, tel: 617/266-7455) and **Longy School of Music** (1 Follen Street, Cambridge, tel: 617/876-0956). Concerts are also held in the **Isabella Stewart Gardner Museum** (▶ 59).

As for rock and pop, you can catch headliners at the **FleetCenter** (tel: 617/624-1000) or one of the college auditoriums. There are small coffee houses, and folk and jazz clubs with live music: two legendary venues in Cambridge are the folk club **Club Passim** (▶ 70) and the **Regattabar** for jazz (Charles Hotel, 1 Bennett Street, Cambridge, tel: 617/876-7777).

**Sport** Boston has three venerable major-league teams: the **Red Sox** (baseball), the **Celtics** (basketball) and the **Bruins** (ice hockey). The **New England Patriots** have made it to the Super Bowl, but never taken the title. Tickets tend to be expensive and hard to come by. For more information about getting tickets for Red Sox games (▶ 14–17). For information on the Celtics and Bruins, contact FleetCenter (tel: 617/624-1000). The New England Patriots play out of town at Foxboro, MA (tel: 508/543-1776).

**Walking Tours** For themed tours, try **Boston by Foot** (77 North Washington Street, tel: 617/367-2345). Foodies will enjoy chef Michele Topor's tour of the Italian North End. Contact **North End Market Tours** (tel: 617/523-6032).

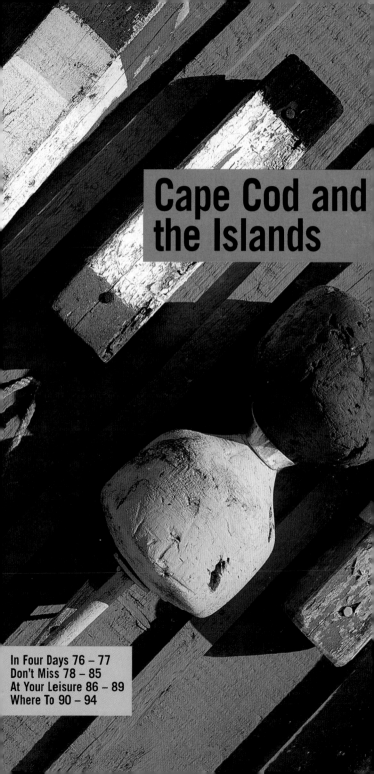

# Cape Cod and the Islands

In Four Days 76 – 77
Don't Miss 78 – 85
At Your Leisure 86 – 89
Where To 90 – 94

# Getting Your Bearings

You're probably not going to have time to do everything you want to on Cape Cod in a single visit. New Englanders have been coming here for years, and still they haven't seen everything. Even the maddening 4-mile tailbacks approaching the Sagamore and Bourne bridges don't deter the faithful, for they know what lies on the other side of those bridges: sparkling white beaches, quaint coastal villages, miles of biking trails, whale-watching cruises and cocktails on the deck overlooking the Atlantic, followed by informal lobster dinners.

Cape Cod is the kind of place people come back to year after year. Many of them rent the same cottage in the same town every summer, go to the same beach and eat at the same restaurants on each visit. And hardly two people will agree on which is the best beach, the best restaurant, even the best town. One thing is certain: you can have a great time weighing all the evidence.

To reduce your choices from the overwhelming infinite to a merely tantalizing multitude, this chapter concentrates on four areas where you might choose to spend a Cape Cod vacation. Chatham, located at the elbow of the Cape, is off the main drag and requires some finding, which means that nobody is there by accident. It still has the flavor of a small-time New England fishing village. Provincetown, at the very end of the Cape, has both

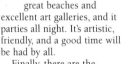

great beaches and excellent art galleries, and it parties all night. It's artistic, friendly, and a good time will be had by all.

Finally, there are the islands of Martha's Vineyard and Nantucket. In general,

**Previous page: Fishing buoys
Left: Getting away from it all –
island life on Nantucket**

Race Point Beach
**Provincetown** 4
Herring Cove Beach
5
North Truro
Head of the Meadow Beach
Truro
*Cape Cod Bay*
6
**Cape Cod National Seashore** 3
Wellfleet
Marconi Beach
South Wellfleet
Nauset Light Beach
Eastham
Coast Guard Beach
Orleans
Brewster
Nickerson State Park
124
Nauset Beach
**Cape Cod Rail Trail** 6
Dennis
6A
*Pleasant Bay*
rmouth Port
134
39
28
stable
South Dennis
**Chatham & Monomoy National Wildlife Refuge** 2
Chatham
hyannis
Harwich
North Monomoy Island
South Yarmouth
nis rt
Monomoy National Wildlife Refuge
South Monomoy Island

*Sound*

Great Point

Muskeget Island
Wauwinet
Dionis Beach
Jetties Beach
Nantucket
**Nantucket** 7
Maddaket
Sanford Farm
Siasconset
Surfside

the Vineyard is bigger, busier, showier and more liberal, whereas Nantucket is farther away, smaller, slower, old-monied, and more conservative. Accommodations can be tight in all of the aforementioned towns, so plan ahead. If you get shut out, the larger, more commercial towns of Hyannis and South Yarmouth have hundreds of motel-style lodgings: what they lack in charm, they make up for in lower prices.

## At Your Leisure

1 Heritage Plantation ► 86

2 Chatham and Monomoy National Wildlife Refuge ► 86

5 Whale watching cruises ► 87

6 Cape Cod Rail Trail ► 88

8 Martha's Vineyard ► 88

Above right: A dolphin weather vane in Chatham celebrates Cape sealife

## ★ Don't Miss

3 **Cape Cod National Seashore** ► 78

4 **Provincetown** ► 81

7 **Nantucket** ► 83

The following itinerary provides a whirlwind tour of the best the Cape has to offer. But don't worry if you end up spending all four days in the same place. It's been known to happen to many people before you.

# Cape Cod and the Islands in Four Days

## Day One

### Morning
Take the picturesque driving tour of **Historic Route 6A** (➤ 178–180). If you do nothing else en route, stop at the **Heritage Plantation** in Sandwich (➤ 86) and visit the car collection, art museum and antique carousel.

### Afternoon
Have lunch at a clam shack anywhere along the Mid-cape – try Brewster's Fish House (2208 Main Street, Brewster, tel: 508/896-7876) – or pack a picnic lunch and visit one of the beautiful beaches on **Cape Cod National Seashore** (above, ➤ 78–80). Nauset Light Beach in Orleans, with its impressive dunes, is the most convenient to the end of the driving tour.

### Evening
Find somewhere to stay in Chatham and head to Christian's (➤ 92) to enjoy your first seafood dinner on the Cape.

## Day Two

### Morning
Drive out to the lively resort of **Provincetown** (left, ➤ 81–82) at the end of the Cape, rent a bicycle and start to explore. Pack a picnic lunch and prepare to spend the first half of the day at the beach.

### Afternoon
Bicycle back into town after lunch, grab a jacket or a sweatshirt and catch a **whale-watching cruise** (➤ 87).

### Evening
Head back to your accommodations in time for dinner. Try Martin House
(➤ 93), which has log fires in winter and a terrace for fine weather. Then
sample the nighttime scene along Commercial Street. Stay overnight in
"P-town," as the locals call it.

# Day Three

### Morning
Drive to Hyannis and catch a
passenger ferry to **Nantucket**
(left, ➤ 83–85). Don't bring
your car (in fact, unless you
have made a reservation in
advance, you can't).

### Afternoon
Check in at your guesthouse
or inn on the island, then
rent bikes again or take the
bus out to Maddaket, at the
western tip of the island, and
watch the sun set.

### Evening
Head to the fun, informal
Lobster Trap (23 Washington
Street, tel: 508/228-4200)
for a lobster dinner with all
the trimmings.

# Day Four

### Morning
Rent a jeep and go four-wheeling on the sand out to Great Point. It's an
expensive proposition, but allows you the freedom to pick your own private
beach.

### Afternoon
Have lunch at Something
Natural (50 Cliff Road,
tel: 508/228-0504). Then
wander around Nantucket
Town (right). Shop for big-
ticket items like jewelry and
lightship baskets, or less
expensive gifts like T-shirts
and hats.

### Evening
Catch the last ferry back to
Hyannis.

# Cape Cod National Seashore

For many people, Cape Cod doesn't begin until you turn the corner at Orleans onto the Outer (also called the Lower) Cape. That's because this is the beginning of the federally protected Cape Cod National Seashore. Less than a year into his term, President John F. Kennedy declared this 40-mile strip a national seashore, forever forbidding development along the sands. The National Park Service does a fine job of administering and maintaining the area, which extends from Chatham in the south all the way to the tip of Provincetown, though it cedes management to local towns at several of the beaches along the way.

Biking, hiking, fishing and even hunting (in some places) take place within the confines of the National Seashore, but it is the miles and miles of unspoiled beaches that attract the most visitors. Everybody has a favorite beach, and no two are exactly the same. Where you end up spreading out your towel and turning the pages of your summer beach novel will probably have more to do with where you are staying than anything else. If you're centered in Chatham, Harwich, Orleans or Brewster, you will most likely choose **Nauset Beach**, a thin finger of sand unconnected to the rest of the National Seashore, and accessible only by a single road through East Orleans. It has no restrooms or changing facilities.

**Sunsets at the west-facing beach at North Truro can be spectacular**

## Near Eastham

If you're staying in Eastham, you can choose between two National Park Service-managed beaches: Coast Guard Beach and Nauset Light Beach. Both have restrooms, showers and changing facilities, and soft golden sands. Of the two, **Nauset**

**Light** is easier to get to by car and is thus usually more crowded, the parking fee notwithstanding. But if you like dunes, this is the beach to visit. Cliffs 100 feet high tower over the beach, which is reached down a long flight of wooden stairs. **Coast Guard Beach** has satellite parking (you have to take a shuttle bus from a remote lot), which is a pain, but the beach is also accessible by an easy, pretty bike trail. This inconvenience discourages people who see easy-in, easy-out parking as a necessity.

Cliffs, lighthouses, broad sands: It could only be the Cape Cod National Seashore

## Near Wellfleet

Wellfleet boasts several town-managed beaches, as well as **Marconi Beach**, named for radio inventor Guglielmo Marconi, who built his radio tower (now the historic Marconi

Wireless Station Site) just up the road. North of Wellfleet, the town of Truro manages several beaches along its eastern shore, one of which is no more than a few feet away from the Park Service's **Head of the Meadow Beach.** The same access road takes you to both the town beach or Head of the Meadow; the fee for Head of the Meadow Beach is only slightly more than the parking fee at the town beach (you get

You don't have to look too far to find your own stretch of sand overlooking the Atlantic

restrooms, showers and changing facilities for the difference). The Truro beaches get a little more seaweed washed up on shore than beaches farther north, but they have gentler waves.

## Near Provincetown

Finally, there are the Provincetown beaches, Race Point and Herring Cove. **Herring Cove** is popular with families and people with motor homes because of the long, thin parking lot that runs parallel to the sands. You can park your car in the lot, and then park yourself on the beach right in front of it. **Race Point** may be the crown jewel of the National Seashore. It's got everything: steep dunes, soft sand, inviting surf, amenities like restrooms and showers, and a nearby visitor center to answer any questions about the local flora and fauna. For many people, a favored way to spend the day is to bicycle to Race Point from Provincetown along the paved Province Lands bike trail up and down through the surrounding dunes.

The waves at Herring Cove are gentle enough for children

### TAKING A BREAK

Try **On the Creek Café** (55 Commercial Street, Wellfleet, tel: 508/228-8886), overlooking Duck Creek, where home-cooked snacks and light meals are served with European flair.

**Park Headquarters**
- 206 E2
- 99 Marconi Site Road, Wellfleet, MA 02667
- (508) 349-3785
- Mon.–Fri. 8–4:30
- Beach parking per day: moderate (good for any Park Service beach until midnight)

**Salt Pond Visitor Center**
- 206 E2
- Route 6 and Nauset Road, Eastham
- (508) 255-3421
- Daily 9–4:30. Extended hours in summer months. Closed Dec. 24

**Province Lands Visitor Center**
- 206 E3
- Race Point Road, Provincetown
- (508) 487-1256; web: www.nps.gov/caco
- Daily 9–4:30, mid-Apr.–Thanksgiving. Extended hours in summer months

## CAPE COD NATIONAL SEASHORE: INSIDE INFO

**Top tip** On busy summer weekends (especially the Fourth of July and Labor Day), parking at any beach can be a nightmare. If you can, do yourself a favor and bike to the beach.

**In more detail** If you're staying in any of the towns around Hyannis, it's worth the extra few minutes driving to go out to the National Seashore beaches. The public beaches along the Upper Cape are often very crowded.

# Provincetown

Ask some people about Provincetown and they'll tell you it's the gay resort town at the end of Cape Cod. But they're only partly right. Yes, Provincetown is gay-friendly, but it's just as friendly as it is gay. Gays, lesbians, straights, couples and families love Provincetown because it is tolerant to all comers. The only people not welcome here are those who have a problem with all that tolerance. If you're not willing to live and let live, then Provincetown isn't for you. If, on the other hand, you don't care who is kissing whom, then come join in the fun.

There are several Provincetowns. There's the beach Provincetown, which is where most people can be found during summer days, sunning themselves on the sands, swimming in the ocean, sailing around the bay, biking along the bicycle paths or the quiet roads, or flying a kite on the beach.

Then there's the gallery Provincetown. Dozens of art galleries thrive here, most of them in the town's east end. Charles Hawthorne started his Cape Cod School of Art in 1899, and "P-town" has been an artist's colony ever since. Painters were not the only artists attracted to the area's natural beauty; Eugene O'Neill began his career as a playwright here, where the rules weren't as strict as those on Broadway.

**Commercial Street (below) at the heart of picturesque Provincetown (above) welcomes shoppers by day and revelers by night**

Other Provincetown alumni include John Dos Passos, Sinclair Lewis, Tennessee Williams and Robert Motherwell. The best among current works of art are to be found at the Provincetown Art Association and Museum (460 Commercial Street, tel: 508/487-1750), the Rice/Polak Gallery (430 Commercial Street, 508/487-1052) and the Berta Walker Gallery (208 Bradford Street, tel: 508/487-6411).

**No visit is complete without a trip to the Portuguese Bakery**

Finally, there is the action-packed Provincetown. Narrow-as-a-driveway Commercial Street, with its narrow-as-an-escalator sidewalks teems with people every summer night, and on weekends in other seasons. Only the occasional presence of a bicyclist or a slow-moving car reminds you that this isn't one giant pedestrian mall. This is where all the action is, often late into the night. Many stores don't even open until 4 o'clock in the afternoon (so their owners can spend the day at the beach), but then stay open until around midnight to capture customers even after they've had dinner. The strip is crowded, as people walk from one end to the other, browsing in the quirky stores, watching the performers in the clubs or on the streets, or just people-watching. There's definitely a gay singles scene going on here, but it's not dominant and you may not even notice it.

**People watching is a prime P-town activity**

### TAKING A BREAK

Try the traditional Portuguese breads and cakes on sale at the **Provincetown Portuguese Bakery & Coffee Shop** (299 Commercial Street, tel: 508/487-1803), just a few steps west of the wharf.

---

**Provincetown Chamber of Commerce**
🏠 206 E3
✉ 307 Commercial Street, MacMillan Wharf, Provincetown, MA 02657
☎ (508) 487-3424; web: www.ptownchamber.com

---

## PROVINCETOWN: INSIDE INFO

**Top tips** If you are looking for somewhere to rent a bicycle, **Arnold's Bikes** (329 Commercial Street, tel: 508/487-0844) is reliable and centrally located.
• The **Pilgrim Monument and Provincetown Museum** (High Pole Hill, tel: 800/247-1620), a 252-foot granite tower overlooking the town, commemorates the Pilgrims' landing here in 1620 (they couldn't find a source of fresh water, so continued on to Plymouth Rock). It provides an interesting diversion for a rainy day, but could never lure you from the beach on a sunny day.

**Hidden gem** If you can't decide between the beach and the arts, consider **Art's Sand Dune Tours** (Commercial and Standish streets, tel: 508/487-1950, web: www.artsdunetours.com), which brings together the best of both worlds. These hour-long tours take you by four-wheel-drive through the Provincetown dunes of Cape Cod National Seashore. Along the way, you get to see the dune shacks where artists and writers, among them Eugene O'Neill, Jack Kerouac and Jackson Pollock, found inspiration. Tennessee Williams is said to have written *A Streetcar Named Desire* while summering in one such shack. Tours are from April to November and cost around $12 per person.

# Nantucket

Unlike some places that are famous for what they have, Nantucket is appealing for the things it doesn't have. Traffic lights, for instance: There isn't a single one on the island. Every now and then, that makes for an infuriating intersection, especially when a ferry unloads another 30 vehicles ashore, but for the most part, the lack of traffic lights is a welcome reminder of Nantucket's lazy island pace.

**Nantucket's cranberry harvest turns the island into an ocean of red**

There are few places as close to civilization and yet as away from it all as Nantucket. The island is a 2½-hour ferry ride from Hyannis, meaning that day-trippers are another thing it doesn't have. If you're coming to Nantucket, you're staying, and if you're staying, you'd better have reservations, because hotel rooms are hard to come by in the summer season – and expensive, even in the simplest guesthouse-standard rooms.

Most people willingly pay the inflated rates (also charged at the island's shops and restaurants) for what Nantucket does have: space. It may be the only place in New England where even in the middle of a holiday weekend, you can still find a stretch of deserted beach to call your own. Nantucket has 110 miles of beach, all of it public, but only a few thousand hotel rooms, inns and private homes. That works out to no more than 100 people per square mile. When you consider that several hundred people are usually crowded into the single square-mile center of Nantucket Town, shopping for jewelry or traditional Nantucket crafts, eating ice cream, trying on T-shirts or just enjoying a cool drink on a breezy patio, the remainder of the island can feel downright empty.

A few days on Nantucket truly feels like an escape from it all; the minute you arrive, you're on island time. The cobblestoned streets in **Nantucket Town** look much the same as they did when this was the whaling capital of the world from 1740 to 1830. Only the multitude of gigantic sport-utility vehicles on the narrow streets reminds you that you're not in the 18th century. Automobile traffic moves slowly not only because of the rough roads, but also because of the pedestrians and bicycles clogging up the streets.

**Siasconset** (pronounced 'Sconset') and **Maddaket** are described by some as towns, but neither is little more than a couple of stores and a bus stop. Around the island, most houses have that gray, weathered look that comes from Cape Cod sea air spraying against cedar shingles for years on end.

Digging for clams, a Cape specialty

Then there are the beaches, which also have the timeless look of summer about them. Children's Beach, Jetties Beach and Dionis Beach, all on the north (Nantucket Sound) side of the island, are popular with families for their soft sand, mild surf and plentiful facilities like lifeguards and restrooms. Jetties even has a food stand, volleyball nets and beach-chair rentals, as well as Fourth of July fireworks festivities.

Nantucket's south side, facing the Atlantic Ocean, has stronger surf and fewer families with small children along its sands. Surfside Beach is popular with teenagers and young adults, whereas Maddaket (at the west end of the island) and Siasconset (on the east end) are quieter options. All three have lifeguards, and Surfside and Maddaket have facilities. Strong crosscurrents at Maddaket and Siasconset make swimming difficult, but not exceedingly dangerous.

Beyond these beaches are the hundreds of miles of shoreline with no names at all. Most of these are strewn along either side of the long finger of sand that leads to **Great Point**. You need a four-wheel drive vehicle (you can rent one in town for the day), but out here, you just drive until you see a spot you like, park on the sand and revel on your own private beach.

Scrimshaw, a craft originated by whalers, recalls the island's days as a whaling center

An especially lovely time on Nantucket is the middle of October, during the cranberry harvest. Farmers flood the **cranberry bogs**, turning them into a brilliant blood-red sea, then collect the fruits as they naturally float to the top. To see this stunning spectacle, contact the Nantucket Chamber of Commerce, which runs buses from the center of town to and from the cranberry bogs on the weekend after Columbus Day. While at the bogs, feel free to listen to the people from Northland Cranberries explain how they harvest 900 tons of cranberries, or simply wander around on your own. An added bonus: Nantucket is rarely crowded at this time of year and you probably won't even need hotel reservations.

## TAKING A BREAK

At **Espresso Café** (40 Main Street, tel: 508/228-9630), right in the heart of Nantucket Town, you can have a quick coffee or soup and a sandwich. In summer there are tables outside at the back. Alternatively, try **The Rope Walk** (1 Straight Wharf, tel: 508/228-8886). You can't beat the setting at the end of the pier, overlooking the water.

Is it 1890 or 1990? On Nantucket it hardly matters

**Nantucket Chamber of Commerce**
🔳 206 E1
✉ 48 Main Street, Nantucket, MA 02554-3595
☎ (508) 228-1700; web: www.nantucketchamber.org

## NANTUCKET: INSIDE INFO

**Top tips** Be smart and **leave your car in Hyannis**. Many of the island's attractions are within walking distance, and cabs and efficient public transportation serve the remoter areas. If you do decide to take a car, you'll need to arrange a ferry passage far in advance.

• The island has 20-plus miles of well-maintained **bicycle trails**. The Nantucket Bike Shop (tel: 508/228-1999), at the end of the ferry dock, will rent you wheels for the day, week or season.

• **Four-wheel-drive vehicles** are expensive to rent, but sell out quickly nonetheless. Budget (tel: 800/527-0700), Hertz (tel: 800/654-3131) and National (tel: 800/227-7368) all have offices at the airport. Local options include Nantucket Jeep Rental (tel: 508/228-1618) and Affordable Rentals (tel: 508/228-3501). You also need a permit to drive on the dunes to Great Point; they cost around $15 and are available at the entry gate.

**Hidden gem** Sanford Farm is a nature preserve with more than 6 miles of walking trails to a deserted beach. The flat 3-mile walk from the parking lot to the beach takes about an hour, just long enough to deter 99 percent of visitors. You can also reach the same beach by driving to the end of Hummock Pond Road and walking west about a half mile, but hardly anybody does this.

# At Your Leisure

## ❶ Heritage Plantation

Part museum, part formal gardens and part miscellaneous collection, Heritage Plantation has no unifying theme, and there's nothing particularly Cape Cod about it, but so what? It has what it has – from Tlingit Indian artifacts to Currier and Ives lithographs – and you will probably find something you like somewhere within the confines.

The antique automobile museum is housed in a replica of the round barn from Hancock Shaker Village (► 104). There's a 1913 Model T, a 1930 Duesenberg Model J and several other vehicles dating back to when cars were called horseless carriages. All are in pristine condition. In the myriad gardens, something is almost always in bloom, be it daylilies, heather or the famous Dexter rhododendrons. Young kids will love riding the restored 1912 carousel (which is free!) and their parents will marvel at the antique wooden animals on display – not just lions and tigers and bears, but the more unusual pigs, deer, ostrich, zebras, cats and frogs.

➕ 206 E2 ✉ 67 Grove Street, Sandwich, MA 02563-2147 ☎ (508) 888-3300; web: www.heritageplantation.org ⊙ Daily 10–5, early May to mid-Oct. ⚑ Moderate. Half-price for children aged 6–18, children under 5 free. Free parking ❚❚ Carousel Café until 4:30

## ❷ Chatham and Monomoy National Wildlife Refuge

Tucked away at the very bottom of the elbow of the Cape is the upscale town of Chatham. Nobody passes through Chatham on their way to somewhere else – you'd never find the town if you weren't looking for it – and that's one reason so many people love it.

Chatham feels like an authentic Cape Cod town. It still supports a viable (though struggling) commercial fishing fleet, and its Main Street still has more quirky, individually owned shops than T-shirt emporiums.

Every Friday night in summer, there's a free band concert in Kate Gould Park. The talent is mostly local musicians, but the crowds (often in the thousands) come from all over. Vacationers from around the Cape make a special trip for these concerts, so come early.

Chatham is also the jumping-off point for the Monomoy National Wildlife

**Refuge.** This is serious bird-watching territory, attracting more than 300 species of migratory birds. Harbor seals also favor the area; you can't help but see them.

You can take a ferry to Monomoy Island, but you get a better appreciation of the wildlife if you go with a naturalist. The Cape Cod Museum of Natural History offers seal cruises, guided birding tours and even overnight excursions. The Massachusetts Audubon Society's Wellfleet Bay Wildlife Sanctuary also runs guided birding tours.

**Chatham Chamber of Commerce**
206 E2 Main Street, Chatham, MA 02633 (800) 715-5567 or (508) 945-5199; web: www.chathamcapecod.org

**Cape Cod Museum of Natural History**
206 E2 P.O. Box 1710, Brewster, MA 02631 (508) 896-3867; web: www.capecodconnection.com/ccmnh/index.htm

**Massachusetts Audubon Society's Wellfleet Bay Wildlife Sanctuary**
206 E2 291 State Highway, Route 6, Wellfleet, MA 02631 (508) 349-2615; web: www.wellfleetbay.org/monomoy.html

## 5 Whale-watching cruises

There are so many humpback and finback whales feeding in the waters off Provincetown that several whale-watching cruise companies guarantee sightings (you get a free rain check if you don't see one). This doesn't ensure that you'll see a humpback breach 20 feet into the air, but you almost certainly will see whales. You might also see dolphins, seabirds and other marine life along the way.

Several companies offer cruises of varying lengths from MacMillan Pier in Provincetown. Dolphin Fleet has been in business the longest (since 1975). Its ships carry a team of researchers from the Center for Coastal Studies, who serve as guides to the whales and their habitats. As with other cruises, their boats have a well-stocked bar on board.

It can get cold, wet and rough on whale-watching cruises, especially in inclement weather. Bring a rain-jacket, a sweater and motion-sickness pills if you get seasick easily. And don't forget binoculars.

**Dolphin Fleet of Provincetown**
206 E3 MacMillan Pier, Provincetown, MA 02657 (800) 826-9300; web: www.whalewatch.com Daily dawn–dusk, mid-Apr. to Oct. Expensive. Children under 6 free

Every summer humpback whales come to the rich feeding grounds off Provincetown

### 6 Cape Cod Rail Trail

What better fate for an abandoned railroad bed than to be paved over and turned into a bicycle path! The Cape Cod Rail Trail meanders for 25 miles, from Route 134 in South Dennis through Harwich, Brewster, Orleans and Eastham before ending at South Wellfleet. It is one of the prettiest ways to see any or all of these Mid-Cape towns. The trail also intersects other trails that lead to town shopping areas or the beach.

Each of the towns on the Cape has bicycle rental shops, so it is fairly easy to find one no matter where you stay. Idle Times has three locations along the Rail Trail, including one near the midpoint, in Nickerson State Park. They have free parking at all their locations.

➕ 206 E2 ☎ (508) 896-3491 for information; web: www. state.ma.us/dem/parks/ccrt.htm

#### Idle Times Bike Shop

➕ 206 E2 ✉ Town Center Plaza, 4550 Route 6, North Eastham, MA 02651-0176. Summer-only locations in Wellfleet and Brewster ☎ (508) 255-8281; web: www.idletimesbike.com
🕐 Daily 9–5 (summer-only locations Memorial Day–Labor Day) 💵 4-hour, 8-hour, 24-hour and week rental available. Rates become relatively less expensive the longer the rental period. Discounts for children's bikes

### 8 Martha's Vineyard

Martha's Vineyard is bigger, more popular and closer to the rest of Cape Cod than its neighbor island Nantucket – something that can be seen as an advantage or a disadvantage depending on your point of view.

The primary attraction, as on Nantucket, is the beach, and in summer the population swells with folks looking to spend time by the cool ocean breezes. Tourists confine themselves largely to the "down-island" towns of **Vineyard Haven**, **Edgartown** and **Oak Bluffs**. These places cater to a transient audience, with abundant shops along their main streets. There are even some galleries and historic house tours in Edgartown to fill a rainy day.

But you might also want to range farther out on the island to linger on remote beaches known only by

Elaborate Victorian gingerbread cottages at Oak Bluffs, Martha's Vineyard

Vineyard veterans, bike through the seemingly out-of-place Correllus

State Forest, take the even smaller ferry to the even smaller island of Chappaquiddick, or visit the picturesque fishing village of Menemsha. Whatever you do, don't leave without seeing **cliffs at Aquinnah,** a stretch of marvelously colorful clay cliffs on the island's far western shore. At different times of day, the cliffs can appear red, orange, white, and even blue, and erosion often turns the surrounding water a murky cinnamon color.

Getting to the Vineyard requires a ferry ride of around 45 minutes from Falmouth or Woods Hole. The ferry from Hyannis takes an hour longer, but carries cars as well as foot passengers (although advance reservations are needed for cars). Call the Chamber of Commerce for schedules and fares. You can also fly from Hyannis on one of several airlines. It saves about 20 minutes but is more expensive.

**Martha's Vineyard Chamber of Commerce**

✚ 206 D1  ✉ Beach Road, Vineyard Haven, MA 02568 ☎ (508) 693-0085; web: www.mvy.com

**The cliffs at Aquinnah on Martha's Vineyard can appear almost any color**

### For Kids

• The **National Marine Fisheries Service Aquarium** (Albatross Street, tel: 508/495-2001), in Woods Hole at the southern end of the Cape, is a favorite with young kids. They can get their hands wet and feel what's in the ocean around them in the touch tanks, watch the seals being fed, or wander through the other exhibits at the country's oldest aquarium. Admission is free.

• On rainy days, the displays on the local flora and fauna at the **Cape Cod Museum of Natural History** (► 87) will keep young children happy. Older kids might enjoy the weekday morning-talks by the resident archeologist on the dig going on near the beach, which has unearthed evidence of a Native American community that lived here approximately 9,000 years ago.

# Where to... Stay

**Prices**

Expect to pay for two people sharing a double room, excluding taxes

$ under $150 $$ $150–250 $$$ over $250

## SANDWICH

### ◆◆Dan'l Webster Inn $–$$

Inns have stood on this site since 1692, but the old-world atmosphere was re-created in 1971 after a fire. Although most of the 54 bedrooms are practical, there are eight luxury bedrooms, each with a canopy bed, whirlpool tub and fireplace. The Conservatory restaurant serves lobster chowder, salads, and grilled beef and seafood. The Tavern at the Inn serves wood-grilled pizzas.

⊞ 206 E2 ⊠ 149 Main Street, Sandwich MA 02563 ☎ (508) 888-3622 or (800) 444-3566; fax: (508) 888-5156; web: www.danlwebsterinn.com

## CHATHAM

### Chatham Bars Inn $–$$$

This large, ocean-side resort has excellent leisure facilities, including tennis, a swimming pool, nature walks, cruises and golf nearby on the town's nine-hole course. Special programs cater to teenagers and younger children. Only a small proportion of the inn's 205 rooms are in the main building, the rest are in cottages. A treat anytime, but particularly at off-season rates.

⊞ 206 E2 ⊠ Shore Road, Chatham, MA 02633 ☎ (508) 945-0096 or (800) 527-4884; fax: (508) 945-4978; web: www.chathambarsinn.com

## NORTH TRURO

### ◆Sea Gull Motel $

At this small family-run motel, some 7 miles north of Truro Center, a boardwalk arrows out onto the private beach. Rooms have refrigerators, telephones and air-conditioning, and the four two-bedroom apartments are ideal for family vacations. Some guests flop on the sundeck on the beach; others fish for striped bass or rent bicycles to pedal to nearby Provincetown.

⊞ 206 E3 ⊠ 654 Shore Road, North Truro, MA 02652 ☎ (508) 487-9070; web: www.capecodtravel.com/seagull motel

## PROVINCETOWN

### Bradford Gardens Inn $

The inn, in a quiet location a few minutes' walk from Commercial Street and the pier, caters to both families and couples. Twosomes book into the main house, built in 1820, or one of the four cottages.

These stand in the large garden, along with five town houses that are ideal for families. All are typical Cape Cod shingle, and the new buildings blend in with the old.

⊞ 206 E3 ⊠ 178 Bradford Street, Provincetown, MA 02657 ☎ (508) 487-1616 or (800) 432-2334; fax: (508) 487-5596; web: www.bradfordgardens.com

### Fairbanks Inn $

Built as a captain's home in 1776, this historic brick and clapboard house offers much that vacationers look for on the Cape: comfortable rooms furnished with antiques, private bathrooms and pleasant sundecks. With wood-burning fireplaces in most of the 14 bedrooms and the lounges, it is especially snug out-of-season, when the Continental breakfast is served in the dining room.

⊞ 206 E3 ⊠ 90 Bradford Street, Provincetown, MA 02657 ☎ (508) 487-0386 or (800) FAIRBNK; fax: (508) 487-3540; web: www.fairbanksinn.com

### ◆◆◆The Masthead $

In a quiet spot at the west end of town, this family-run motel stands right by the water, with more than 400 feet of private beach, a deck for sunbathing and even grills for barbecues. Most rooms are in apartments and cottages in the cheerful gardens, with a further eight in the motel itself. Guests who arrive by yacht can tie up on the moorings or use the motel's launch service.

✚ **206 E3** ✉ **31–41 Commercial Street, Provincetown, MA 02657** ☎ **(508) 487-0523 or (800) 395-5095; fax: (508) 487-9251; web: www.capecodtravel.com/masthead**

## NANTUCKET

### ◆◆Carriage House $

A former 19th-century carriage house, hidden behind the main street on a narrow island lane made of crushed clamshells, today houses a pleasant bed-and-breakfast. The seven bedrooms have a few antiques and one has a canopy bed. Breakfast

is Continental, usually taken on the patio. The common room, with books, a TV and sofa, becomes the breakfast room in wet weather.

✚ **206 E1** ✉ **5 Ray's Court, Nantucket, MA 02554** ☎ **(508) 228-0326**

### ◆◆◆Seven Sea Street Inn $

In the heart of the historic district of Nantucket Town, this red oak post-and-beam inn, with its widow's walk (rooftop deck) was built in 1986. The owners have successfully re-created an early American atmosphere with carefully chosen reproduction furniture. Enamel gas stoves add a glow to chilly island evenings in some of the eleven bedrooms (two are in the Guest House next door). For Continental breakfast expect cranberry crunch granola and freshly baked coffee cake and muffins.

✚ **206 E1** ✉ **7 Sea Street, Nantucket MA 02554** ☎ **(508) 228-3577 or (800) 651-9262; fax: (508) 228-3578; web: www.sevenseastreetinn.com**

### ◆◆◆Sherburne Inn $

Although this handsome building near Steamboat Wharf has been an inn since the mid-19th century, its origins go back to merchant days when it was the headquarters of the Atlantic Silk Co. in 1835. In the eight bedrooms, fine old paintings and Oriental rugs; one has a fireplace. The favorite is Room 8, with its high king-sized bed, claw-foot bath, and private balcony overlooking the old town. Continental breakfast is served.

✚ **206 E1** ✉ **10 Gay Street, Nantucket, MA 02554** ☎ **(508) 228-4425 or (888) 577-4425; fax: (508) 228-8114; web: www. sherburneinn.com**

### ◆◆Tuckernuck Inn $

Bedrooms at the Tuckernuck have a modern New England look, with plain walls, frilly curtains and patterned quilts. Upstairs rooms at the back are the best, with partial views of the harbor. Out of season, a Continental breakfast is served,

but in summer, the hotel's popular American Bounty restaurant is open, serving a full breakfast. In chilly weather, the small library and sofa are tempting. The inn is just one block from the harbor beach and four blocks from downtown.

✚ **206 E1** ✉ **60 Union Street, Nantucket, MA 02554** ☎ **(508) 228-4886 or (800) 228-4886; fax: (508) 228-4890; web: www.tuckernuckinn.com**

## MARTHA'S VINEYARD

### Ashley Inn $

This 19th-century sea captain's home, a couple of blocks away from the downtown bustle, has an old-fashioned air, with four-poster beds and fireplaces. Guests can relax in the small but pleasant yard, where there are hammocks and chairs. Light breakfasts are served. In high season there is a three-night minimum stay.

✚ **206 E1** ✉ **129 Main Street, Edgartown, MA** ☎ **(508) 627-9655; fax: (508) 627-6629**

# Where to...
## Eat and Drink

### Prices
Expect to pay per person for a three-course meal, excluding drinks and service
$ under $15  $$ $15–30  $$$ over $30

## SANDWICH

### The Belfry Inne & Bistro $$$
A few minutes from the Sandwich Glass Museum, this Victorian inn was once the rectory for the church next door. The church has been converted into a restaurant with a range of inventive main dishes, such as lobster, scallop and leek strudel and crab cakes with a *remoulade* sauce, or rack of lamb for the less adventurous. Desserts might include Belfry Pillow, a *Bavarois* with fresh berries and a raspberry coulis. Reservations are recommended.

➕ 206 E2 ☒ 8 Jarves Street, Sandwich ☎ (508) 888-8550
🕐 Tue.–Sat. 5–8:30 (also Sat. 8:30–9:30 p.m.), Sun. 10:30 a.m.–1 p.m. Closed Sun. evening and Mon. Off season also closed Tue.–Wed.

## CHATHAM

### Christian's $–$$
Right on the main street of Chatham village, this old house is really two restaurants in one. Upstairs is cozy and informal, with a bar and pianist who plays every night in season, and on weekends the rest of the year. Try one of the homemade pizzas. Downstairs suits those who want to linger over their meal. Seafood fans should try one of the daily lobster and fish specials, using seafood landed on nearby Chatham Pier.

➕ 206 E2 ☒ 443 Main Street, Chatham ☎ (508) 945-3362 🕐 Daily 5–10. Upstairs only: Thu.–Mon. 5–9 (also Sat.–Sun. 9–10 p.m.)

## EASTHAM

### Lobster Shanty $
A fixture, along with the Lobster Pound (its sister restaurant at Orleans), this typical clam shack is decorated with nets and lobster pots. A family-oriented eatery, it offers all-you-can-eat fish and chips throughout the day. Even though the clams are dug from the sands outside and the fish is local, stick to what they do best: lobster, with corn and melted butter.

➕ 206 E2 ☒ 2905 Route 6, Eastham ☎ (508) 255-9394 🕐 Daily 11–10, mid-May through Oct.

## PROVINCETOWN

### Front Street Restaurant $$–$$$
Since the mid-1980s, Donna Aliperti has served Mediterranean-influenced dishes in this old Victorian house. The snug atmosphere is enhanced by bare wood tables, brick walls and high-backed wooden booths. Dishes regularly on the menu include tea-smoked duck and herb-crusted rack of lamb, but try her braised short ribs on chickpea polenta, seared shrimp or maple-grilled salmon. Italian, French and California vintages dominate the wine list. Open for dinner, but the bar is hopping until late.

➕ 206 E3 ☒ 230 Commercial Street, Provincetown ☎ (508) 487-9715 🕐 Wed.–Mon. 6–10:30 p.m., mid-May through Jan. 1 (also Tue. late in Aug.)

### ◆ Gallerani's Café $$
Small, stylish and as popular with the locals as with visitors, Gallerani's, in the West End of

town, focuses exclusively on dinner, using fresh products simply prepared. Fish such as halibut and tuna are regularly on the menu. Sauces are rarely more complex than a beurre blanc; spicy chutneys add life. There is a small but well-chosen wine list, and all the desserts are freshly prepared on the premises. Advance reservations are recommended.

➕ **206 E3** ⊠ **133 Commercial Street, Provincetown** ☎ **(508) 487-4433** 🕒 **Daily 6–10:30 p.m.; closed Mon.–Tue. in winter**

### ◆◆Martin House $$$

The building dates from 1740, but the dishes are strictly 21st century. Start with seared foie gras with a roasted apple and Stilton *galette*, move on to oven-roasted halibut with a crab crust and sage beurre blanc, then finish with an individual angel food cake, served with caramel curds and a milk-chocolate sauce. In summer, sit out on the brick garden terrace overlooking

the harbor; off-season, retreat to the snug, colonial-style rooms complete with blazing fires.

➕ **206 E3** ⊠ **157 Commercial Street, Provincetown** ☎ **(508) 487-1327** 🕒 **Daily 6 p.m.–1 a.m., Apr.–Oct. (kitchen closes at 11 p.m.); Fri.–Mon. 6–10 p.m, Nov.–Mar.**

### ◆◆The Mews $–$$$

At the Mews there are two places to eat: the light, airy restaurant, and the darker café. Both have views of the water and an informal dress code. The menus are about the same, "eclectic American," with filets and baked seafoods for the less adventurous. Be bold and try specials such as a lobster and sweet potato stew or a spice-rubbed rack of lamb with herb polenta. The Sunday brunch is getting to be an institution.

➕ **206 E3** ⊠ **429 Commercial Street, Provincetown** ☎ **(508) 487-1500** 🕒 **Mon.–Fri. 6–10:30 p.m. (6–8:30 p.m. off season), Sat.–Sun.11–2:30, 6–10:30 p.m. (6–9:30 p.m. off season)**

## Moors Restaurant $$

Provincetown still has a Portuguese population, descendants of fisherfolk who emigrated here in the 19th century. The menu at this long-established, unpretentious restaurant (way out of town, almost on the moors), features Portuguese fish dishes as well as the usual steaks and seafood. Try *caldeirada* (with shrimp, fish, mussels and clams in an herby tomato sauce) or *espada cozida* (swordfish cooked with olive oil and garlic).

➕ **206 E3** ⊠ **5 Bradford Street West, Provincetown** ☎ **(508) 487-0840** 🕒 **Daily 5.30–9.30, mid-May to mid-Oct.**

## NANTUCKET

### Black-Eyed Susan's $$

Breakfasters come for Dutch pancakes, omelettes and grits, but the evening crowd rarely knows what to expect from the chef, whose inspiration includes Asian, Indian and South American cuisine.

Malaysian barbecued pork might be served with a scallion pancake and mango slaw. The dessert of the day could be a Key lime pie, for example, with fresh raspberries and coconut cream. Bring your own wine; credit cards are not accepted.

➕ **206 E1** ⊠ **10 India Street, Nantucket** ☎ **(508) 325-0308** 🕒 **Mon.–Sat. 7–1, 6–10 p.m.; Sun. 7–1**

## Boarding House $$$

The Boarding House provides the sort of relaxed sophistication that vacationers from the big city enjoy. You can sit at the bar and eat a light dish, watch the world go by from the sidewalk terrace or go downstairs to the candlelit basement for a romantic meal. Order the exotic: Thai pesto noodles, pecan-crusted scrod and yellow-fin tuna with soy ginger. Reservations essential.

➕ **206 E1** ⊠ **12 Federal Street, Nantucket** ☎ **(508) 228-9622** 🕒 **Mon.–Sat. 6–10 p.m; Tue.–Sat. off-season**

# Where to...
## Shop

**Old King's Highway** In the towns along scenic Route 6A, you will find silver- and goldsmiths, glassblowers, potters, weavers and woodworkers. In Sandwich, the **Stencil Shoppe of Cape Cod** (Merchant Square, tel: 508/888-1124) carries over 3,000 designs. **Blacks** (597 Route 6A, tel: 508/362-3955) in West Barnstable specializes in throws and scarves woven on its own looms.

For antique shops, try **Maps of Antiquity** (1022 Main Street, West Barnstable, tel: 508/362-7169) or **Mark Lawrence Fine Period Antiques** (1050 Main Street, Brewster, tel: 508/896-6381). For more names, check out the **Cape Cod Antique Dealers Association** (www.ccada.com) and the **Cape Cod Potters** (capecodpotters.com).

**Provincetown** Local artists exhibit in the town's many galleries or at the **Provincetown Art Association and Museum** (460 Commercial Street, 508/487-1750). The **Julie Heller Gallery** (2 Gosnold Street, tel: 508/487-2169) follows in the tradition of artists such as Karl Knaths, Ross Moffett and Harry Hensche, who helped put the town on the artistic map. Contemporary work is shown at the **Rice/Polak Gallery** (430 Commercial Street, tel: 508/487-1052) and the **Cortland Jessup Gallery** (432 Commercial Street, tel: 508/487-4479).

**Nantucket** For local crafts, climb the stairs to **Made on Nantucket** (44 Main Street, tel: 508/228-0110) or stop at **Nantucket Glassworks** (28 Centre Street, tel: 508/228 7779). For Nantucket Reds (sailcloth clothes) go to **Murray's Toggery Shop** (62 Main Street, tel: 508/228-0437), and for lightship baskets to **Lightship Shop** (20 Miacomet Avenue, tel: 508/228-4164).

# Where to...
## Be Entertained

**Theater** Cape Cod has a long tradition of summer stock theater at venues such as the **Cape Playhouse** in Dennis (820 Main Street, Route 6A, tel: 508/385-3911) and the **Provincetown Repertory Theater** (336 Commercial Street, tel: 508/487-8673).

**Bicycling** In recent years, cycling on the Cape has taken off, thanks to a series of designated trails, which include the 3.6 mile Shining Sea Bike Trail and the 25-mile Cape Cod Rail Trail (▶ 88). Hiring a bike is easier than it used to be. In Falmouth Heights, **Holiday Cycles** (465 Grand Avenue, tel: 508/540-3549) have tandems as well as regular 10- or 3-speed models. Rent for an hour, a day or the week. Out in Provincetown, **Arnold's** (329 Commercial Street, tel: 508/487-0844) is a 50-year old business. The **Dennis Chamber of Commerce** (tel: 800/243-9920) has free Rail Trail maps.

**Sailing** You can charter a 36-foot sailboat with a skipper or learn to sail yourself with **Cape Cod Sailing** (Eventide, Hyannis tel: 508/771-7918), or keep it simple with a canoe, sail board or sunfish from **Jack's Boat Rentals** in Wellfleet (Gull Pond, tel: 508/349-7553).

**Golf** With 32 public and 12 private courses, the Cape is a delight for golf enthusiasts. For more information, contact the **Cape Cod Chamber of Commerce** (P.O. Box 790, Hyannis MA 02601, tel: 508/362-3225).

# The Berkshires

In Two Days 97
Don't Miss 98 – 102
At Your Leisure 103 – 105
Where To 106 – 108

# Getting Your Bearings

**When the top names in music and dance go on vacation, they head for the Berkshire Hills in western Massachusetts, home to two of the country's premier arts festivals.**

Tanglewood, the summer home of the Boston Symphony Orchestra, has entertained audiences since 1938 with concerts on the lawn almost every night in summer, while Jacob's Pillow Dance Festival attracts the hottest names in classical and modern dance for summer performances in the country air.

July and August are the busiest months in the Berkshires. This is the season for all the cultural events, when rooms double or triple in price and are still hard to come by. You can come at other times of year and find cheaper rates, but it's like visiting the beach offseason.

The Berkshires grew up in the mid-19th century when wealthy New Yorkers and Bostonians (novelists Edith Wharton and Herman Melville and abolitionist Henry Ward Beecher among them) fled here from oppressive urban summers. Their homes are now fine inns welcoming a new breed of wealthy unfazed by the high prices.

If you overdose on culture, you can always revive with a walk along the Appalachian Trail, a shopping trip to Sheffield and Great Barrington. Or just do as the locals do: sit on the porch and watch folks hurry by.

Previous page: Beartown State Forest

## ★ Don't Miss

**1** Tanglewood ➤ 98
**3** The Appalachian Trail ➤ 100
**4** Jacob's Pillow Dance Festival ➤ 102

## At Your Leisure

**2** Norman Rockwell Museum ➤ 103
**5** The Mount ➤ 103
**6** Hancock Shaker Village ➤ 104
**7** Williamstown Theatre Festival ➤ 105

# The Berkshires in Two Days

## Day One

### Morning

Enjoy a leisurely breakfast, then drive down Route 7, the antiques corridor of the Berkshires. Sheffield is the unofficial antiques capital, but equally interesting furniture, collectibles and other assorted treasures can be had in Great Barrington.

### Afternoon

Have lunch at the historic Red Lion Inn in Stockbridge (➤ 107), then cruise over to the **Norman Rockwell Museum** (➤ 103). If the museum itself doesn't appeal, just walk around the picturesque town that inspired the artist's (above) many *Saturday Evening Post* covers.

### Evening

Get yourself to Lenox in time for an early dinner at Gateways Inn (51 Walker Street, tel: 413/637-2532) before heading off for an evening of top-flight classical music at **Tanglewood** (➤ 98–99).

## Day Two

### Morning

Make an early start for a walk on the **Appalachian Trail** (➤ 100–101). John Drummond Kennedy Park is a good local option, with more than 12 miles of trails leading to scenic overlooks. Alternatively, drive to Beartown State Forest in Stockbridge (left) for the 4-mile loop around Benedict Pond, or the link to the Maine-to-Georgia Appalachian Trail.

### Afternoon

Grab a quick lunch in Lee at Cactus Café (54 Main Street, tel: 413/243-4300), an informal Mexican restaurant. Then catch a matinee performance at **Jacob's Pillow** (➤ 102), which is to dance what Tanglewood is to music. Tickets for top performers sell out, so order them in advance.

### Evening

After the performance at the Pillow, you can treat yourself to a fine dinner at the Federal House Inn in Lee (Route 102, tel: 413/243-1824) or, if you have the stamina, drive up to Williamstown for a performance of the **Williamstown Theatre Festival** (➤ 105).

# Tanglewood

A blanket big enough for two spread out on a rolling green lawn. A picnic basket filled to the flaps with freshly baked bread, delicious cheeses, inventive salads and gourmet pasta dishes. A bottle of fine wine to be sipped on a moonlit night. What could be more perfect? Music, you say? Okay. How about the Boston Symphony Orchestra?

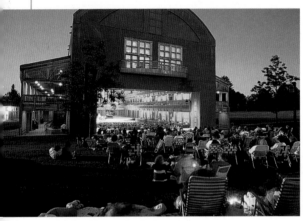

**Smaller concerts are held at the Seiji Ozawa Hall**

**Sir André Previn is frequently a guest conductor at Tanglewood**

If it sounds too good to be true, then it must be Tanglewood, the nation's premier summer music festival, and the main reason the Berkshire Hills are what they are today. In the era before air-conditioning, the Boston Symphony Orchestra decided that its urban home was too hot for concerts in July and August, and took up summer residence in the Berkshires, where the temperature and humidity were more bearable, especially at night. The location, 2 hours from Boston and 3 hours from New York, immediately appealed to wealthy patrons of the arts in these two cities, who continue to come here in droves each summer. The top names in classical music find Tanglewood almost as enticing as the audiences do.

Picnicking on the lawn is the romantic way to go, but those who prefer an actual seat will have to plan ahead. You pay more for an assigned seat in the 5,000-seat Koussevitsky Music Shed (designed in 1938 by noted architect Eliel Saarinen and later named for the BSO's erstwhile music director, Serge Koussevitsky), but you have an actual view of the stage, and are under cover in case of bad weather.

Tanglewood's schedule is usually announced in late February, and returning visitors get the first chance at the best seats. But there are still plenty of good seats available when tickets go on sale to the general public by the middle of

March, and even if you wait until June, you're likely to find seats for all but the most popular weekend performances. If you're content to sit on the lawn, you can wait until the day and see how the weather turns out before assembling your picnic.

Try to attend a midweek concert, when the 300-acre site is a lot less crowded. You'll have plenty of elbow room and fewer sport-utility vehicles hogging space in the parking lot. And if you prefer a seat in the Shed, you can often get tickets to midweek concerts a few days before (sometimes even the day of) the show.

Wynton Marsalis (above) and Yo-Yo Ma (left) are just two of the internationally acclaimed musicians who make room for Tanglewood in their summer schedules

### TAKING A BREAK

You can get gourmet picnic fixings at various delicatessens in town. Try **Perfect Picnics** (72 Church Street, Lenox, tel: 413/637-3015).

✚ 206 A3
✉ West Street, Lenox, MA 01240. From Lenox, take Route 183 1.4 miles west. Mailing address: Symphony Hall, 301 Massachusetts Avenue, Boston, MA 02115
☎ Box office and general information: (413) 637-1600; concert dates and information: (413) 637-5165; web: www.bso.org
💵 Tickets range from around $12.50 for seats on the lawn to $82 for seats in the Koussevitsky Music Shed. Lawn tickets for children under 12 are free. No children under 5.
🕐 Evenings, mid-Jun. to first weekend in Sep.

### TANGLEWOOD: INSIDE INFO

**In more detail** Smaller concerts are held in the 1,180-seat **Seiji Ozawa Hall**, named for the BSO's music director, who stepped down in 1999 after a 25-year run. Lawn seats are also available for performances in Ozawa Hall.
• Once or twice a month, Tanglewood stages **opera** in a venue known simply as "the Theatre." It, too, attracts the top names, from Jessye Norman to Kiri Te Kanawa. Prices range from around $20 to $100. Note there are no lawn seats for opera performances.

**One to miss** Don't bother trying to see **Hawthorne Cottage**; the building is a replica of the one where author Nathaniel Hawthorne lived while writing *The House of the Seven Gables* (1851) and isn't open to the public.

# The Appalachian Trail

The Appalachian Trail is arguably the finest hiking trail in the United States. Built by volunteers from 1921 to 1937 and designated a National Scenic Trail in 1968, it snakes 2,158 miles from Maine all the way down to Georgia. Each year, hundreds of hardy souls set out to hike the trail from one end to the other – a journey of five to six months – and quite a few of them finish the trek.

But not everybody need go to such extremes. The trail meanders through the Berkshires, so you can pack a picnic lunch and make a day hike of it. Although the trail scales heights of 5,000 to 6,000 feet at times, the highest summits in the Berkshires are no more than 3,500 feet.

The best place to catch up with the Appalachian Trail is at **Beartown State Forest** (from Great Barrington, take Route 7 north to Monument Valley Road, then turn left onto Stony Brook Road and follow it about 5 miles to the Benedict Pond visitor area). Here you will find a placid lake where you can swim, fish or take an hour-long stroll around the circumference of its shores. About halfway around the trail that loops the pond, you come to the intersection with the Appalachian Trail (marked by white blazes on the trees). From here, you can hike 5 miles or 50. In the course of your day hike, you may cross paths with one or more hikers taking aim at the trail's entire length. In May and June, you'll meet optimistic trekkers on the early part of their journey south; in late summer, you'll encounter slightly scraggier hikers looking to make it north to Maine before the first frosts of fall.

Another Appalachian Trail crossroads lies in **October Mountain State Forest** (take Route 20 east to East Street and turn left, then turn right on Willow Hill Road and follow the signs to the main entrance). Ask at the park headquarters how to get to the Appalachian Trail, or see which of the dozen other trails in the park best matches your ability. The Appalachian Trail is linear: how far you go is how far you have to come back.

The trail wends through forest (above) and pastureland (left) on its way across New England

## THE APPALACHIAN TRAIL: INSIDE INFO

**Top tip** Bring **insect repellent** to combat the gnats and mosquitoes. *Deep Woods Off* is particularly effective, as are *Avon's Skin So Soft* lotions and oils. Powdered garlic capsules are also reportedly effective.

**In more detail** There are 31 hiking trails of varying difficulty at **John Drummond Kennedy Park** in Lenox. Walk or drive up Main Street just past the Church on the Hill (you can park in the lot any time except Sunday morning). In winter, these trails are used by cross-country skiers.

The 4-mile loop around Benedict Pond is a shorter, less hilly option to the Appalachian Trail itself

## TAKING A BREAK

Make up a picnic lunch at **Guido's Marketplace** in Great Barrington (760 Main Street, tel: 413/528-5775).

### Beartown State Forest
➕ 206 A3  ✉ 69 Blue Hill Road, Monterey, MA 01245 ☎ (413) 528-0904; web: www.state.ma.us/dem/parks/bear.htm

### October Mountain State Forest
➕ 206 A3  ✉ 317 Woodland Road, Lee, MA 01238-9563 ☎ (413) 243-1778; web: www.state.ma.us/dem/parks/octm.htm

# Jacob's Pillow Dance Festival

What began as dance pioneer Ted Shawn's attempt to legitimize dance as an honorable career for men has resulted in the country's premier summer venue for dance. All the biggest names in American dance have performed here – Twyla Tharp, Mark Morris, Merce Cunningham, the Dance Theater of Harlem and, of course, Martha Graham, who was a regular every summer.

At the end of the festival's first summer in 1933, the crowds were so big that Shawn had to turn people away. By 1942 the first permanent theater had been built, and despite wartime rationing, the crowds climbed the hill on foot and on horseback to see performances in ballet, folk and modern dance.

Today, the audiences arrive via station wagons and sport-utility vehicles rather than horses, and the quality of the performers has kept pace. The festival is a hot ticket, especially on summer weekends. If you want to see a popular show, get your seats as far in advance as possible. The summer schedule is first announced in February and tickets go on sale May 1. You can order them over the phone or on the Internet.

If the performances alone don't sate your appetite, consider the free pre- and post-performance discussions, as well as the Saturday lecture series.

The **Pillow Café** (tel: 413/637-1322) offers dining under a tent, but reservations are a must. **Pillow Pub,** which serves sandwiches and salad and has a snack bar for tea, coffee and cookies, is another option. Alternatively, you can take a picnic. Ask at your inn or bed-and-breakfast if they'll make one for you (some places pride themselves on their gourmet picnic baskets), or call 24 hours in advance to order one from Jacob's Pillow itself.

---

✚ 206 A3
✉ P.O. Box 287, Lee, MA 01238. From Route 7, take Route 20 east approximately 8.3 miles. Turn left onto George Carter Road. Travel half a mile and make a right at the entrance to Jacob's Pillow
☎ (413) 637-1322 or (413) 243-0745 for the box office; web: www.jacobspillow.org
🕐 Season: most days, late Jun.– Aug. 31. Performances at the Ted Shawn Theatre: 8 p.m. Tue.–Thu., 8:30 p.m. Fri.–Sat., 2 p.m. and 8:30 p.m., 2 p.m. Sun. Performances at the Doris Duke Studio Theater: 8:15 p.m. Thu.–Fri., 5 p.m. Sat.–Sun.

# At Your Leisure

## 2 Norman Rockwell Museum

If, while strolling along Stockbridge's Main Street, you feel like you've walked into a painting, it's because you have. The artist Norman Rockwell, of *Saturday Evening Post* fame, called Stockbridge home from 1953 until his death in 1978, and if he were to return today, there is little he wouldn't recognize.

The largest collection of Rockwell's work is housed in this museum just outside of Stockbridge. Some people love Rockwell's visions of the common events of people's lives, such as visits to the doctor, sibling rivalry and rain disrupting a baseball game. Others dismiss Rockwell's Americana as too sentimental to be considered serious art.

From time to time, the museum collects all 321 of Rockwell's *Saturday Evening Post* covers (dating from 1916 to 1963) in a single exhibit. Other draws are Rockwell's studio itself (relocated here, along the banks of the Housatonic River) and the Mirror on America exhibit, which includes the artist's more serious works. His "Four Freedoms" series was intended to create support for World War II, while several portraits done in the 1960s and 1970s reveal a political side few knew about.

🕂 206 A3 ⊠ Route 183, Stockbridge, MA 01262 ☎ (413) 298-4100; web: www.nrm.org 🕐 Museum: daily 10–5, May–Oct.; Mon.–Fri. 10–4, Sat.–Sun. 10–5, Nov.–Apr. Closed Jan. 1, Thanksgiving and Dec. 25. Studio: daily 10–5, May–Oct. 💵 Moderate. Discounts for children aged 6–18; children under 6 free.

## 5 The Mount

The Mount is home to **Shakespeare & Co.**, a company staging admirable productions of the Bard's work, as well as that of lesser playwrights – not to mention puppet shows, dance programs and student productions. Works by the Pulitzer Prize-winning author Edith Wharton, who lived here from 1902 to 1911, are also produced regularly. The actors are strictly summer stock, but every now and then a big national name joins the crew.

Wharton fans may wish to tour the white Georgian-style mansion, which she designed. She was no dilettante when it came to home design. Following the publication of her best-selling novel, *The House of Mirth*, she wrote: "Decidedly, I'm a better landscape gardener than novelist, and this place, every line of which is my own work, far surpasses *The House of Mirth*." It is one of only a handful of National Historic Landmarks designed by a woman.

🕂 206 A3 ⊠ 2 Plunkett Street, Lenox, MA 01240 ☎ The Mount: (413) 637-1899. Shakespeare & Co.: (413) 637-1199 or box office (413) 637-3553; web: www.shakespeare.org 🕐 The Mount: daily 9–3, May–Oct. 💵 Tickets range from moderate for student productions to expensive for Saturday night Shakespeare performances. The Mount: moderate

## 🄺 Hancock Shaker Village

Ask any high school student what he or she remembers about the Shakers and the invariable one-word answer is: celibacy. This community, so named for its fervor during religious rites, led an ascetic life, believing that spirituality could be attained by performing routine tasks to perfection. Shaker communities prospered from 1744 to the mid-19th century, gaining a reputation for their craftsmanship and ingenuity, and the simple, ordered lifestyle attracted followers until about 1960.

The Shaker community in Hancock was one of the most important, and when the religious movement died out it became an outdoor museum of Shaker life in America. Some 21 buildings are located on more than 1,200 acres here, with special events, programs and even Shaker meals on offer.

The most impressive building on the property is the 1870 Round Stone Barn, designed so that one person standing in the middle could feed more than 50 cows at once, and milk them nearly as easily. The original Brick Dwelling, built in a swift 10 weeks in 1832 by 100 Shaker men and women, is also of interest. Shaker Sisters staffed the huge communal kitchen downstairs. Upstairs, dormitory-style "retiring rooms" housed men on one side of the building and women on the other

**The Round Stone Barn (top), the most famous building at Hancock Shaker Village, is noted for its ingenious interior design (above)**

(with separate entrances on opposite sides of the building). The sexes came together only during meals and meetings.

The Barn and the Brick Dwelling are the only must-sees among the buildings. Three others – the Trustees Office and Store, the Laundry/Machine Shop and the Meetinghouse – are on the guided tour. If you want to see more (or less) than this, go in summer, when you can take a self-guiding tour.

✚ 204 A1 ✉ P.O. Box 927 (at the intersection of routes 20 and 41), Pittsfield, MA 01202-0927 ☎ (413)

443-0188 or (800) 817-1137; web:
www.hancockshakervillage.org
🌐 Daily 9:30–5, Memorial Day weekend–Oct.; 10–3, Apr.–Memorial Day
weekend and late Oct.–Nov. Winter
Week in February, with 90-minute
guided tours leaving on the hour
💰 Expensive. Reductions for children
under 18 and families

## 7 Williamstown Theatre Festival

Every summer, the college town of
Williamstown
hosts an 11-

**7**
**Williamstown**
**Theatre Festival**
1064m
Mount ▲ Mt Greylock
Greylock
State ○ Adams
Reservation
New
Ashford ○
7
116
Appalachian Trail
Lanesborough ○
8
Dalton ○
20 □ Pittsfield
20 **6** □ Hancock
Shaker Village
8
43

week theater festival, with 11 different productions of classic and new
plays, readings and workshops. The
festival, which was begun in 1955 to
draw tourists to this sleepy part of
the northern Berkshires, has become
a model for summer theaters around
the country and attracts top-name
Broadway and Hollywood actors and
directors. Many festival productions
have later gone on to Broadway.
➕ 204 A1 ✉ 1000 Main Street, Route
2, P.O. Box 517, Williamstown, MA
01267-0517. Take Route 7 north to
Williamstown. The Adams Memorial
Theatre is at the junction of Route 7
and Route 2 east, next to the Williams
College admissions building ☎ 24-
hour information: (413) 597-3399. Box
office (summer only): (413) 597-3400;
web: www.wtfestival.org 🌐 Season:
mid-Jun. to mid. Aug. Main Stage
performances: Tue.–Fri. 8 p.m., Sat.
8:30 p.m. Matinees Thu. and Sun.

### Berkshire Towns

With the exception of Williamstown,
the Berkshire towns described in this
chapter are all within easy reach of
one another. Lenox has the best
dining scene; Stockbridge the best
shops and two fine historic homes,
**Chesterwood** (tel: 413/298-3579)
and **Naumkeag** (tel: 413/298-3239);
and Sheffield the best antiques.
Great Barrington is the commercial
center. If you go to Williamstown for
the Theatre Festival, the **Sterling and
Francine Clark Art Institute** (225 South
Street, tel: 413/458-2303) is worth
a visit. The fine collection includes
works by Renoir, Degas and Gauguin,
as well as 17th- and 18th-century
paintings.

#### Great Barrington's Southern Berkshire Chamber of Commerce
➕ 206 A3 ✉ 362 Main Street, Great
Barrington, MA 01230 ☎ (413) 528-
1510; web: www.greatbarrington.org

#### Lee Chamber of Commerce
➕ 206 A3 ✉ P.O. Box 345, Park
Place, Lee, MA 01238-0345
☎ (413) 243-0852;
web: www.leechamber.org

#### Lenox Chamber of Commerce
➕ 206 A3 ✉ P.O. Box 646, Lenox,
MA 01240 ☎ (413) 637-3646;
web: www.lenox.org

#### Stockbridge Chamber of Commerce
➕ 206 A3 ✉ P.O. Box 224, Elm
Street, Stockbridge, MA 01262
☎ (413) 298-5200;
web: www.stockbridgechamber.org

#### Williamstown Chamber of Commerce
➕ 204 A1 ✉ Box 357, Williamstown,
MA 10267 ☎ (413) 458-9077;
web: www.williamstownchamber.com

2 p.m., Sat. 4 p.m. 💰 Main Stage
production tickets: $20 to $37
depending on date and seat location

# Where to... Stay

## Prices
Expect to pay for two people sharing a double room, excluding taxes

$ under $150  $$ $150–250  $$$ over $250

### ◆◆◆Inn at Stockbridge $$

The inn, once a millionaire's summer home, is separated from Stockbridge by the Massachusetts Pike. The owners have renovated the modern Georgian-style building throughout and added a cottage at the rear, with four themed bedrooms: St. Andrew's, which has a display of clubs, is ideal for golf fans; Provence is for romantics. The swimming pool is a bonus.

✚ 206 A3 ✉ 30 East Street, Stockbridge, MA 01262 ☎ (413) 298-3337 or (888) 466-7865; fax: (413) 298-3406; web: www.stockbridgeinn.com

### ◆◆◆The Gables Inn $-$$

Writer Edith Wharton stayed here before it became an inn and much is made of the Wharton connection, with a re-creation of her octagonal library and a floral bedroom with four-poster bed named for her. Other themed bedrooms include the Teddy Wharton and the U.S. Presidents. This is a great place to relax, with a garden and terrace, tennis court and a solar-heated swimming pool.

✚ 206 A3 ✉ 103 Walker Street, Lenox, MA 01240 ☎ (413) 637-3416; web: www.gableslenox.com

### ◆◆◆Brook Farm Inn $-$$

This converted 19th-century farmhouse stands in a residential area just off the Old Stockbridge Road. The two rooms at the front are the most attractive, with canopy beds and antique furnishings. All 12 rooms have their own bathrooms. The owners put out a new "poem of the day" to inspire their guests each morning, and at 4 p.m. they serve tea in the sitting rooms.

✚ 206 A3 ✉ 15 Hawthorne Street, Lenox, MA 01240 ☎ (413) 637-3013 or (800) 285-7638; fax: (413) 637-4751; web: www.brookfarminn.com

### Walker House $

Walker House, a 19th-century Federal-style building behind a neat white fence, is within easy reach of Tanglewood. Owner Richard Houdek was a music critic and his wife Peggy an opera singer, and bedrooms are named for composers such as Mozart, Beethoven and Handel (this last with a handsome brass bed). Breakfast is taken outdoors on the veranda in summer, or in among the antiques and plants in the dining room.

✚ 206 A3 ✉ 64 Walker Street, Lenox, MA 01240 ☎ (413) 637-1271 or (800) 235-3098; fax: (413) 637-2387; web: www.walkerhouse.com

### Field Farm Guest House $$

Spare, square Field Farm comes as a surprise after the predominantly colonial architecture of rural Massachusetts. Built in 1948 in the American Modern style, it has five bedrooms (three with private decks), lawns and views of the Taconic Mountains. Furnishings are in keeping: American modern art and Scandinavian Modern chairs and tables. All this and Belgian waffles with berries for breakfast. It is now run by a preservation society.

✚ 204 A1 ✉ 554 Sloan Road, Williamstown, MA 01267 ☎ (413) 458-3135; fax: (413) 458-3135; web: www.thetrustees.org

# Where to...
# Eat and Drink

## Prices
Expect to pay per person for a three-course meal, excluding drinks and service

$ under $15  $$ $15–30  $$$ over $30

---

### GREAT BARRINGTON

## Castle Street Café $$

Traditional New England dishes are mixed with European imports for a truly eclectic menu. In the fall, menus include dishes like butternut squash soup, French cassoulet and warm cranberry cobbler. French vintages are a feature of the wine list. There is live jazz at weekends and six nights a week in summer.

➕ 206 A3 ⊠ 10 Castle Street, Great Barrington ☎ (413) 528-5244
◷ Daily 5–10 (also Fri.–Sat. 10–11 p.m.); off-season: daily 5–9 (also Fri.–Sat. 9–10 p.m.)

---

### STOCKBRIDGE

## ◆◆◆ Red Lion Inn $$–$$$

The historic Red Lion still welcomes one and all. In the formal main dining room modern dishes are served, ranging from skillet-roast spiced chicken to marinated grilled tuna with clams. The Tavern is more casual, while the downstairs pub serves local brews and lighter fare. Drinks and cocktails are served all day on the famous front porch.

➕ 206 A3 ⊠ Main Street, Stockbridge ☎ (413) 298-5545
◷ Daily 7 a.m–9 p.m.

---

cakes, pan-roasted chicken with pumpkin flan, or rustic beef stew served with caramelized fall vegetables. Take time over the excellent wine list. Reservations are recommended.

➕ 206 A3 ⊠ 65 Church Street, Lenox ☎ (413) 637-2745 ◷ Daily 11:30–2, 5:30–9; closed Sun.–Mon., Nov.–May

---

### LENOX

## Apple Tree Inn and Restaurant $$

With Tanglewood just across the street, reservations here are essential during the season. The hilltop hotel is set in 22 acres and there are grand views to the south from the circular dining room. In summer, you can sit out on the deck. Dishes include filet mignon, baked salmon, roast duck and, in season, apple pie made from the apples growing right outside. Desserts are served after concerts.

➕ 206 A3 ⊠ 10 Richmond Mountain Road, Lenox ☎ (413) 637-1477
◷ Daily 5.30–9, in season; closed Mon.–Wed., rest of year

## Church Street Café $$$

A strong local following has built up for the "eclectic American" cooking served here and whether you wear shorts or a suit and tie, you are made welcome. Signature dishes include sauteed Maine crab

---

## ◆◆◆ Lenox House $$

Despite the pressure of crowds during the summer concert and fall foliage seasons, Lenox House (just a few minutes from the center of town) maintains consistent levels of well-prepared food and attentive service. The country-style dining room is known for its popovers. Along with familiar beef and chicken dishes, regular favorites include chicken amandine and veal Oscar. Families are made particularly welcome here.

➕ 206 A3 ⊠ 55 Pittsfield–Lenox Road, Lenox ☎ (413) 637-1341
◷ Daily 11:30–10

# Where to... Shop

**Antiques** The villages along Route 7, which parallels the New York State border as it runs north from Connecticut through Massachusetts to Vermont, are known for their antiques shops. Expect everything from folk art and painted furniture to quilts and paintings.

In Great Barrington, take time to explore **Coffman's Country Antiques Market** (Jenifer House Commons, Route 7, tel: 413/528-9282), as well as the **Berkshires Art Gallery** and a tempting microbrewery. Sheffield, Stockbridge, Lenox and Williamstown are also good hunting grounds.

**Crafts** Look out for **Fellerman & Raabe Glassworks** (534 South Main Street, Route 7, Sheffield, tel: 413/229-8533), where glass sculptures and vases are made in front of you. At **All Fired Up!** in West Stockbridge (6 Harris Street, tel: 413/232-4666), you can make your own paperweights.

Try **Hancock Shaker Village** for crafted wood items (Routes 20 and 41, Pittsfield, tel: 413/443-0188 or 800/817-1137), **MASS MoCA** (87 Marshall Street, North Adams, tel: 413/664-4481) for chunky, industrial-look jewelry; and the **Sterling and Francine Clark Art Institute** (225 South Street, Williamstown, tel: 413/458-9545) for an astonishing array of art books, posters and related material.

**Outlet Shops** In Lee, catch a bargain at the **Berkshire Outlet Village** (Route 20 East, tel: 413/243-8186). The **Berkshire Pendleton and Outlet Store** (100 Williamstown Road, tel: 413/443-6822) in Lanesborough has a fine array of patterned Indian blankets and pillows, as well as sportswear.

# Where to... Be Entertained

**Hiking and Bicycling** The natural beauty of the Berkshire Hills makes them ideal for hiking or bicycling. For maps and more information contact the Department of Environmental Management (tel: 617/626-1250).

At **Bartholomew's Cobble**, a nature reserve near Ashley Falls, there are 6 miles of marked trails. At **Monument Mountain**, high above Great Barrington, 3 miles of trails lead to fine views of Devil's Pulpit. On a clear day, you can see five states from the top of **Mount Greylock**, which at 3,487 feet is the highest point in Massachusetts. For more energetic hikes, sign up with a specialist outfitter such as **Greylock Discovery Tours** (tel: 413/499-9648) or **Zoar Outdoors** (tel: 800/532-7483).

**Historic Homes** After visiting the Norman Rockwell Museum (▶ 103), you can drop by **Chesterwood** (4 Williamsville Road, off Route 183, Stockbridge, tel: 413/298-3579), the vacation home of sculptor Daniel Chester French. **Naumkeag** (Prospect Hill Road, Stockbridge, tel: 413/298-3239), another "summer cottage," is also worth a visit. The 23-room mansion has a delightful garden, the highlight of which is the elegant birch walk.

**Fall Foliage** Although the displays in Vermont and New Hampshire are better known, the Berkshires can be equally impressive. **Route 2**, or the Mohawk Trail, between North Adams and Orange, is popular with leaf-peepers in October.

# Vermont

In Four Days 112 – 113
Don't Miss 114 – 120
At Your Leisure 121 – 124
Where To 125 – 130

# Getting Your Bearings

There is something special about Vermont. Maybe it's the fact that the entire state has only one city with more than 20,000 people. Maybe it's the law banning billboards from marring the beautiful Green Mountain landscape. Maybe it's the cheese from the hundreds of dairies and creameries. Whatever it is, it's wonderful, and while you may not be able to put your finger on exactly what makes Vermont so special, you will notice it almost as soon as you cross the state border.

Woodstock and Manchester are two of the state's top resort destinations. Manchester, in southwestern Vermont, boasts some of the state's finest inns and some of the best fishing in the northeastern United States. Woodstock is in central Vermont, at the center of countless different kinds of outdoor activities. The driving tour on pages 181–183 shows a scenic route between the two areas. The tour, indeed all of Vermont, is at its most gorgeous during fall foliage season, but that's also when rates are highest at lodgings throughout the state.

Summer is the time when all of Vermont's wares are on display. The state has only two limited-access highways, but hundreds of byways, dirt roads and hiking trails. There are scant few multiplexes where you can see a movie, but thousands of bucolic spots for a picnic. In Vermont, you trade in your briefcase for a backpack, your cell phone for a fishing pole, and your laptop for a trail map; you might travel

**Laid back and leisured: life in Vermont**

via horseback or bicycle from one inn to another, or you might spend all day fishing for trout in the stream behind your hotel. It's an early-to-bed, early-to-rise kind of state; once the sun goes down, deer outnumber people on most roads, and nightlife is pretty tame – the exception being the access roads to downhill ski resorts across the state, where in winter the aprés-ski parties continue late into the night.

**Previous page: Fall foliage**
**Left: West Barnet, a quintessential Vermont town**

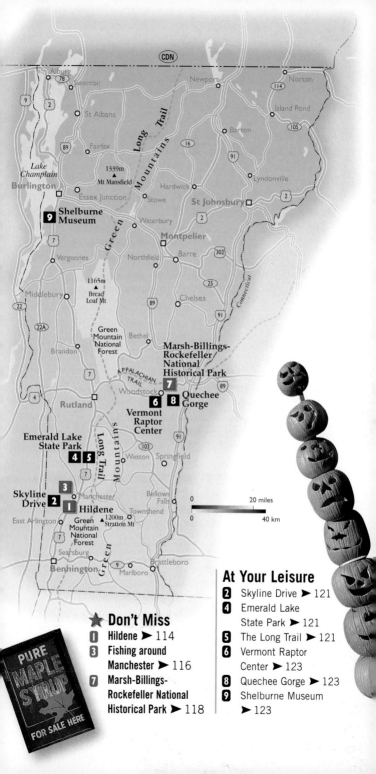

CDN

Alburg
Swanton
St Albans
Fairfax
Lake
Champlain
**Burlington**
Essex Junction
Stowe

**9** Shelburne
Museum

Waterbury

Vergennes
Middlebury

Northfield

1165m
▲
Bread
Loaf Mt

Brandon

Green
Mountain
National
Forest

Rutland

**Emerald Lake
State Park**

**4** **5**

**Skyline
Drive**

**2** **1**

**Hildene**

East Arlington

Searsburg

**Bennington**

Newport
Norton

Island Pond

Barton

Hardwick

**St Johnsbury**
Lyndonville

**Montpelier**

Barre

Chelsea

Bethel

**Marsh-Billings-
Rockefeller
National
Historical Park**

Woodstock
**7**
**6** **8** Quechee
Gorge

**Vermont
Raptor
Center**

Weston
Springfield

Manchester

Bellows
Falls
Townshend

1200m
▲
Stratton Mt

Green
Mountain
National
Forest

Marlboro
Brattleboro

Long Trail

Green Mountains

APPALACHIAN TRAIL

Connecticut

1339m
▲
Mt Mansfield

0        20 miles
0           40 km

## ★ Don't Miss

**1** Hildene ► 114
**3** Fishing around
Manchester ► 116
**7** Marsh-Billings-
Rockefeller National
Historical Park ► 118

## At Your Leisure

**2** Skyline Drive ► 121
**4** Emerald Lake
State Park ► 121
**5** The Long Trail ► 121
**6** Vermont Raptor
Center ► 123
**8** Quechee Gorge ► 123
**9** Shelburne Museum
► 123

PURE
MAPLE
SYRUP
FOR SALE HERE

The best of Vermont is seen along its dirt paths, hiking trails and back roads. Try fly-fishing on a quiet lake near Manchester, hike part of the Long Trail and stop at one of the multitude of picturesque Vermont towns.

# Vermont in Four Days

## Day One

### Morning
Make your way from your base in Manchester to **Hildene** (➤ 114–115), the historic home of Robert Todd Lincoln (left). In winter, you can cross-country ski on the grounds. In summer, the lawns and gardens are amazing.

### Afternoon
Have lunch at the Little Red Rooster Café in Manchester (➤ 128), then stroll down Main Street toward the outlet stores. Learn to fly-fish at **Orvis** headquarters (➤ 116), or drive out to **Emerald Lake State Park** (➤ 121) for the afternoon. If you're feeling energetic, you could hike part of the **Long Trail** (➤ 121–122), one of New England's prettiest hiking paths.

### Evening
Have dinner at one of the fine inns or at the Black Swan in Manchester Village (➤ 127). Nightlife here is pretty tame, but the clear Vermont air and rural countryside make for great stargazing from your hotel porch or balcony.

## Day Two

### Morning
Head north to the Woodstock area, following the first half of the **Vermont driving tour** (➤ 181–183). The route takes you through some of Vermont's finest scenery (right), passing the ski resorts of Stowe and Killington.

### Afternoon
Stop for lunch in Weston at the Bryant House Restaurant (tel: 802/824-3184), just a few steps from the Vermont Country Store. If you arrive in Woodstock early enough, visit the **Vermont Raptor Center** (➤ 123), with its magnificent birds of prey, or visit the Kedron Valley Stables (➤ 130).

### Evening
Settle in at your Woodstock accommodations, then head to Bentley's for dinner. The food is good, desserts are even better, and on Friday nights half the town shows up for the DJ and dance tunes (➤ 128).

# Day Three

### Morning

Spend the day at the various parts of the
**Marsh-Billings-Rockefeller National Historical
Park** (➤ 118–120). Start by hiking to the
top of **Mount Tom** (➤ 118) for a commanding
view of the entire Woodstock area.

### Afternoon

Visit **Billings Farm and Museum**
(➤ 118–119), a working dairy farm where
you can watch cows being milked, introduce
yourself to week-old calves and pet sheep.
Across the street is the historic mansion that
was home to both Marsh and Billings, as well
as Mary and Laurance Rockefeller.

### Evening

Drive east along Route 4 to the nearby town of Quechee. If there's still
daylight, check out **Quechee Gorge** (above, ➤ 123). Or watch glassblowers at
work at the Simon Pearce Studio. Dine at the Simon Pearce Restaurant
(➤ 128), overlooking a waterfall on the Ottaquechee river.

# Day Four

Drive north on I-89 to the town of Shelburne, home of the **Shelburne Museum**
(below, ➤ 123–124), a veritable cornucopia of art and architecture from all
over New England and New York. It's almost like the region's attic. Break the
journey in Montpelier and sample the work of student chefs from the New
England Culinary Institute at the casual Main Street Grill and Bar (118 Main
Street, tel: 802/229-9209).

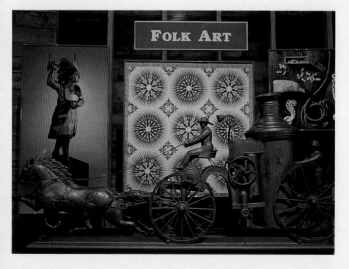

FOLK ART

# Hildene

Vermont isn't usually known for its historic homes – most of the state's pleasures are to be found outdoors, not in. The exception that proves the rule is Hildene, a majestic 24-room Georgian Revival mansion overlooking hundreds of acres of the choicest land in Manchester.

Hildene was built in 1905 as a summer home for Robert Todd Lincoln, the only son of President Abraham Lincoln to survive to adulthood. The younger Lincoln loved Vermont and was a frequent visitor for more than 40 years before building his estate here. By that time, aged 62, he had amassed a small fortune as a lawyer, Secretary of War, ambassador to Great Britain, and president of the Pullman Palace Car Company.

**Robert Todd Lincoln (above), only son of Abraham Lincoln, built Hildene (top) as a summer home**

The house is opulent by any definition, but compared to the extravagant "cottages" built around the same time in Newport by the Astors and Vanderbilts, it is on a much more human scale. What is extraordinary, however, is the 1908 Aeolian organ, with its 1,000 pipes. The house is literally built around the organ, with the pipes cleverly concealed in air shafts within the sweeping staircase. When the organ is played (and it will be if you take the tour), music suffuses the air, permeating every corner of the house – it's better than the surround sound at your local movie theater. Behind the home are the luxurious formal gardens, laid out in a grid formation in imitation of a stained-glass window.

Lincoln summered here until his death in 1926, and his descendants (all of whom were female) occupied the home until 1975, when they donated it to the Church of Christ

**Rooms at Hildene, such as the library (above), are authentically furnished, and feature much Lincoln memorabilia**

Scientist. It was later sold to the Friends of Hildene, which still cares for the site today.

Tours of Hildene begin every half hour and last about an hour. They include a short film, a performance on the organ, and visits to the downstairs common rooms, a few bedrooms (including the one where President Taft slept) and servants' quarters. After the tour, you're welcome to stroll around the grounds and formal gardens for as long as you like, or simply sit and enjoy the view the Lincolns had of the surrounding Green Mountains.

### TAKING A BREAK

The **Marsh Tavern**, within the historic Equinox resort (➤ 125), is a special place for a casual meal.

🚩 204 A2 ✉ Route 7A, Manchester, VT 05254 ☎ (802) 362-1788; web: www.hildene.org 🕐 Tours daily, 9:30–4, mid-May–Oct. 💰 Moderate. Half-price for children aged 6–14; free for children aged under 6

## HILDENE: INSIDE INFO

**Top tips** Entry just to Hildene's **lawns and gardens** costs half the full admission price. In summer, the gardens are a popular site for evening weddings (don't worry – festivities start after the last tour leaves).

• In winter, the grounds are ideal for **cross-country skiing**, with over 10 miles of groomed trails for skiers of all abilities. The carriage house turns into a warming hut, where you can rent skis or escape the cold for a cup of hot chocolate.

# Fishing around Manchester

The Manchester area is a hot spot for fishing aficionados of all ability levels, not only because of its multitude of lakes, rivers and streams, but also because of its outfitters and instructors. There is even a museum devoted to fly-fishing.

The headquarters of **Orvis,** in Manchester Village, is the place for fishing enthusiasts, stocking equipment, clothing, flies, books, videos and knickknacks that only a fisherman could love. A river literally runs right through the store, and the pond behind the showroom is stocked with trout, making it the perfect place to show beginners how to cast a fly rod, identify feeding patterns, and otherwise outsmart Vermont trout. Even rank amateurs should make Orvis their first stop. From mid-April through to mid-October, the store runs short fly-fishing courses that can teach even the most inexperienced angler to land the big ones. Classes are not cheap, but the fee includes equipment, lunches and fishing licenses.

Once you have stocked up on the latest gear, your hardest decision is choosing where to fish. You can wade hip deep into Manchester's Batten Kill River for trout, drive north to Lake St. Catherine for bass and pike, head east to the Connecticut River for walleye and shad, or go south to the Harriman Reservoir for perch.

Fly-fishing fanatics will delight in the **American Museum of Fly-Fishing.** It has every imaginable piece of lore about fly-fishing, as well as myriad exhibits of painstakingly tied flies.

**The streams near Manchester are perfect for those seeking solitude**

Learn to cast a line or stock up on the latest fishing gear: Orvis in Manchester

You'll find everything you need to out-smart the Vermont trout in Manchester

## TAKING A BREAK

For the makings of a glamorous picnic, try the **Gourmet Café** (4961 Main Street, tel: 802/362-1254) in Manchester Center.

### Orvis

🏠 204 A2 ✉ Route 7A, Manchester, VT 05254 ☎ (802) 362-3750; web: www.orvis.com 🕐 Daily 9–6. Two-day fly-fishing classes every other Mon.–Tue., Thu.–Fri., or Sat.–Sun., mid-Apr.–mid-Oct. 💰 $370 for two-day classes, including all equipment. Special 2½ day classes start on Monday or Friday and cost $430

### American Musuem of Fly Fishing

🏠 204 A2 ✉ Route 7A in Manchester Village, one block north of the Equinox Hotel ☎ (802) 362-3300. 🕐 Daily 10–4, May–Oct.; Mon.–Fri. 10–4, Nov.–Apr. 💰 Inexpensive for adults, free for children under 12

### Vermont Fish & Wildlife Department

🏠 204 B4 ✉ 103 South Main St., Waterbury, VT 05671-0501 ☎ (802) 241-3700

---

## MANCHESTER: INSIDE INFO

**Top tip** Students at Orvis fly-fishing classes are eligible for special rates on lodgings at the Equinox Hotel (► 125) or at the Inn at Willow Pond. Call (800) 239-2074 ext. 784 for more information.

**Hidden gems** Though **Somerset Reservoir** is a bit harder to get to than most fishing holes in southern Vermont, the unspoiled wilderness surrounding it makes it worth the trouble it takes to get there. A dirt road that's closed in winter is the only route that goes near it. You might think you'd have such a remote place to yourself, but be prepared to share the solitude with other fishermen. To get there from Manchester, take Route 7 or 7A south to East Arlington. Turn left onto the Kelly Stand Road (see the signs for Kansas) and follow it about 10 miles to the Grout Pond parking area. You'll have to walk about a mile from here. The southern end of the reservoir requires no walking, but a lot more driving. Take Route 7 south to Bennington, turn left onto Route 9 east. About 2 miles past Searsburg, turn left onto Somerset Road and follow it 9 miles to the end.

# Marsh-Billings-Rockefeller National Historical Park

People around Woodstock will tell you that Marsh-Billings is a national park. Don't believe them. At a scant 555 acres, Marsh-Billings doesn't have nearly the acreage to be classified as a national park. There are no buffalo roaming here, no remote cabins in the wilderness, no towering redwoods to marvel at.

Marsh-Billings-Rockefeller is classified instead as a National Historical Park. It is still protected by the federal government, still has plenty of unspoiled forest, and still enjoys prompt maintenance and has lots of helpful rangers to answer questions. Marsh-Billings is actually three sites in one, but unless you stop at the newly opened visitor center, you might not even know they're related.

## Mount Tom Forest

Frederick Billings (Billings, Montana, is named for him) planted thousands of trees and built a 20-mile network of carriage roads and hiking trails on what used to be farmland here in the 1870s. It remains today one of the country's best examples of managed forests. Trails starting at Faulkner Park in town lead to a small lake known to locals as "the Pogue." Other paths ascend gently up the slopes of Mount Tom to its peak, where the reward is a panoramic view of the entire town below, including, in the right weather, several covered bridges over the Ottauquechee River. In winter, the carriage trails become groomed cross-country skiing trails (operated by a private company, the Woodstock Ski Touring Center).

The panoramic view of Woodstock from Mount Tom is well worth the 3-mile walk

## Billings Farm and Museum

Kids will love the working farm, and they might even take an interest in the museum portion of the property, which displays the self-sufficient lifestyle of the 19th-century hill-farms that shaped Vermont's landscape. In the dairy barn, they can watch the herd of Jersey cows being milked, or they can go next door to pet calves as young as one day old. They can visit chickens in the chicken coop, sheep in the pasture

**Hikers can enjoy almost complete solitude at Mount Tom Forest**

and horses in the barn. Then they can cool off with some ice cream that was in all likelihood made with cream from the very same cows.

The Billings Farm House won't appeal as much to kids, but their parents might like to tour the ahead-of-its-time 1890 abode. It had indoor plumbing, hot and cold running water, and a multitude of rooms for a simple farm house. Most interesting is the basement creamery, where the fresh milk was used to make butter and cream.

## Marsh-Billings-Rockefeller Mansion

The third part of the park is the residential complex, built for the family of George Perkins Marsh in 1805. Marsh, a noted writer and conservationist, grew up in this home,

**Antiques at the Billings Farm and Museum**

but sold it to Frederick Billings in 1869. The Billings family renovated the mansion twice before finally selling it to Mary F. and Laurance S. Rockefeller in 1954.

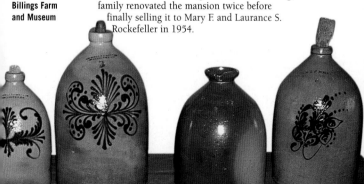

## MARSH–BILLINGS–ROCKEFELLER NATIONAL HISTORICAL PARK: INSIDE INFO

**Hidden gem** The **Prosper Road entrance** to Mount Tom Forest is well known to locals. The hiking trails from this end of the park are a little longer and a little more interesting than the switchbacks that go up the front side of the mountain from Faulkner Park. From the center of Woodstock, take Route 12 north across the Iron Bridge over the Ottauquechee River and turn right to stay on Route 12. Bear left at the first fork (don't go to Billings Farm) and left again at the next fork a half mile later. Look for signs for Prosper Road on your left. Turn left onto Prosper Road and continue up the hill for about a half mile. After the cemetery, there is a small parking lot on the left. Trails begin here.

**In more detail** The **Woodstock Ski Touring Center** (tel: 802/457-6674) maintains cross-country skiing trails in Mount Tom Forest in winter. If you want to ski the forest, you need to get a pass from them. They can also provide trail maps and rental skis. The center is located on Route 106, just south of town.

**At Billings Farm you can watch cows being milked. The working farm produces its own ice cream in summer**

The interiors are lavishly furnished with period furniture and more than 500 paintings by artists such as Albert Bierstadt and Asher B. Durand.

In 1992, the Rockefellers donated the forest land, the homes and the farm to the U.S. government, which turned it into a National Historical Park.

Entrance to Mount Tom Forest is free; mountain bikes, snowmobiles and other motorized vehicles are prohibited. There are separate admission charges for Billings Farm and Museum and for the Marsh-Billings-Rockefeller Mansion.

### TAKING A BREAK

Head to **Bentley's** in Woodstock (➤ 128) for a light lunch.

---

✚ 204 B3 ✉ 54 Elm Street, Woodstock, VT 05091 ☎ (802) 457-3368 ◉ Daily 10–5, late-May–Oct. 🎫 Guided tours of the Marsh-Billings-Rockefeller mansion, the grounds and gardens: moderate. Tours of Mount Tom Forest: free.

**Billings Farm and Museum**
✚ 204 B3 ✉ P.O. Box 489, Route 12 and River Road, Woodstock, VT 05091-0489 ☎ (802) 457-2355; web: www. billingsfarm.org ◉ Daily 10–5, May–Oct; 10–4 Sat.–Sun., Dec (also some winter activity weekends). 🎫 Moderate. Reduced price admission for children aged 5–17, children under 5 free

# At Your Leisure

## 🮂 Skyline Drive

If you want to see the views from atop one of the Green Mountains, but you don't want to spend all day hiking just to get there, get behind the wheel and head up to Skyline Drive. The entrance is on Route 7 just south of Manchester. There is a fee but you'll quickly make it to the 3,816-foot summit of Mount Equinox. The road to the top is about 5 miles long, and the views are stunning, though as you would expect from somewhere with a paved road, you won't have the place entirely to yourself.

➕ 204 A2 ✉ Box 2411, Arlington, VT 05250 ☎ (802) 362-1114 🕐 Daily 8 a.m.–10 p.m., May–Oct. 🮲 Moderate. Charges per car, with an additional fee per passenger

## 🯤 Emerald Lake State Park

The lake at this 430-acre park, 8 miles north of Manchester, isn't quite the color of emeralds, but the park is a gem nonetheless. Motors are prohibited on the lake, making it a quiet spot for swimming, fishing

Covered bridges are common in Vermont. Woodstock alone has three

and boating, and there are excellent camping facilities. And for those who want to get away from car campers, several hiking trails meander through the hills above the lake.

➕ 204 B2 ✉ Route 7, North Dorset, VT 05253 ☎ (802) 362-1655; web: www.state.vt.us/anr/fpr/parks/emerald/index.htm 🕐 Daily 8 a.m.–10 p.m. mid-May to mid-Oct

## 🯥 The Long Trail

This 270-mile-long trail is the oldest hiking path in the United States, predating even the Maine-to-Georgia Appalachian Trail that overlaps some of the same territory. Carved between 1910 and 1930 by the Green

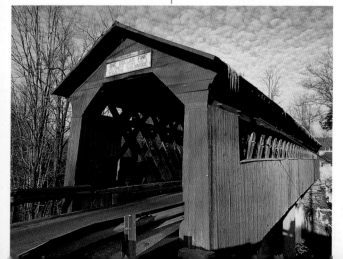

## Off the Beaten Track

At **Grafton** you can see what a Vermont village might have looked like in 1700. The foundation that sponsored the town's preservation even went so far as to bury the power lines. While you're here, check out the cheese-making process at Grafton Village Cheese Co. (tel: 800/472-3866) or simply sample some of its excellent wares. If you're here in winter, you can strap on boards or snowshoes at the Grafton Ponds Cross-Country Ski Center (tel: 802/843-2400).

Mountain Club, the Long Trail runs the length of Vermont from Massachusetts to Canada. The Appalachian Trail joins the Long Trail for its first 100 miles in southern Vermont, making this portion more traveled and more populated. The trails diverge at Sherburne Peak (just north of Killington), but the beauty of the Long Trail is so great that it has lured away many a hiker who had intended to follow the Appalachian all the way to Maine.

Along the way are more than 70 huts, lean-tos and other primitive campsites. But you can also enjoy a day hike almost anywhere on the length of the path. Near Manchester, the best way to access the trail is by taking Route 11 approximately 6 miles east of Manchester Center. Take the turnoff on the left side to the trailhead. From there, you can hike 3 miles north to Bromley Mountain, 10 miles south to Stratton Mountain, 40 miles south to Massachusetts, or 230 miles north to Canada.

Whichever way you decide to go, wear comfortable shoes, bring plenty of water and insect repellent, and don't forget your camera. In addition to rugged mountain peaks and pristine ponds peeking through the thick green hardwood forests, you might see deer, raccoons and, if you're lucky, a rare peregrine falcon. The Green Mountain Club publishes the *Long Trail Guide*, which has detailed maps and descriptions.

204 B4 ⊠ The Green Mountain Club, 4711 Waterbury-Stowe Road, Waterbury Center, VT 05677 ☎ (802) 244-7037; web: www.greenmountainclub.org

**The Vermont Raptor Center rehabilitates injured peregrine falcons and other predatory birds**

## 6 Vermont Raptor Center

Kids may be disappointed when they hear that this 78-acre nature preserve is not a dinosaur playground, but they will still enjoy a trip. The center, dedicated to rehabilitating and learning more about birds of prey, has over 30 species of raptor, among them hawks, bald eagles, snowy owls and peregrine falcons. All the residents have been injured and are treated by the center's staff until they can be returned to the wild. There are self-guiding walking trails on the property from where you can see these and other birds in a natural setting.

➕ 204 B3 ✉ Church Hill Road, Woodstock, VT 05091 ☎ (802) 457-2779 🕐 Daily 10–4, May–Oct.; Mon.–Sat. 10–4, Nov.–Apr. 💲 Moderate. Discounts for students and children. Guided tours available Mon.–Sat., Jun.–Oct.

## 8 Quechee Gorge

Don't believe the hype: Quechee Gorge is not the Grand Canyon of the east, though it is still impressive. The 165-foot-deep gorge was carved thousands of years ago by the glacial erosion of the Ottauquechee river. A pleasant half-mile walking trail takes you from the side of the road down to water level, where there's even a refreshing swimming hole. You can also get a fine view of the gorge from the pedestrian sidewalk on the bridge that spans the chasm.

➕ 204 B3 ✉ Route 4, Quechee, VT. Park in the Quechee Gorge Gifts parking lot on the north side of the road

## 9 Shelburne Museum

Though the museum is 80 miles from Manchester (a good 2-hour drive), its unique collection makes it worth the trip, especially on a cool or rainy day. Founded in 1947 by Electra Havemeyer Webb, Shelburne is known as "New England's Smithsonian" for good reason. In addition to paintings and other arts, it has the finest collection of American folk art and architecture in northern New England.

Among the museum's 80,000 exhibits are decoys, quilts, weather vanes and other Americana. These compete for space with more traditional museum fare like paintings and prints by artists as diverse as Rembrandt, Andrew Wyeth, Grandma Moses, Monet, Winslow Homer and Degas.

**At Shelburne Museum, many of the 80,000 exhibits are complete buildings, moved in their entirety to the site**

## An Antiques Corridor

If you're an antiques hound, head for **Route 30,** from Brattleboro to Townshend. There are dozens of antique shops along this 12-mile strip, as well as a Sunday flea market just north of the town of Newfane. Most of what you'll find is early American, but there are some good English and French collectibles here as well.

The collection is distributed among 37 buildings on the museum's 45-acre site, many of which are attractions in their own right. There's an 1890 railroad station, a one-room schoolhouse, a **1901 Vermont round barn**, a **lighthouse**, a jail and an 18th-century general store. Perhaps the most curious piece is the steamboat, *Ticonderoga,* a designated National Historic Landmark, "moored" nowhere near water.

➕ 204 A4 ✉ Route 7 Shelburne, VT 05482 ☎ (802) 985-3346; web: www.shelburnemuseum.org ⊙ Daily 10–5, late May–late Oct.; late Oct.–late

May 90-minute tour of selected buildings daily (except holidays) at 1 p.m. Reservations recommended 💰 Expensive. Discounts for children aged 6–14. Family pass available

## Maple Syrup

Want to know how maple syrup gets from the depths of the forest to the top of your pancakes? Vermont is the perfect place to find out: The state makes more maple syrup than any other in the country, producing half a million gallons each year. And dozens of sugarhouses are open to the public.

Sugaring is extremely weather-dependent. Temperatures have to be above freezing during the day, and below freezing at night in order to stimulate movement of maple sap from the roots to the budding leaves of the trees. In Vermont, that usually happens as early as late February and as late as early April. Sugarers tap small spouts into the trees to siphon off some of the sap, then back at the sugarhouse, they use huge wood-fired furnaces to evaporate water and turn the sap into syrup. It's an expensive, time-consuming process, especially when you consider that you need 40 gallons of sap to make a single gallon of maple syrup.

In the Manchester area, you can visit a sugarhouse at Merck Forest and Farmland Center. At Woodstock, both Kedron Sugar Makers and Sugarbush Farm are open to the public. For a complete list of sugarhouses, contact the Vermont Department of Agriculture.

### Merck Forest and Farmland Center
✉ Off Route 315, near Manchester, VT ☎ (802) 394-7836; web: www.merckforest.com

### Kedron Sugar Makers
✉ Sugarhouse Road, Woodstock, VT ☎ (802) 457-3015

### Sugarbush Farm
✉ At Route 4 in Taftsville, leave main road, cross Red Covered Bridge and go 3 miles up Hillside Road ☎ (800) 281-1757 or (802) 457-1757

### Vermont Department of Agriculture
✉ 116 State Street, Drawer 20, Montpelier, VT 05620-2901 ☎ (802) 828-2416; web: www.state.vt.us/agric/sugarhouses.htm

# Where to... Stay

## Prices
Expect to pay for two people sharing a double room, excluding taxes

$ under $150  $$ $150–250  $$$ over $250

## ◆◆◆The Equinox and Charles Orvis Inn $$$

Behind the long pillared porch, this rambling 1769 hotel has the luxurious add-ons of a top-class resort: concierges, a falconry school, a Land Rover "university" and a golf course. Many of the 183 bedrooms are modern rustic, with pale wood furniture contrasting with dark burgundy walls and floral quilts. Choose from three sophisticated dining areas. The 19th-century inn next door, with suites named for fly-fishing flies, was once run by Charles Orvis of fishing fame; it's now a luxurious inn-within-an-inn.

**☐ 204 A2 ☒ Historic Route 7A, Manchester Village, VT 05254
☎ (802) 362-4700 or (800) 362-4747; fax: (802) 362-4861; web: www.equinoxresort.com**

## 1811 House $$

The Duff family has transformed the 1811 House by going back in time. By stripping out Victorian additions and installing English and American antiques, they have re-created an early 19th-century look, complete with billiard table and help-yourself decanters of port and sherry in the public rooms. The 14 bedrooms are spacious, with four-posters and oriental rugs. Breakfast only is served.

**☐ 204 A2 ☒ Historic Route 7A, Manchester Village, VT 05254
☎ (802) 362-1811 or (800) 432-181; fax: (802) 362-2443; web: www.1811.com**

## Seth Warner Inn $

This small bed-and-breakfast on the southern outskirts of town, well away from the bustle of the outlet stores, dates from the early 1800s. The colonial-style interior includes four-poster beds, antique furniture and, thankfully, air-conditioning. The bedrooms at the back overlook the pretty garden. Guests can come and go as they please, with space to relax in the small library, which stocks a selection of books on local history.

**☐ 204 A2 ☒ Historic Route 7A, Manchester Center, VT 05255
☎ (802) 362-3830; fax: (802) 362-1268; web: www.sethwarnerinn1.bizonthe.net**

## ◆◆◆Village Country Inn $$$

Using plenty of antiques, fresh flowers and lace, the owner has transformed this century-old house into a frilly French-style country inn. The most romantic of the 33 bedrooms are La Fleur and Rose Noire, with canopy beds and views over the garden. The restaurant has a fine reputation and guests tend to book in for dinner, bed and breakfast. Dishes might include pan-seared Long Island duck breasts or charcoal-grilled Atlantic salmon.

**☐ 204 A2 ☒ 3835 Main Street (Historic Route 7A), Manchester Village, VT 05254 ☎ (802) 362-1792 or (800) 370-0300; fax: (802) 362-7238; web: www.villagecountryinn.com**

## West Mountain Inn $

Set high on a hillside above the Batten Kill River but still within easy reach of Manchester, the West Mountain Inn combines New England rustic charm with modern practicalities. The Rockwell Kent Suite, "half living room, half library," is particularly popular with families. The wood-paneled restaurant always seems to be busy, in contrast to the carefully tended, peaceful gardens and fields.

☐ 204 A2 ☒ West Mountain Inn Road, Arlington, VT 05250 ☎ (802) 375-6516; fax: (802) 375-6553; web: www.westmountaininn.com

## DORSET

### ◆◆◆ Inn at Westview Farm $

The informal 10-bedroom inn stands on the edge of town. Although there are some attractive antiques, decoration and furnishings are stylish rather than folksy. In the Auberge restaurant, imaginative dishes range from walnut-crusted rack of lamb to sesame shrimp. The lively Clancy's Tavern serves lighter, but still well-prepared meals.

☐ 204 A2 ☒ 2928 Route 30, Dorset, VT 05251 ☎ (802) 867-5715 or (800) 769-4903; fax: (802) 867-0468; web: www.vtweb.com/innatwestviewfarm

## WOODSTOCK

### ◆◆◆ Kedron Valley Inn $

The 28-room inn in the pretty Kedron Valley, 5 miles south of Woodstock, has all the classic ingredients: rural peace, antique quilts on the walls, even its own swimming hole. Room 31, with a downstairs sitting room, king-size bed and double tub, is particularly romantic. The restaurant uses the best Vermont-grown produce to create unfussy American dishes.

☐ 204 B3 ☒ Route 106, South Woodstock, VT 05071 ☎ (802) 457-1473 or (800) 836-1193; fax: (802) 457-4469; web: www.innformation.com/vt/kedron

### ◆◆◆ Village Inn of Woodstock $

The gabled Victorian house, just east of village center, recently celebrated its 100th birthday. The eight bedrooms are attractive, particularly Room 9 under the eaves, with its cherrywood four-poster, garden view and fireplace. In the popular ground-floor restaurant, chef-owner Kevin Clark serves pasta dishes and New England favorites such as lobster pie or roast turkey with all the trimmings.

☐ 204 B3 ☒ 41 Pleasant Street, Woodstock, VT 05091 ☎ (802) 457-1255 or (800) 722-4571; fax: (802) 457-3109; web: www.villageinnof woodstock.com

### ◆◆◆ Winslow House $

A mile from Woodstock proper, in the hamlet of West Woodstock, this four-bedroom guest house in a converted farmhouse is a real gem. The larger bedrooms are Room 3, with mahogany furniture, and Room 4, furnished in lighter oak. Both have private sitting rooms and bathrooms. Breakfast is taken seriously: home-baked breads, French toast and four sorts of pancakes.

☐ 204 B3 ☒ 492 Woodstock Road, Woodstock, VT 05091 ☎ (802) 457-1820; web: www.pbpub.com/winslow house

### ◆◆◆ The Woodstocker Bed-and-Breakfast $

In the heart of the village and within easy reach of all the amenities, but with Mount Tom on the doorstep, the Woodstocker is popular with hikers and cross-country skiers. The atmosphere is relaxed and informal. Of the nine bedrooms, families prefer the suites, which have small sitting rooms, while romantics go for the canopy room with its queen-size bed. Breakfast is a generous buffet, backed with waffles, pancakes and egg dishes.

☐ 204 B3 ☒ 61 River Street, Woodstock, VT 05091 ☎ (802) 457-3896; fax: (802) 457-3897; web: www. scenesofvermont.com/woodstocker

### ◆◆◆ Woodstock Inn and Resort $$$

With standards of comfort and cuisine that would grace a city hotel, this is no cozy village inn. Everything is on a grand scale, from the grand piano in the lounge to the 144 bedrooms. Most guests

# Where to...
## Eat and Drink

### Prices

Expect to pay per person for a three-course meal, excluding drinks and service

$ under $15 $$ $15–30 $$$ over $30

## MANCHESTER

### ◆◆Bistro Henry $$

Although the food is described as Mediterranean, there are interesting variations – crispy sweet potato arrives with walnut ricotta and grilled onion with three-mushroom hash. Main courses might be Moroccan chicken with couscous or braised lamb shank with garlic mashed potatoes and Merlot gravy. The rich desserts are superb.

🏠 204 A2 ⊠ Route 11/30, Manchester ☎ (802) 362-4982 🕒 Tue.–Sun. 5–10 ; Tue.–Sat. in winter

### ◆◆◆Black Swan $$$

Chef-owner Richard Whisenhunt once worked at New York's Le Cirque. A favorite since 1985, the Black Swan offers carefully prepared dishes, but no great surprises: Crab cakes come with an avocado-pepper mayonnaise, rack of lamb with a lingonberry-mint sauce, and fried chicken with pan gravy and garlic mashed potatoes. Start with cocktails on the garden patio, then move into the candlelit dining room.

🏠 204 A2 ⊠ Route 7A, Manchester Village ☎ (802) 362-3807 🕒 Thu.–Tue. from 5:30; Thu.–Mon. in winter

come for the sports facilities, which include tennis courts, a golf course, squash and spa facilities. In winter, guests have free access to the hotel's ski touring center, just south of the village. The elegant dining room has an award-winning New England menu.

🏠 204 B3 ⊠ 14 The Green, Woodstock, VT 05091 ☎ (802) 457-1100 or (800) 448-7900; fax: (802) 457-6699; web: www.woodstockinn.com

## QUECHEE

### ◆◆◆The Quechee Inn at Marshland Farm $

Away from the Quechee Gorge, but overlooking the Ottauquechee river, this 18th-century farmhouse has been transformed into a comfortable inn. Of the 24 bedrooms, those in the old house with river views have the most atmosphere. Guests come here to get away from it all. Breakfast is a help-yourself affair, but dinner is more elegant.

Dishes include duck, salmon and beef, and there is always a vegetarian option on the menu.

🏠 204 B3 ⊠ Quechee Main Street, Quechee, VT 05059 ☎ (802) 295-3133 or (800) 235-3133; fax: (802) 295-5587; web: www.quecheeinn.com

## SHELBURNE

### The Inn at Shelburne Farms $–$$

This grand mansion on the edge of Lake Champlain was once home to the Webb family, founders of the Shelburne Museum. Here you can experience how the upper crust spent their summers. The 24 bedrooms are comfortable without being fancy, and the dining room serves modern American dishes made from local produce. Profits go back into the farm and the inn.

🏠 204 A4 ⊠ 1611 Harbor Road, Shelburne, VT 05482 ☎ (802) 985-8498; fax: (802) 985-1233; web: www.shelburnefarms.org

### ◆◆Chanteleer $$$

It is hard to believe that Michel Baumann's cozy French restaurant was once a barn. Dishes are quite complex. Artichokes are not only stuffed with crab, but also served with a horseradish and bacon cream sauce; spaetzle are livened with black pepper and rosemary; and the massive mixed grill of lamb, venison and veal sausages is glazed with a raspberry and port sauce. Desserts are even more elaborate. It may be expensive, but for a special occasion it's well worth the money.

🚹 204 A2 ⊠ Route 7A North, Manchester ☎ (802) 362-1616 ⏰ Wed.–Mon. 6–9.30 p.m.; Wed.–Sun. in winter

### Little Red Rooster Café $

This unpretentious spot with little tables and cheerful service has an imaginative lunch menu: fresh Maine crab cakes, grilled fresh tuna salad Niçoise as well as soups.

🚹 204 A2 ⊠ Route 7A, Manchester ☎ (802) 362-3496

### Mistral's $$$

Expect classic French starters, from onion soup to snails, and entrees such as tournedos of veal with wild mushrooms, and sweetbreads with a mustard sauce. Some contemporary dishes have been introduced, among them grilled tuna with ginger cream. The well-chosen wine list has a French bias. Reservations are important on weekends.

🚹 204 A2 ⊠ Toll Gate Road, Manchester ☎ (802) 362-1779 or (800) 279-1779 from VT only ⏰ Thu.–Tue. from 6 p.m.; Thu.–Mon. in winter

### WOODSTOCK

### Bentley's $-$$

You'll find old-fashioned charm and a lively atmosphere here. Antique prints of old Woodstock decorate the restaurant and a carved lion observes the coffee shop. Order steaks, burgers or vegetarian dishes. There is live music on the weekend, and Sunday brunch during the winter. The coffee shop serves breakfast and light lunches.

🚹 204 B3 ⊠ 3 Elm Street, Woodstock ☎ (802) 457-3232 ⏰ Daily 8 a.m.–9.30 p.m. (also Fri.–Sat. 9:30–10 p.m.)

### ◆◆◆The Prince and the Pauper $$-$$$

Its statewide reputation for excellent food and fine wines mean it is worth dressing up for a meal here. Cocktails are served from 5 p.m., dinner from 6 p.m. The menu includes European classics, such as veal with a mushroom sauce, and Modern American dishes like seared tuna with Cajun spicing. Guests in a hurry or on their own can eat in the stylish wine bar.

🚹 204 B3 ⊠ 24 Elm Street, Woodstock ☎ (802) 457-1818 ⏰ Daily 5–9.30 p.m.

### ◆◆Spooner's Steakhouse $-$$

Strictly for nonvegetarians, this old-time, informal steak house, near the fire station, is in a former farmhouse, where original wooden walls complete the rustic feel. Start with copious salads or grilled coyote shrimp (Cajun-style) before tackling your favorite cut of beef.

🚹 204 B3 ⊠ on Route 4 East at Sunset Farm Barn, Woodstock ☎ (802) 457-4022 ⏰ Daily 5–9.30 (also Fri.–Sat. 9:30–10 p.m.)

### QUECHEE

### ◆◆◆Simon Pearce Restaurant $$$

Set along one side of a converted mill, overlooking the river and covered bridge, the restaurant is as stylish as Pearce's glass and pottery creations (▶129). The menu includes full-flavored dishes such as cod crusted with horseradish, chicken scented with cumin, and roast duckling with a mango chutney sauce. Breads are homemade; the wine list award-winning.

🚹 204 B3 ⊠ The Mill, Quechee ☎ (802) 295-1470 ⏰ Daily 11:30–2:45, 6–9 p.m.

# Where to... Shop

Shopping in Vermont is surprisingly varied, ranging from traditional products like cheese and maple syrup through antiques, right up to discounted designer fashions.

**General Stores** These country shops once satisfied every need in rural communities, from food to clothes and farm implements to household goods. Several have survived to fuel the nostalgia for days gone by. The most famous is the **Vermont Country Store** (Route 100, tel: 802/824-3184) in Weston, which looks like something out of a movie set. There is also a branch in Rockingham (Route 103, tel: 802/463-2224). There are several less commercial stores, used by locals more than visitors, but call ahead for directions to save time negotiating the back roads. Try **J. J. Hapgood Store** (off Route 11 in Peru, tel: 802/824-5911), which enjoyed 15 minutes of fame in the Diane Keaton movie "Baby Boom"; the **Red Cupboard**, a general store in West Woodstock (tel: 802/457-3722); and the **Taftsville Country Store** (tel: 802/457-1135) in tiny Taftsville.

**Traditional Produce** You can buy cheese and maple syrup at country stores, but it is more fun to go to farms where they are made. Finding your way can be difficult, so phone ahead for directions and opening times. **Cabot Creamery** (2870 Main Street, Cabot, tel: 802/563-2231) has built a worldwide reputation over some 80 years, and its New England mature cheddar is even exported to England, where the cheese originated. Weekday tours are available. **Sugarbush Farm** (Hillside Road, Woodstock, tel: 802/457-1757) makes and sells seven varieties of hand-waxed cheese, plus maple syrup from its own sugarhouse. Other picturesque outlets include: the **Sugar Shack** at Arlington (tel: 802/375-6747), **Highland Farms**, South Woodstock (tel: 802/457-5895), the **Richardson Farm** near Woodstock (tel: 802/457-2674) and **Palmer's Sugarhouse** at Shelburne (tel: 802/985-5054).

**Crafts** Vermont has an abundance of skilled craftsmen and women. The **Vermont State Craft Center** at Frog Hollow showcases the best of local talent, as well as work by international artists living in the state. There are other branches in Middlebury, Burlington and Manchester (Route 7A, opposite the Equinox Hotel, tel: 802/362-3321). One of the state's best-known craftsmen, **Simon Pearce**, works at the **Mill in Quechee** (Route 4, Quechee, tel: 802/295-2711 or 800/774-5277). Here, world-class potters and glassblowers work in the converted 19th-century riverside mill, which doubles as a showroom for everything from handsome furniture to elegant glasses. At the **Vermont Teddy Bear Company** (Route 7, tel: 802/985-3001), you can see how teddy bears are "born."

**Outlet Shopping** If it's up-to-the-minute fashion that you want, then the factory stores in **Manchester Center** have a wide selection of big-name labels, including Armani, Brooks Brothers, Burberry's, Calvin Klein, Christian Dior and Versace. Advertisements insist that discounts can be up to 70 percent. The attractive village, with 35 factory stores, plus restaurants, is geared to browsing and makes a welcome change to echoing city malls. Footwear, handbags, accessories, books, cards and CDs, as well as jewelry and furniture are heavily discounted. Phone ahead for information (tel: 800/955-SHOP).

# Where to...
## Be Entertained

In summer, Vermont's Green Mountains are popular with hikers and cyclists but the area comes into its own in winter, attracting 5 million skiers to some 20 resort areas.

**Hiking and Bicycling** Three companies put together self-guiding hiking tours in the area, with prearranged routes and accommodation tailored to time and ability: **Country Inns Along the Trail** (tel: 802/247-3300) in Brandon; **Walking-Inn-Vermont** (tel: 802/228-8799) based in Ludlow; and **Merrell Hiking Center** (tel: 802/422-6708) in Killington.

Several companies provide bicycle tours. They arrange accommodations and take your luggage from inn to inn. Try **Vermont Bicycle Touring** (tel: 802/453-4811) or

**POMG Bike Tours of Vermont** (tel: 802/434-2270). Contact **Bike Vermont** (tel: 802/457-3553) for rental only.

**Skiing** Top-class skiers head for **Killington** (tel: 800/621-MTNS), where there are miles of trails for every type of skier. Families love **Okemo** (tel: 800/78-OKEMO) for its warm welcome and organization, while stylish **Stratton** (tel: 800/STRATTON) is packed with New Yorkers. Farther north, picturesque **Stowe** challenges the best skiers with its "Front Four" twisting double-diamond runs. The excellent **Stowe Mountain Resort Ski and Snowboard School** (tel: 802/253-3000) is renowned.

Vermont has a host of centers for cross-country skiing. For 50 miles of groomed trails through the trees and real solitude, get a room at **Blueberry Hill Inn** in Goshen (tel: 800/448-0707), deep in Green Mountain National Park.

**Watersports** Fishing, canoeing and sailing are readily available along the shores of **Lake Champlain**. At **BattenKill Canoe** (6328 Route 7A, Arlington, tel: 800/421-5268) canoes are at the ready on the banks of the Batten Kill river. They can suggest easy paddles only 2 hours long, or organize a trip paddling from inn to inn.

**Fishing** Visitors aged 15 and over need a license, available from any Town Clerk's office, some commercial outlets and fish and game wardens. The Vermont Fish and Wildlife Department issues the Vermont Guide to Fishing as part of their Vermont's Fishing kit (tel: 802/241-3701). **Battenkill Anglers** (tel: 802/362-3184) is a full-service outfitter dedicated to fly-fishing.

The **Hawk Inn and Mountain Resort** (tel: 802/672-3811) near Ludlow is another that maintains an extensive fly-fishing program on its trout-filled stretch of the Black River, as well as two lakes for bass.

**Horseback Riding** At **Kedron Valley Stables** (Route 106, South Woodstock, tel: 802/457-1480 or 800/225-6301), they organize easy trail rides or more demanding 4-day inn-to-inn rides covering about 25 miles a day. **Cavendish Trail Horse Rides** (tel: 802/226-7821), near Proctorsville, offers trail riding through woods and meadows from May to October. No experience is needed to ride with their Western saddles, and there are ponies for children under eight years old.

**Golf** There are over 60 well-maintained courses and, best of all, low green fees and plentiful tee times. Contact **Vermont Golf Journal** (tel: 800/639-1941; web: www.golf-vermont.com) for details.

# Newport and Southeastern Connecticut

In Three Days 134 – 135
Don't Miss 136 – 140
At Your Leisure 141 – 145
Where To 146 – 148

# Getting Your Bearings

At just over 1,200 square miles, Rhode Island is America's smallest state geographically, but because most of the state is coastline, it offers an endless number of waterside attractions. It's not called the Ocean State for nothing.

Almost all of Rhode Island's attractions come together in the upscale village of Newport, which bills itself as America's first resort. Founded in 1639, it was frequented in its early days by ship's captains and traders. Back in the late 19th century, when a million dollars really meant something, Vanderbilts, Astors and the rest of America's millionaires flocked here for the beaches, the yachting regattas, the lawn tennis and the society parties. The indescribably opulent mansions they built for themselves remain in their wake and provide Newport with an even bigger attraction: tours of these extravagant homes draw millions of visitors each year.

Newport is at its best, and its most crowded, in the summer months (especially weekends), when the weather is warm, the beaches are inviting and the seafood at its most delicious. But because so many of the attractions are indoors, any time is a good time to visit. It's about a 90-minute drive from Boston, making it a popular weekend getaway.

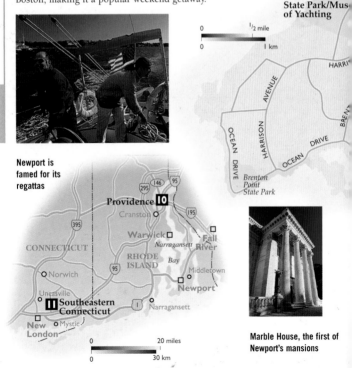

*Narraga
Bay*

**Fort Adams 9
State Park/Mus
of Yachting**

HARRI

AVENUE

HARRISON

OCEAN DRIVE

BRENT

OCEAN DRIVE

*Brenton
Point
State Park*

0      ½ mile

0      1 km

**Newport is
famed for its
regattas**

146
295
95
**Providence 10**
Cranston
195
395
**Warwick** *Narragansett* **Fall
River**
**CONNECTICUT**
**RHODE
ISLAND** *Bay*
95
Middletown
Norwich
**Newport**
Uncasville
**11 Southeastern
Connecticut** Narragansett
New
London Mystic

0      20 miles

0      30 km

**Marble House, the first of
Newport's mansions**

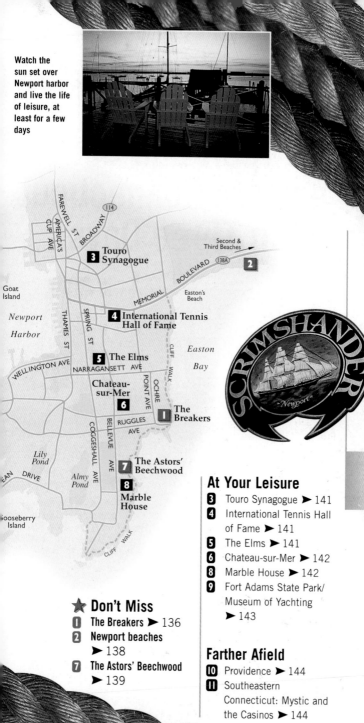

Watch the sun set over Newport harbor and live the life of leisure, at least for a few days

SCRIMSHANDER
*Newport*

## ★ Don't Miss

1 The Breakers ➤ 136
2 Newport beaches ➤ 138
7 The Astors' Beechwood ➤ 139

## At Your Leisure

3 Touro Synagogue ➤ 141
4 International Tennis Hall of Fame ➤ 141
5 The Elms ➤ 141
6 Chateau-sur-Mer ➤ 142
8 Marble House ➤ 142
9 Fort Adams State Park/ Museum of Yachting ➤ 143

## Farther Afield

10 Providence ➤ 144
11 Southeastern Connecticut: Mystic and the Casinos ➤ 144

Just about anything that you'd want to do in Rhode Island can be found in Newport. Similarly, the best of Connecticut is crowded into the southeastern corner of the state.

# Newport and South-eastern Connecticut in Three Days

## Day One

### Morning
Make your way to **The Breakers** (above, ➤ 136–137), Newport's most magnificent mansion. The tour is unforgettable, but gets crowded later in the day. Spend the rest of the morning following the **Cliff Walk** (➤ 184–186) to get an overview of the luxurious mansions on Bellevue Avenue and the stunning ocean view that initially attracted their super-rich owners to Newport.

### Afternoon
If the weather's great, put together a picnic lunch and squander the rest of the day at one of Newport's **beaches** (➤ 138). If it's cold or rainy, stop for lunch at La Forge Casino Restaurant (186 Bellevue Avenue, tel: 401/846-3474), then tour the interior of one of the mansions, perhaps the **Elms** (➤ 141) or **Chateau-sur-Mer** (➤ 142).

### Evening
Head to Lower Thames Street in the early evening so you can catch a little shopping there before stores close. Choose a spot for dinner beforehand – the long wait for tables at the award-winning seafood restaurant Scales and Shells (527 Thames Street, tel: 401/846-3474) is definitely worth it. Bars and clubs along this same stretch provide post-dining entertainment.

# Day Two

## Morning

Take the guided tour of the **Astors' Beechwood** (➤ 139–140). Its period-costumed actor-guides (left) make this mansion unlike the others. If there is any time left before lunch, visit the **International Tennis Hall of Fame** (➤ 141) to pay homage to the great stars of the game.

## Afternoon

Have lunch at the lively Red Parrot (➤ 147) at the heart of Newport's waterfront, then drive over to **Fort Adams State Park** (➤ 143), where you can lie on the beach or play frisbee on the large lawns. Alternatively, visit the **Museum of Yachting** (➤ 143).

## Evening

Walk around the Washington Square historic district and the waterfront to see where colonial-era ships came and went, bringing Newport the riches that made it so famous. Dine at the White Horse Tavern (➤ 147), America's oldest surviving restaurant, or the Brick Alley Pub and Restaurant (➤ 147).

# Day Three

## Morning

Head west across Rhode Island and follow Route 1 along the Connecticut coast to the town of Mystic. Tour the **Mystic Aquarium** (➤ 145).

## Afternoon

Join fans of the movie "Mystic Pizza" for lunch at the pizzeria of the same name (➤ 147), then visit **Mystic Seaport** (below, ➤ 145), a re-creation of a 19th-century whaling village, complete with a museum and period shops. It is also still a working shipyard.

## Evening

Head to one of the nearby **casinos** (➤ 145), for a night of entertainment. Alternatively, enjoy the food and the stunning views over Long Island Sound at the Flood Tide Restaurant (at the intersection of routes 1 and 7, tel: 203/536-9604).

# The Breakers

This massive stone palace occupies an acre of land and is surrounded by 10 more acres of lawns and gardens. It was built between 1892 and 1895 by Richard Morris Hunt for Cornelius Vanderbilt II, grandson of Commodore Cornelius Vanderbilt I, the richest man in American history. Money was no object, and Cornelius thought nothing of spending the family fortune on every conceivable luxury.

Opulence oozes from every corner, with scores of crystal chandeliers hanging from gold-encrusted ceilings, red alabaster columns framing 12-foot-high windows and miles of oriental rugs. There is even hot and cold running and fresh sea water in each of the 23 bathrooms. You can't help but try to add up the cost of everything in the dining room alone, and your jaw will drop at the sight of the marble-sheathed great hall, which measures 50 feet in every direction.

**When Cornelius Vanderbilt II (above) commissioned The Breakers no expense was spared**

**Left: The dining room, noted for its red alabaster columns**

The Grand Salon, one of two rooms that were custom-made in Paris and shipped to Newport in their entirety, is so immense that it makes the grand piano within it look like a spinet. Red velvet and gold leaf compete for space on the walls, the moldings, the curtains, the furniture and even the intricately detailed ceiling.

The Breakers took some 2,000 workmen 3 years to build, and constant concerns over the intricate details demanded by the Vanderbilts were believed to have sent its architect (who did not live to see its completion) to an early grave.

You can tour the mansion in less than an hour (not counting waiting time), although you may be tempted to laze around the huge lawn overlooking the ocean long after your tour of the interior ends.

## TAKING A BREAK

Choose coffee and cookies, or a sandwich and some fruit from **The Market on the Boulevard** (43 Memorial Boulevard, tel: 401/848-2600), a popular combination bakery, café, deli and grocery store.

Many of the 40 servants employed at The Breakers worked in the kitchen

🔒 206 D2
✉️ Ochre Point Avenue near Bellevue Avenue, Newport, RI 02840
☎️ (401) 847-1000; web: www.NewportMansions.org
🕐 Daily 10–5, Apr.–Oct.; Sat.–Sun. and holidays 10–4, Nov.–Jan. 2
💲 Expensive. Discounts available for tours of more than one mansion; call (401) 847-1000 for details, or check the web at www.NewportMansions.org.

## THE BREAKERS: INSIDE INFO

**Top tips** This is the most popular of all the mansions and it can get crowded quickly. To **avoid the crowds,** go early in the morning, or late in the afternoon.
• The Preservation Society of Newport County, which runs The Breakers, operates 10 mansions in all and offers **discounts** on visits to more than one house. They offer tours of Chateau-sur-Mer, Chepstow, The Elms, Green Animals, Hunter House, Isaac Bell House, Kingscote, Marble House and Rosecliff (▶ 142–143 for information on other mansions). Not every house is open all year, and Chepstow is open for tours by reservation only.

**Hidden gem** The Breakers Stable and Carriage House, on Coggeshall Avenue, was also designed by Richard Morris Hunt. More than a dozen different horse-drawn vehicles are on display here, including Alfred Gwynne Vanderbilt's famous *Venture*. Admission is free with a ticket stub from any Preservation Society mansion.

# Newport beaches

Newport's long beaches are what originally attracted the former owners of the lavish estates, and they continue to draw those of more modest means to the area today.

Sachuest Beach (left) and Easton's Beach (below left) are among Newport's most popular

Everybody's favorite beach is **Easton's Beach**, also known as First Beach because even first-time visitors can find it without a map. It's on Memorial Boulevard just below the entrance to the Cliff Walk. Lockers, bathhouses, restrooms, a snackbar and a carousel are open from Memorial Day to Labor Day.

There's a small bay beach at **Fort Adams State Park** (► 143) that's good for swimming, as well as areas for boating, sailing and fishing. Admission to the park is $4 per car. **Brenton Point State Park**, near Hammersmith Farm, has gentle waves and conditions conducive to fishing, kite-flying and scuba diving.

Newport's two other great swimming beaches are actually in the neighboring city of Middletown, where many of the more affordable accommodations are also located. **Sachuest Beach,** or Second Beach, is on Sachuest Point Road, about 2 miles east of Easton's Beach. It's popular with those who favor sand dunes, which is apparently a lot of people – the parking lot holds 1,000 cars, and on sunny August weekends it fills up quickly.

Just on the other side of Sachuest Point is **Third Beach.** Part of this beach is private, but the public part is favored by sailors and windsurfers. A plus for solitude-seekers: this is usually the least-crowded beach.

---

Parking at First Beach is $8 weekdays, and $10 weekend days ($6 if you arrive before 9:30 a.m.). At Second and Third beaches, it's $10 on weekdays, $15 on Saturdays and Sundays. Beach parking is free from Labor Day to Memorial Day weekend at all three beaches

# Astors' Beechwood

At the Astors' Beechwood mansion, costumed actors taking the roles of the Astor family and staff show you around the home. You play the role of a guest invited to an 1891 dinner party at the mansion – don't worry, neither acting skills nor evening gowns are required for admission. It may seem corny, but it works. Your guides never break character, but they impart as much factual information, and a great deal more insight into the life of leisure enjoyed by the Astors, as any conventional tour guide.

Beechwood is not as large or ornate (or garish, some might say) as most of its neighbors, but it was the social center of its day. Mrs. Astor, the woman who determined who was who in late 19th-century society, held

*Costumed guides re-create the life led by the Astors*

court here, admitting only members of "The 400" to her company. To be a member of this elite group, you had to have $1 million for every member of your family, have three generations of wealth, and never have worked a day in your life. It is said that the list was limited to 400 people because that's exactly the number that could fit in the ballroom (Newport's largest at the time).

    One of the first rooms that you enter in the mansion is the ornately paneled drawing room. Here, as in times past, you present a calling card on the tray, which a footservant takes to her ladyship. Depending on who you are and how you present your card – there were all kinds of codes about

folding and bending corners of calling cards – Mrs. Astor will either admit you to her company or, to your eternal shame, not receive you.

Mrs. Astor's presence is still felt throughout the house, particularly in the ballroom, where her countenance graces the cove moldings looking down on her assembled guests.

Tours of Beechwood last about 45 minutes and include all the downstairs rooms (including the kitchen) as well as several bedrooms and servants' quarters. Wear whatever you like, but be aware that the actors are likely to comment on your outfit, especially women showing a racy bit of ankle.

### TAKING A BREAK

**Annie's** (176 Bellevue Avenue, tel: 401/849-6731), a welcoming coffee house serving breakfast and lunch, is a great place to take time out from sightseeing.

Tours give an insight into life below stairs (above), as well as that enjoyed by Mrs. Astor's guests (below)

✚ 206 D2
✉ 580 Bellevue Avenue, Newport, RI 02840
☎ (401) 846-3772; web: www.astors-beechwood.com
🕐 Daily 10–5, mid-May through Oct.; Fri.–Sun. 10–4, early Feb. to mid-May. Tours leave approximately every 20 minutes (every 30 minutes in the off-season) 💲 Moderate. Discounts for children aged 6–12, students and seniors (over 60). Children under 6 free

## THE ASTORS' BEECHWOOD: INSIDE INFO

**Top tip** Tours of Beechwood are at their best when guests participate. Don't be afraid to get into the act, talk to the performers, and even pretend you are landed gentry. Everybody on your tour will have a lot more fun if you all loosen up and play along.

**Hidden gem** Special events run at the mansion at night. On Tuesday evenings, put on your finest (or come as you are) for the **Astor Ball**, a re-creation of a Victorian fete. If you've left your tux and evening gown at home, come Thursday night for a **Murder Mystery** tour of the mansion. Both events are popular, so reserve in advance.

# At Your Leisure

## 3 Touro Synagogue

The oldest extant synagogue in the United States dates to 1763, some 100 years after the first Jews emigrated here from Portugal. George Washington visited the synagogue in 1790 and promised the congregation that the new nation would cherish religious freedom by giving "bigotry no sanction; to persecution no assistance." It is said that Thomas Jefferson, who visited with Washington, was so inspired by the building's portico that he used the design for his own estate, Monticello, in Virginia.

The simple exterior belies a much more ornate interior. Of particular note are the 500-year-old Torah, which accompanied the first Jews to Newport from Portugal, and the trap-door below the central pulpit, a reminder of the days when freedom of worship was not guaranteed.

Touro was designated a National Historic Site in 1946 and still holds services for a dedicated membership.

➕ 206 D2 ✉ 72 Touro Street (at Spring Street), Newport, RI 02840 ☎ (401) 847-4794; web: www.tourosynagogue.org 🕐 Tours operate every 30 minutes Sun.–Fri. 10–5, Jul.–Sep.; Mon.–Fri. 1–3, Sun. 11–3, May–Jun. and Sep.– late-Oct.; Sun. 11–3, Nov.–Apr. 💲 Free

## 4 International Tennis Hall of Fame

The first U.S. National Lawn Tennis Championships (forerunner of the U.S. Tennis Open) were played on the grass court here in 1881, when this building was better known as "The Casino." It was built only a year earlier as a social club by architect Stanford White of McKim, Mead and White. In fact, it was Mr. White's first commission.

The Tennis Hall of Fame moved to the location in 1954, and all the

greats of men's and women's tennis are now enshrined here, from Bill Tilden and Helen Wills Moody to Bjorn Borg and Evonne Goolagong. John McEnroe joined the rolls in 1999. The exhibits on the history of the game are what you might imagine, but the interactive displays where you can test your own abilities are better than expected.

Every July, the Hall of Fame plays host to Newport Tennis Week, during which top players compete in the only tournament in the United States still played on grass. You, too, can play on any of the complex's 13 grass courts (the only public lawn tennis courts in the U.S.), just by calling ahead and reserving a court any time from May through October.

➕ 206 D2 ✉ Newport Casino Lawn Tennis Club, 194 Bellevue Avenue, Newport, RI 02840 ☎ (800) 457-1144 or (401) 849-3990; web: www.tennis fame.org 🕐 Daily 9:30–5. Closed Thanksgiving and Christmas 💲 Moderate. Discounts given for children under 13 and students and seniors

## 5 The Elms

Now a National Historic Landmark, The Elms was built in 1901 for coal magnate Edward J. Berwind in the style of an 18th-century French chateau. Its unique Gilded Age Tour gives a behind-the-scenes look at the

The aptly named Gold Ballroom at the Vanderbilt's opulent Marble House

service parts of the mansion, including the basement, the laundry room, the wine cellar and even the steam room, where the full-time staff kept operations humming through countless demands, social engagements and blowout parties enjoyed by Newport's elite. You also get to see the showpiece rooms of the house. Advance reservations are required for the Gilded Age Tour.

➕ 206 D2 ✉ Bellevue Avenue next to the Astors' Beechwood ☎ (401) 847-1000; web: www.NewportMansions.org ⏰ Daily 10–5, May–Oct.; call for opening times at other times of year

## 6 Chateau-sur-Mer

This granite Victorian mansion, built in 1852 for merchant William Shepard Wetmore, was the biggest house in town until the Vanderbilts moved in. Wetmore's son, George Peabody Wetmore, held his inaugural ball here in 1889 upon becoming Governor of Rhode Island. Despite its name, Chateau-sur-Mer is significantly more removed from the sea than the other mansions – you can't even see it from the Cliff Walk.

➕ 206 D2 ✉ Bellevue Avenue next to the Astors' Beechwood ☎ (401) 847-1000; web: www.NewportMansions.org ⏰ Daily 10–5, May–Oct.; call for opening times at other times of year

## 8 Marble House

The 1892 home of Mrs. William K. (Alva) Vanderbilt, constructed entirely of marble on the outside, drips with gold inside. The dining-room chairs, made of solid bronze, are so heavy that two footmen were required to seat each dinner guest. The mansion is immediately identifiable from the Cliff Walk – just look for the Chinese Tea House. Built for Mrs. Vanderbilt in 1914 on the lawn overlooking the ocean, it looks like a pagoda made out of Lego bricks.

➕ 206 D2 ✉ Bellevue Avenue next to the Astors' Beechwood. ☎ (401) 847-1000; web: www.NewportMansions.org ⏰ Daily 10–5, May–Oct., call for opening times at other times of year

## For Kids

**Green Animals Topiary Garden** contains 80 sculpted trees and hedges, including 21 in the shape of animals. There's a giraffe, a donkey, a lion and an elephant, not to mention a policeman and a sailboat. The estate is 10 miles north of Newport in Portsmouth, but the tour is on the Newport Preservation Society combination ticket.

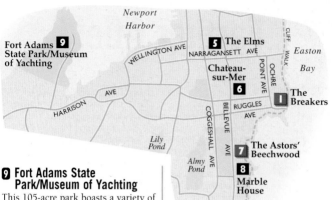

Newport
Harbor

**5** The Elms

Easton
Bay

Chateau-
sur-Mer **6**

**I** The
Breakers

Fort Adams **9**
State Park/Museum
of Yachting

WELLINGTON AVE
NARRAGANSETT AVE
AVE
HARRISON AVE
POINT AVE
OCHRE
CLIFF WALK
RUGGLES AVE
BELLEVUE AVE
COGGESHALL AVE
ALMY AVE

Lily
Pond

Almy
Pond

**7** The Astors'
Beechwood

**8**
Marble
House

## **9** Fort Adams State Park/Museum of Yachting

This 105-acre park boasts a variety of activities, from swimming and sailing to bicycling and fishing. The rolling lawns are also home each August to the Ben & Jerry's Folk Festival and the JVC Jazz Festival (call 401/847-3700 for information about schedule and performers for either venue). Within the park is the **Museum of Yachting**, which has an interesting exhibit on the history of the America's Cup races.

➕ 206 D2 ☎ (401) 847-2400
🕐 Park: dawn–dusk, year round (staffed only from Memorial Day to Labor Day). Museum: daily 10–5, mid-May–Oct. 💲 Park: free (overnight parking inexpensive), Memorial Day to Labor Day only. Museum inexpensive. Children aged 2–12 free

Below: A celebration of yachting at Newport's museum

## Off the Beaten Track

Though it shouldn't be the first house you tour, **Chepstow** (Narrasausett Avenue, tel: 401/847-1000) makes a nice change of pace. By most people's standards it is still closer to a mansion than a cottage, but in comparison to Newport's other mansions it is tiny. So small, in fact, that tours are available by reservation only.

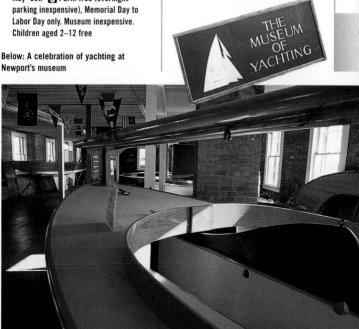

# Farther Afield

## ⑩ Providence

Rhode Island's capital city was once a farming center, hence the official state name: Rhode Island and Providence Plantations. Today, this working-class city is still a busy seaport, but it is also beginning to acquire something of a reputation for its burgeoning restaurant scene. It gets the same quality seafood and other ingredients as restaurants in nearby New York and Boston, but prices here are a fraction of those charged in the bigger cities.

The city spans both sides of the Providence River, with most places of interest to visitors found on the east side. The exceptions are the **Arcade,** a 19th-century shopping mall, and the **Rhode Island State House,** which boasts the world's largest golden dome (and is not a little reminiscent of St. Peter's in Rome).

The east side is home to two of the best universities in the country within shouting distance of each other in the fashionable, wealthy College Hill neighborhood. **Brown University,** built in 1764 and a member of the elite Ivy League, is the larger of the two. For many years, its University Hall was the only building on campus, and during the Revolutionary War, it served as a barracks for French and American soldiers. The **Rhode Island School of Design** (RISD), just down the road, is one of the top art and design schools in America. The collection of art at its **museum** spans the last millennium, with works from around the globe, as well as special exhibitions by RISD faculty. The most popular galleries are those where works of European masters like Monet, Cezanne, Matisse, Picasso and Rodin hang. The American wing features the works of Gilbert Stuart and John Singer Sargent.

From RISD, you can walk south along narrow Benefit Street, where stately old colonial homes rub shoulders with lovingly restored Victorian houses. Turn left at Power Street to see John Brown House, ironically home to an 18th-century slave trader and revolutionary, not the abolitionist of the same name. The collection of china, glassware and colonial furniture contained within the house is museum quality.

**Providence Warwick Convention and Visitors Bureau**
✚ 206 C2 ✉ One West Exchange Street, Providence, RI 02903 ☎ (404) 274-1636 or (800) 233-1636; web: www.providencecvb.com

## ⑪ Southeastern Connecticut

For the first-time visitor, the best of Connecticut, the nation's second smallest state, is found in its southeastern corner, where the Thames River flows into the Atlantic. The top things to see are within a short drive of each other.

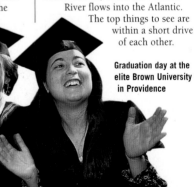

**Graduation day at the elite Brown University in Providence**

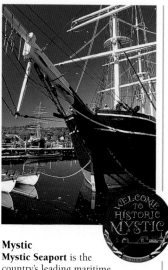

## Mystic

**Mystic Seaport** is the country's leading maritime museum. Part museum, part working shipyard and part 19th-century village, it brings to life the days when Mystic was the center of the whaling industry. More than 400 ships are on display here, and you can board three of them, including the 1841 wooden whaleship *Charles W. Morgan*.

In the village, you can look around the shops and businesses that typically supported the whaling industry, including a ship's chandlery and craftsmens' shops. Kids will be interested in the one-room schoolhouse and the Children's Museum, where they can take part in the same games played by whaling-era kids.

At nearby **Mystic Aquarium**, kids will clamor loudest to see the Atlantic bottlenose dolphins, seals and penguins, but the whales are the real stars. At a new 1-acre outdoor exhibit, visitors can watch beluga whales from above or below the water's surface through giant underwater viewing windows.

### Mystic Seaport
🏛 206 C1 ✉ 75 Greenmanville Avenue, Mystic, CT 06355-0990
☎ (860) 572-5315 or 888-9-SEAPORT
🕐 Ships and exhibits: daily 10–4. Museum grounds: daily 9–5. Closed Dec. 25 🎟 Two-day admission: expensive. Half price for children aged 6–12, children under 6 free

### Mystic Aquarium
🏛 206 C1 ✉ 55 Coogan Boulevard, Mystic, CT 06355-1997 ☎ (860) 572-5955 🕐 Mon.–Fri. 10–5, Sat.–Sun. 9–5, Sep.–Jun.; Mon.–Fri. 10–6, Sat.–Sun. 9–6, Jul.–Labor Day. Closed Jan. 1, Thanksgiving and Dec. 25 🎟 Expensive. Discounts for seniors (over 60) and children aged 3–12, children 2 and under free

## The Casinos

Though Mystic Seaport and Aquarium have long drawn visitors to this part of Connecticut, the area really took off when gambling was legalized on Native American reservations. In 1992, the Mashantucket Pequot tribe opened **Foxwoods**, at the time the largest casino in the world. Four years later, the Mohegan built the **Mohegan Sun** casino in the town of Uncasville, just across the Thames River. It attracts an average of more than 15,000 people a day and has been so successful that the tribe is already building more casino space.

### Foxwoods
🏛 206 C2 ✉ Route 2, Ledyard, CT 06339 ☎ 800-752-9244 or 800-PLAY-BIG; web: www.foxwoods.com

### Mohegan Sun
🏛 206 C1 ✉ 1 Mohegan Sun Blvd., Uncasville, CT 06382 ☎ 888-226-7711; web: www.mohegansun.com

**The Mashantucket Pequot tribe's Foxwoods casino attracts thousands of visitors**

# Where to... Stay

**Prices**
Expect to pay for two people sharing a double room, excluding taxes
$ under $150 $$ $150–250 $$$ over $250

## NEWPORT

### ◆◆ Brinley Victorian Inn $$

The inn, on a quiet street just a short stroll from the harbor, has 16 bedrooms decorated in Victorian style. Accommodations are split between two houses, so there are two parlors and two porches, plus a paved courtyard and a library. Beds and furniture are antique; some rooms have fireplaces and whirlpool tubs. Breakfast is a full Continental spread.

✚ 206 D2 ☒ 23 Brinley Street, Newport, RI 02840 ☎ (401) 849-7645 or (800) 999-8523; web: www.brinleyvictorian.com

### ◆◆◆ Hydrangea House Inn $$

A small, elegant inn at the north end of Bellevue Avenue, Hydrangea House is furnished with fine fabrics, original paintings and antiques. Guests can take afternoon tea in what the owners call the common room or relax in front of the fire. For a real treat, reserve either the Hydrangea Suite, with a whirlpool bath and king-size bed, or the newest suite, which was added in 1999.

✚ 206 D2 ☒ 16 Bellevue Avenue, Newport, RI 02840 ☎ (401) 846-4435 or (800) 945-4667; fax: (401) 846-6602; web: www.hydrangeahouse.com

### ◆◆ James B. Finch House $–$$

Champlin Mason, architect for some of Newport's grand mansions, designed this seven-room bed-and-breakfast. Room 4, with its whirlpool tub and king-size bed, is a favorite. At weekends, a chef comes in to prepare special breakfasts; in summer, guests sit out in the gardens, sipping lemonade.

✚ 206 D2 ☒ 102 Touro Street, Newport, RI 02840 ☎ (401) 848-9700 or (800) 235-1274; fax: (401) 848-9311

### ◆◆ Melville House $–$$

Melville House, in the heart of the historic district, maintains a colonial feel, with antique furnishings and no telephones or TVs in the bedrooms. Locally made woolen rugs brighten the hall and stairs. Breakfasts are hearty, with home-made granola and hot dishes such as raspberry-stuffed French toast.

✚ 206 D2 ☒ 39 Clarke Street, Newport, RI 02840 ☎ (401) 847 0640; fax: (401) 847-0956; web: www.melvillehouse.com

## MYSTIC

### ◆◆ Old Mystic Inn $–$$

The 18th-century inn in Old Mystic is quintessentially New England in style, with a handsome porch and a log fire in the sitting room. The bedrooms are named for New England authors, and copies of their works are left by the beds. Guests enjoy a full country breakfast of bacon, eggs and home fries, waffles or pancakes.

✚ 206 C1 ☒ 52 Main Street, Old Mystic, CT 06372 ☎ (860) 572-9422; fax: (860) 572-9954; web: www.visitmystic.com/oldmysticinn

### ◆◆ Steamboat Inn $$

Within walking distance of the popular attractions, this is a good central choice. Rooms are cheerful, light and relaxing, and all but one have views of the Mystic River and the sleek schooner moored outside.

✚ 206 C1 ☒ 73 Steamboat Wharf, Mystic, CT 06355 ☎ (860) 536-8300; fax: (860) 572-1250; web: www.visitmystic.com/steamboat

# Where to...
# Eat and Drink

**Prices**
Expect to pay per person for a three-course meal, excluding drinks and service

$ under $15  $$ $15–30  $$$ over $30

## NEWPORT

### ◆◆Brick Alley Restaurant $–$$

This has been one of Newport's most popular dining spots for over 20 years, thanks to its simple menus. Once you have loaded up at the fine salad bar, you can choose from gourmet pizza and pasta, steaks and ribs. It is always worth checking out the daily fresh fish special. The Sunday brunches are busy, so reservations are essential.

🚹 206 D2 ⊠ 140 Thames Street, Newport 🕾 (401) 849-6334 🕒 Mon.–Fri. 11:30–10, Sat.–Sun. 11–10:30

### The Red Parrot $

Known for its weekends of live jazz, but lively most evenings, this pub has a Caribbean atmosphere, with frozen drinks and exotic dishes.

🚹 206 D2 ⊠ 348 Thames Street, Newport 🕾 (401) 847-3140 🕒 Daily 11–11 (also Fri.–Sat. 11 p.m.–midnight)

### West Deck $$$

It is worth making time for chef James Mitchell's French-influenced cooking. Signature dishes include filet mignon with a port and Stilton sauce, potato-crusted salmon and raspberry bread pudding. During the season, eat outdoors on the waterfront patio. Sunday brunch is popular from November into May.

🚹 206 D2 ⊠ 1 Waites Wharf, Newport 🕾 (401) 847-3610 🕒 Daily noon–10, mid-May to Labor Day; Wed.–Sun. 6–10 p.m., day after Labor Day to mid-May

### ◆◆◆White Horse Tavern $$$

The tavern was first licensed to sell liquor in 1687 and is still the stuff of legend – patrons have included pirates, state legislators and director Steven Spielberg and his film crew during the shooting of "Amistad." The formal dining room is known for its local seafood, and there is a sophisticated champagne brunch on Sundays. Dinner is expensive but lunch, Sunday brunch and drinks are not if you just want to stop in and soak up the atmosphere.

🚹 206 D2 ⊠ 26 Marlborough Street, Newport 🕾 (401) 849-3600 🕒 Daily noon–3, 6–10 p.m.; closed Tue. lunch

## MYSTIC

### ◆Abbott's Lobster in the Rough $

Although lobsters are the main attraction at this archetypal lobster shack in the picturesque village of Noank, Abbot's also serves excellent steamed clams, steamed mussels and crab rolls. If you don't like fish, you can order chicken, grilled cheese sandwiches or a fresh vegetable platter. Simple, but fun.

🚹 206 C1 ⊠ 117 Pearl Street, Noank 🕾 (860) 536-7719 🕒 Daily noon–9, May–Labor Day; Sat.–Sun. noon–7, day after Labor Day to mid-Oct.

### Mystic Pizza $

Expect a cheerful welcome from the Greek owners of this restaurant (on which the movie "Mystic Pizza" was based). Pizzas have a Greek twist: one is topped with moussaka. A short stroll from Mystic Seaport.

🚹 206 C1 ⊠ 56 West Mystic Street 🕾 (860) 536-3700 🕒 Daily 10 a.m.–11 p.m.

# Where to... Shop

**Newport** Rhode Island has a fine history of furniture-making, and in and around Newport **antique** shops abound. The art galleries and specialist shops of Brick Market Place, Thames Street and America's Cup Avenue make the city a shopping destination. Try **Ball and Claw** (55 America's Cup Avenue, tel: 401/848-5600), which sells works by furniture-maker Jeffrey Greene (whose pieces grace the grand mansions); **Thames Glass** (688 Thames Street, tel: 401/846-0576), where glassblower Matthew Buechner fashions elegant vases and witty fish at his studio, or silversmith **J. H. Breakell** (132 Spring Street, tel: 800/767-6411), whose small lighthouse pins and silver quahog (clam) bracelets are small masterpieces. Over at **Newport**

**Scrimshanders** (14 Bowen's Wharf, tel: 401/849-5680 or 800/635-5234), Brian Kiracofe carves bone just as sailors once did.

**Mystic** At Olde Mistick Village, shops specialize in gifts and souvenirs. **Raining Cats and Dogs** (tel: 860/536-4941) sells everything to do with pets, including weathervanes shaped like your favorite breed of pooch. **Zeke's Ship Shop** (tel: 860/536-9313) concentrates on the nautical: prints, brass bells, lamps and weather instruments. Across the street are Mystic's more contemporary factory outlets. For handmade goods, follow the trail that links the **Connecticut Craft Centers** (tel: 1-888 CT CRAFT).

**Providence** Enjoy indoor shopping at the 1828 **Arcade** (65 Weybosset Street). You can't miss the temple-like frontage; inside, under a glass roof are three levels of stores and restaurants, with decorative banners and iron railings.

# Where to... Be Entertained

**Sailing** The Newport County **Convention and Visitors Bureau** (23 America's Cup Avenue, tel: 800/326-6030) has details of yacht charters lasting from a couple of hours to a week. It also has details of the many schools in the area where you can learn to sail, kayak and fish. At **International Yacht Restoration School** (449 Thames Street, tel: 401/848-5777) you can watch experts and apprentices at work restoring classic wooden yachts.

**Horseback Riding** For a romantic ride along one of Newport's beaches contact **Newport Equestrian Academy** (tel: 401/847-7022).

**Festivals** The city hosts a wide range of festivals from the **Great Chowder Cook Off** (June) to the **Black Ships Festival** (July), which commemorates the state's cultural links with Japan.

In July, classical musicians from around the world perform against a backdrop of the great mansions. Details from the **Newport Visitor Information Center** (23 America's Cup Avenue, tel: 401/845-9123 or 800/976-5122). Then it's off with the black ties and on with the electric guitars, as America's leading rhythm and blues artists hit town. In August, the **folk festival** is a prelude to the world famous JVC **jazz festival**. Both are held in the grounds of Fort Adams State Park.

Other highlights in an ever busy program include the **men's pro tennis tournament**, played each July on the grass courts at the International Tennis Hall of Fame.

# Coastal Maine to the White Mountains

In Six Days 152 – 153
Don't Miss 154 – 164
At Your Leisure 165 – 167
Where To 168 – 172

# Getting Your Bearings

Maine has statewide air-conditioning. When the rest of New England reaches its boiling point in July and August, the traffic swells up Route 95 like mercury in a thermometer. Everyone is in search of cool nights, a wealth of outdoor activities and, if they're lucky, a glimpse of a moose.

Don't worry about Maine becoming uncontrollably crowded in summer. At 21,000 square miles, it is bigger than all the other New England states combined, so there is more than enough solitude to go around.

In everybody's rush to get to the coolest place in the northeast, New Hampshire often gets overlooked. On your way from Boston to Maine, you pass through the Granite State for little more than half an hour, but New Hampshire rises to the same heights that Maine does: Mount Washington, the tallest peak in the northeast, is in the New Hampshire portion of the White Mountains. New Hampshire also boasts a midsize city, Portsmouth, that's as attractive as anything in all of New England.

Maine has more than 3,000 miles of coastline, New Hampshire less than 50, yet they enjoy about the same amount of beachfront. New Hampshire's beaches are small and often crowded in summer, as are the southernmost Maine beaches. Maine's beaches are all clustered together between the New Hampshire border and Portland, the state's largest city; the northernmost of these beach communities, Kennebunk and Kennebunkport, are the least crowded.

North of Portland – not a tourist attraction, but with enough indoor attractions to fill a rainy day – the coast turns rocky. Although this makes for poor sunbathing, it does make for stunning snapshots. The northeast coast is simply picturesque, as are the handful of towns sprinkled along the way – Camden, Castine, Blue Hill, Belfast, Port Clyde. Each has its own charms that can be experienced only by walking or bicycling through the uncrowded streets. The most dramatic scenery is to be found in and around Acadia National Park, near Bar Harbor.

Finally, there are the White Mountains, which stretch across the top third of New Hampshire and poke into Maine's interior. This is the land of blue lakes and blueberries, of wild rivers and wild moose. There's no gorgeous rocky coast here, but there are thousands of miles of wilderness to explore. The most celebrated terrain can be found within the confines of Maine's extremely remote Baxter State Park, but an away-from-it-all experience is easily within the reach of anybody with a picnic lunch, a bottle of water, and the gumption to get off the road and into the woods.

**Pick your own apples near Canterbury**

Previous page:
Pemaquid Point

Above right:
Fishing buoys

Far right:
The Mount
Washington
Cog Railway is
a sight to
behold

⭐ **Don't Miss**

❶ Portsmouth and
Strawbery Banke
► 154

❷ Kennebunk and
Kennebunkport ► 155

❻ Acadia National Park
► 158

❾ The White Mountains
► 161

## At Your Leisure

❸ Portland Head Light and
Museum ► 165

❹ L.L. Bean ► 165

❺ Maine Maritime Museum
► 165

❼ Baxter State Park
► 165

❽ Allagash Wilderness
Waterway ► 166

❿ Lake Winnipesaukee
► 166

⓫ Canterbury Shaker
Village ► 167

Travel up the coast from Boston, passing through the historic town of Portsmouth and the picturesque villages of Kennebunk and Kennebunkport. Follow Maine's spectacular rocky coastline to Acadia National Park, then turn inland to the White Mountains.

# Coastal Maine to the White Mountains in Six Days

## Day One

Drive north from Boston, stopping in **Portsmouth** for lunch. Spend the afternoon looking around the town and visit historic **Strawbery Banke** (➤ 154). Continue north to the **Kennebunks** (➤ 155–157), arriving in time for your first (of many) lobster dinners. Overnight in Kennebunkport (right).

## Day Two

Spend the day at one of the beaches in Kennebunkport. Goose Rocks Beach, just north of town, is a favorite, and not too crowded. If it's not beach weather, visit the Seashore Trolley Museum or just wander around the stores and galleries of Kennebunkport and Kennebunk lower village. Have dinner at the sophisticated White Barn Inn (➤ 168).

## Day Three

Stop in Portland for a quick visit to the **Portland Head Light and Museum** (➤ 165), then continue up the coast to Freeport, where you should allot plenty of time for browsing through the multitude of wares at **L.L. Bean's** (➤ 165) flagship store, as well as the hundreds of other outlet stores here. Don't spend too much time here, however. You still want to get to Bar Harbor tonight so you can have a full day to explore Acadia National Park.

# Day Four

Spend all day at **Acadia National Park** (left, ➤ 158–160). Hike the trail around Jordan Pond, rent a bicycle and cruise the carriage trails, take a sea kayak into Somes Sound, or just sit on a rock and soak up the superb scenery. Have dinner at Abel's Lobster Pound (tel: 207/276-5827), where you can feast on lobsters in the shade of towering pines that preside over the waters of a magnificent fjord.

# Day Five

Head west through Maine to the **White Mountains** (➤ 161–164). Take Route 3 to west Augusta, jog north on Route 27, then Route 2 west to Gorham. Along the way, you'll pass through almost every kind of scenery New England has to offer: rocky coast, tidal flats, rolling farmland, rural villages and White Mountain National Forest. Ascend **Mount Washington,** or, especially in October, drive across the **Kancamagus Highway.** Get out and hike one of the countless trails, or just stop and have a picnic lunch. Spend the night at one of the White Mountain towns, or continue south to **Lake Winnipesaukee** (right, ➤ 166).

# Day Six

Spend the day on the lake, boating, fishing, swimming or just sunning yourself. On your way back to Boston, stop at **Canterbury Shaker Village** (below, ➤ 167), for a glimpse of life in a Shaker community.

# Portsmouth and Strawbery Banke

In 1958, the citizens of Portsmouth made a crucial decision about the city's future. When urban renewal plans promised to demolish the Strawbery Banke neighborhood (the area of original settlement), a group of local residents fought back and succeeded in turning the area into a 10-acre outdoor museum, preserving historic homes, a colonial tavern and more than two dozen other historic buildings.

A bastion against urban sprawl: the lovely New Hampshire town of Portsmouth

Named for the wild strawberries found on the banks when the English first arrived in 1630 (before spelling was standardized), Strawbery Banke is still a work in progress. While work on renovating the houses and buildings continues, visitors can spend time savoring the fruits of the preservation efforts. The tavern and nine historic homes dating back to the 1790s, which form the museum, are open to the public for a single admission charge.

Besides saving individual buildings from the wrecking ball, the Strawbery Banke restoration helped Portsmouth rediscover its past. It prevented the kind of urban renewal so popular during the late 1950s, which almost assuredly would have destroyed the city's charm. Today, Portsmouth is a harmonious mix of old and new. It is a lovely place to spend an afternoon shopping or just strolling the streets. Strawbery Banke has also made historic home renovation something of a cottage industry here. In addition to the outdoor museum, half a dozen other historic homes in Portsmouth open their doors to the public, though you'd have to be a fanatic about traditional decor to want to see them all.

## Greater Portsmouth Chamber of Commerce
➕ 205 E2 ✉ 500 Market Street, Portsmouth, NH 03801 ☎ (603) 436-1118; web: www.portcity.org

## Strawbery Banke
➕ 205 E2 ✉ Macy Street, Portsmouth, NH 03802 (temporary entrance on Hancock Street) ☎ (603) 433-1100; web: www.strawberybanke.org 🕐 Daily 10–5, Apr.–Oct. 💵 Expensive. Discounts for children aged 7–17, children under 7 free

# Kennebunk and Kennebunkport

Even before former President George Bush put the
Kennebunks (as Kennebunk and Kennebunkport are
collectively known) on the map, these two blue-blood
villages on opposite sides of the Kennebunk river were
among the most charming on the Maine coast. Of the two,
Kennebunkport is the more precious, with hardly a store or
gas station open past 10 p.m. Kennebunk is equally sleepy,
though a few essential services cater to those who don't rise
and set with the sun.

The population here doubles in summer, and nearly triples on
summer holiday weekends, when it's risky to venture to a
restaurant without a reservation and downright impossible to
find a hotel room. The flood of tourists strangles traffic
negotiating the two-lane bridge across the river, but it also
provides the stores with enough business to keep them afloat
through the cold Maine winters. As with most resort towns,
many stores cater purely for a tourist clientele, but there is
also a good selection of crafts, clothing, pottery and art.

The excellent beaches, with calm waters and long expanses
of soft white sand, are the reason people come to the

**White clapboard
homes and
churches make
Kennebunkport
one of Maine's
most idyllic
towns**

Kennebunks. The water is usually too cold for swimming except for the heartiest souls on the hottest days, but it makes for a bracing dip between sunbathing sessions. Getting to the beach, however, can be problematic. Each beach requires its own permit to park along the surrounding streets. The permits are different for each beach and are not available at the beaches themselves; you have to buy them at the local police station, town hall or Chamber of Commerce. For the fee, you might expect some amenities but, except at Mother's Beach, all you get is the beach. So make sure you pack a lunch, carry a chaise, and bring plenty of water, because you can't get any of these things on the beach.

**Gooch's Beach,** which parallels Beach Avenue in Kennebunk, is perhaps the most popular stretch of sand. It's easy to find and has calm surf and ample parking. Permits are available from the Chamber of Commerce or at Kennebunk Town Hall (on Summer Street near Green Street).

**Mother's Beach,** located west of Gooch's Beach in Kennebunk, has a similar stretch of sand, a similar view, and the same parking restrictions. It's a bit more remote than Gooch's, but it is the only beach with a bathroom.

**Goose Rocks Beach** is in a residential neighborhood north of Kennebunkport, just off Route 9. At high tide, this 4-mile-long ribbon of sand easily accommodates the relatively few numbers that make the 10-minute drive out here. At low tide, it becomes a massive tidal flat where you can walk for hours in ankle-deep ocean. To get there, take School Street (Route 9) from Kennebunkport. Stop at the police station for a parking permit. Then continue along Route 9 to Dyke Road and turn right. At the fork in the road, turn left and park inside the white lines.

On rainy days, the most popular attraction (besides heading an hour south to outlet shops in Kittery, or an hour north to L.L. Bean in Freeport) is the **Seashore Trolley Museum.** Kids love to ride the working trolley back through time: The historical dioramas and real-life displays re-create an era

**Above: Wedding Cake House is among Kennebunkport's many historic buildings**

**Top: Exclusive boutiques and charming inns draw visitors to Kennebunkport year-round**

when trains, trams and trolleys, rather than cars, took people everywhere.

## TAKING A BREAK

For the real Maine experience, try the informal **Nunan's Lobster Hut** (➤ 169), 2 miles from Kennebunkport. It's well worth the short drive.

Above: Taste life from a past era at the Seashore Trolley Museum

### Kennebunk – Kennebunkport Chamber of Commerce

🕀 205 E2 ✉ Routes 9 and 35, Kennebunk, ME 04043 ☎ (800) 982-4421 or (207) 967-0857; web: www.kkcc.maine.org

### Seashore Trolley Museum

🕀 205 E2 ✉ 195 Log Cabin Road, Kennebunkport, ME 04046 ☎ (207) 967-2800; web: www.trolleymuseum.org ⏰ Daily 10–5, late May to mid-Oct. Tours leave approximately every half hour 🎟 Moderate. Discounts for children aged under 17

## THE KENNEBUNKS: INSIDE INFO

**Top tips** Colony Beach in Kennebunkport overlooks the same patch of ocean as Gooch's Beach, and though it's not very long and gets crowded early, has two distinct advantages. It is within walking distance of several of the accommodations along Ocean Drive, and it has a small lot where you can park for free without a permit. Get there early before it fills up.

**In more depth** If you can't find accommodations in the Kennebunks, the town of Ogunquit (above), about 10 miles south, is also attractive, with a 3-mile-long beach and no parking permit nonsense. Ogunquit has more affordable motels and restaurants than the Kennebunks, but isn't as commercial as Wells, its neighbor to the north. Ogunquit is popular with gay travelers, though neither the town nor the travelers advertise this.

# Acadia National Park

Acadia was the first national park east of the Mississippi River when it was established in 1919 and is still the only one in the northeast quarter of the country. Even though at 40,000 acres it's one of the smallest parks in the system, Acadia is one of the most popular, drawing more than 2.7 million visitors annually.

If this sounds crowded, take solace in the fact that the vast majority of visitors do little more than drive the park loop road and never leave their cars except to have lunch at the Jordan Pond House restaurant. This means that there are 39,999 other acres for you to explore by bicycle, canoe, kayak or on foot. Whichever you choose, you can't go wrong. The most popular choice is two-wheeling. John D. Rockefeller, who purchased more than 11,000 acres of pristine land at the beginning of the 19th century, carved out a 45-mile network of carriage trails and linked them with 16 hand-cut stone bridges. Hiking and horseback riding are also popular carriage-trail pursuits, but the multitude of bicycle rental shops in the nearby town of Bar Harbor, the gateway to the park, will give you an idea of the preferred method of transportation on these byways.

Hiking in Acadia is a treat, since many of the trails were cut by the same stonemasons who built the carriage roads: in

**The park loop road is the most popular drive at Acadia National Park**

Acadian land-
scapes: long
stretches of
rocky coast

other words, carved, rather than just hacked out of the
mountains. There are more than 120 miles of hiking trails in
addition to the carriage trails, and most get no more than a
few visitors per day. The 3.3-mile loop around Jordan Pond is
the most popular, though many people turn around when
they see they will have to scramble across a section of low,
jagged boulders. (It's inconvenient, but not
difficult.) Check in at the Hulls Cove Visitor
Center for a list and map of the park's
hiking trails.

Sea kayakers of all ability levels will love
the waters in and around Acadia, from the
bathtub-still **Somes Sound**, a true geological
fjord, to the stronger surf of the open ocean.
Several outfitters, most located on Cottage
Street in Bar Harbor, run trips which range
from a few hours to a full-day voyage to an
offshore island.

Even the less active are able to take in the beauty of Acadia
with a drive to the top of **Cadillac Mountain** (1,530 feet), a
beautiful spot for watching the dawn of a new day. Of course,
if the thought of a 4:30 a.m. start doesn't appeal, you can
come later in the day. It's almost as exhilarating at sunset, and
not nearly as tiring.

Mount Desert Island (pronounced like *dessert*, though just
as often mispronounced) is the lobster claw-shaped island on
which most of the park sits (two areas in other nearby
peninsulas are also under federal protection). Bar Harbor, the
major town, is more a tourist strip than a typical Maine town.

The Maine coast
is home to a
variety of sea-
life, including
Northern
Starfish

## TAKING A BREAK

**Jordan Pond House** (Park Loop Road, tel: 207/288-5592), on the park's main circuit, is an institution, serving excellent light lunches, afternoon tea (the popovers are a must) and home-made ice cream. It's not off the beaten track, so don't expect to be alone.

✚ 203 E2
✉ Park Headquarters, P.O. Box 177, Bar Harbor, ME 04609
☎ (207) 288-3338; web: www.acadianationalpark.com
⊙ Hulls Cove Visitor Center, 3 miles west of Bar Harbor on Route 233: daily 8–4:30, mid-Apr. to Jun. and Oct.; daily 8–6, Jul.–Aug.; variable hours Sep. Winter visitor center, at park headquarters: daily 8–4:30, Nov. to mid-Apr.
💰 May–Oct.: Moderate, half-price for bikers and walkers (good for unlimited entries and exits for seven days).

From the top of Cadillac Mountain, early-risers can be the first in the U.S. to greet the dawn

## ACADIA NATIONAL PARK: INSIDE INFO

**Top tip** In the peak season (July and August), bike rentals sometimes sell out. To avoid disappointment, call Bar Harbor Bicycle Shop (tel: 207/288-3886) and **reserve a bike** in advance.

**In more detail** There are several other tiny towns on Mount Desert Island. The largest of them are **Northeast Harbor,** on the eastern lobe, and **Southwest Harbor,** on the western lobe. Each is home to a few restaurants, hotels and shops of a slightly more charming variety than those found in Bar Harbor.

# The White Mountains

The White Mountains aren't so much an attraction as an entire region. Covering 780,000 acres, this mountainous area is the size of the entire state of Rhode Island. Yet there isn't a town of more than 10,000 people to be found anywhere in these mountains. Still, you don't come here for the towns. The lure of the White Mountains is the trails for hiking, country roads for biking and rivers for canoeing.

Sounds like too much exertion? You can take a driving tour of the same scenery, ride up the side of the Northeast's highest mountain in a railway car or visit the house where Robert Frost wrote many of his poems.

## Mount Washington

The first stop on any visit to the White Mountains should be **Mount Washington,** at 6,288 feet the tallest mountain in the Northeast. Around New Hampshire you'll often see bumper stickers proudly proclaiming "This Car Climbed Mount Washington." If you can't resist the temptation of a slow, narrow, white-knuckle drive to the top of a mountain, by all means join this lusty club. But you might want to consider some better ways to get to the summit.

The first is hiking. Pick up a copy of the Appalachian Mountain Club's *White Mountain Guide,* which is available in any local bookstore and is regarded as the hikers' bible for this region. The hike is strenuous but rewarding. Allow

*The Swift River courses across the prettiest part of the White Mountains*

3 to 5 hours to get up, and 3 to 4 to make the journey back down, plus some time to enjoy the views from the peak.

If, on the other hand, you read that with alarm, you may prefer to use the **Mount Washington Cog Railway,** which operates from May to October. This 3.5-mile track, laid in 1869, remains a marvelous engineering accomplishment. The steepest part of the climb, Jacob's Ladder, angles upward at an exciting 37 percent grade. The leisurely ride takes about 3 hours round trip.

Finally, there is a van tour up the 8-mile-long **Mount Washington Auto Road,** which you can pick up in Great Glen or Route 16. The rate is only slightly more than the fee to drive the road yourself. The road is only open when weather permits, and not at all between the end October and mid-May.

Regardless of how you get to the top, remember that Mount Washington has worse weather than almost any place in North America. The average temperature at the summit is 30 degrees Fahrenheit, and the winds, which once reached a record 231 m.p.h., are fierce even in summer.

## Kancamagus Highway

The Kancamagus Highway, which parallels the Swift river from Conway to Lincoln, is a less inclement excursion. It's designated a National Scenic Byway and with good reason. On weekends in fall foliage season, this out-of-the-way road is often choked with motorists tootling through the corridor of brilliant ocher and vermilion leaves. The most popular stop on the 34-mile route is **Sabbaday Falls,** just about halfway along, though there are dozens of other worthwhile places where you

can pull over and have a look around at covered bridges, or start off on a day hike through the mountains.

The Kancamagus Highway is wide enough to be a favorite with bicyclists, and steep in only a few portions. Those who prefer mountain biking should head to Great Glen Trails (tel: 603/466-2333), near the entrance to the Mount Washington Auto Road. You can also rent bikes and helmets here.

## Franconia Notch State Park

Hikers gravitate toward the town of Franconia Notch and the state park of the same name. A notch is a mountain pass, and Franconia Notch is barely wide enough to squeeze an 18-wheeler through. That leaves plenty of unspoiled wilderness in which to hike, bike, swim or just enjoy a warm afternoon. Dozens of hiking trails lace the state park, including the

*Below: The lure of the White Mountains is its quiet beauty*

homestretch of the Georgia-to-Maine Appalachian Trail. Were it not for the presence of helpful park rangers, you would never be able to distinguish the state park from the surrounding national forest.

The park is home to two areas of particular note. The first, the **Old Man of the Mountains,** a natural formation of five granite ledges, looks from some angles like a profile view of a 40-foot head. If this face looks familiar – some say it looks like Thomas Jefferson – it may be that you've seen it on state highway signs: it's the New Hampshire state symbol. The best place to see the Old Man is from the marked viewing area at Profile Lake.

*Left: The Mount Washington Cog Railway inches its way up the tallest mountain in New England*

The second landmark is the **Flume,** a 90-foot-deep gorge through which Flume Brook cascades. You can walk the 2 miles of well-maintained trails, bridges and boardwalks that crisscross the area.

In the nearby town of Franconia is the literary highlight of the White Mountains, **Frost Place.** Robert Frost spent 19 summers here from 1921 to 1940, and wrote as many as half of his poems in this house. The simple 1859 farmhouse contains several signed first editions.

### North Conway

Finally, if the White Mountains can be said to have a commercial center, it must be North Conway. Like mushrooms after a rainfall, outlet shops keep cropping up along the major intersection in this town, causing big-time traffic jams on gray Saturdays. The surrounding area is much prettier, however, as evidenced by the existence of the **Conway Scenic Railroad** (tel: 603/356-5251), which takes passengers on rides through the Mount Washington Valley. Trips vary in length from 1 to 5 hours, priced accordingly.

### TAKING A BREAK

For gourmet sandwiches, stop in Franconia at **Dutch Treat** (Main Street, tel: 603/823-8851). Fillings range from steak or grilled vegetables to ostrich!

---

**White Mountains Tourist Office**
➕ 204 C3 ✉ P.O. Box 10 GB, North Woodstock, NH 03262. Visitor Center at Exit 32 on I-93 in North Woodstock. ☎ (603) 745-8720; web: www.VisitWhiteMountains.com

**Frost Place**
➕ 204 C4 ✉ Ridge Road, Franconia ☎ (603) 823-5510 🕐 Wed.–Mon. 1–5, Jul.–Oct.; Sat.–Sun. 1–5, May–Jun.

**Franconia Notch State Park**
➕ 204 C3 ✉ Franconia Notch Parkway, Franconia ☎ (603) 823-5563 🕐 Mid-May to mid-Oct.

**Mount Washington Cog Railway**
➕ 205 D4 ☎ (800) 922-8825

**Mount Washington Auto Road**
➕ 205 D4 ☎ (603) 466-3988

**Conway Scenic Railroad**
➕ 205 D3 ☎ (603) 356-5251

---

## THE WHITE MOUNTAINS: INSIDE INFO

**Top tip** The major towns of the White Mountains form a near-perfect rectangle, with Mount Washington above the top right-hand corner. Interstate 93 connects the towns of Franconia Notch and Lincoln (and North Woodstock). Conway and North Conway are linked by Route 16, which continues north to Mount Washington. The 34-mile-long Kancamagus Highway (Route 112) runs east-west between Conway and Lincoln, and Route 302 connects North Conway and Franconia Notch, though the mountainous terrain forces it to take an extremely circuitous route.

**Hidden gem** The town of Jackson, nestled in its own corner of the White Mountains, is much more picturesque than North Conway, its more commercial neighbor. A 93-mile network of cross-country skiing trails, one of the finest in the country, makes it an especially fine place to visit in winter.

# At Your Leisure

early five-masted schooners to the first paddlewheel steamships. You can even visit the historic shipyard where the largest wooden ship ever built in America was constructed. The museum sponsors cruises (some of them on windjammers) along the Kennebec river or out to nearby offshore islands.

**All things maritime are on display at the Maine Maritime Museum**

## 🔢 Portland Head Light and Museum

This was one of the first lighthouses in the country, and it is still one of the most picturesque. It was a working lighthouse as recently as 1989, when it went fully automated. The former keeper's quarters have been converted into an excellent museum, and the surrounding Fort Williams Park is a fine place for a picnic overlooking Casco Bay.

➕ 205 F3 ✉ 1000 Shore Road (Route 1 North to Oak Hill, then right onto 207, and left on Route 77. Turn right onto Shore Road) ☎ (207) 799-2661; web: www.portlandheadlight.com 🕐 Daily 10–4, Memorial Day to mid-Oct.; Sat.–Sun. 10–4, mid-Apr. to Memorial Day and mid-Oct.–Dec. 25 💵 Inexpensive. Children aged under 6 free

## 🔢 L.L. Bean

Bean's headquarters is the catalog come to life, with helpful salesfolk who really know their boots from their boats. Best of all, it's open 24 hours (► 24–25).

➕ 205 F3 ✉ Main Street, Freeport, ME 04033 ☎ (800) 221-4221; web: www.llbean.com

## 🔢 Maine Maritime Museum

Everything you might expect in a museum on Maine's maritime history is located in this one place, from

In Bath's 19th-century glory days, the nearby Bath Iron Works was a shipbuilding center. It still builds and repairs ships for the U.S. Navy.

➕ 205 F3 ✉ 243 Washington Street, Bath, ME 04530. (Follow Washington Street 1.6 miles past the Bath Iron Works) ☎ (207) 443-1316 🕐 Daily 9:30–5; closed Jan. 1, Thanksgiving, Dec. 25 💵 Moderate. Discounts for families, seniors and children aged 6–16, children under 6 free

## 🔢 Baxter State Park

Baxter State Park, closer to Quebec than it is to Portland, is truly a hike. Even people who live in Maine consider Baxter a long way away. The reward for venturing so far afield, of course, is solitude and wilderness –

A spray-spectacular at Allagash Falls

miles and miles of wilderness, 20,000 acres in all, topped by Mount Katahdin, one of the most challenging ascents on the Appalachian Trail. Less adventurous souls can brave other trails among the 180 miles offered here, canoe the several ponds and lakes, or go whitewater rafting down the west branch of the Penobscot river. Several outfitters offer packages.

Baxter is truly away from it all. The terrain is as untamed as it was when Governor Percival Baxter deeded the land to the state in 1931 and decreed that it be "forever left in its natural wild state." Lodging options range from your own tent to simple cabins and bunkhouses (you'll need a permit: call far in advance to get one). And keep your eyes peeled for moose.

🚩 202 C4 ✉ 64 Balsam Drive, Milinocket, ME 04462 ☎ (207) 723-5140 🎒 Moderate. Camping permits inexpensive; bunkhouses also available

## 8 Allagash Wilderness Waterway

Canoeists, take note: The Allagash Wilderness Waterway is one of the best trips in the country. The Allagash is designated a Wild and Scenic River and development is forbidden for 500 feet on either side of the 92-mile corridor between Telos Dam, the put-in point, and Allagash, the take-out point farther north. The entire trip takes 7 to 10 days, with campsites along the route. Several outfitters in the town of Greenville offer guided tours of the waterway, as well as equipment packages.

**Maine Bureau of Parks and Recreation**

🚩 202 C5 ✉ Department of Conservation, State House 22, Augusta, ME 04333 ☎ (207) 289-3821

## 10 Lake Winnipesaukee

The paucity of ocean beaches goes somewhat unnoticed in New Hampshire, largely because of the abundance of sandy lake beaches in

## Off the Beaten Track

**Hanover,** on the Connecticut River near the Vermont border, is the home of Dartmouth College, the oldest member of the Ivy League, and the only one without any graduate schools. Hanover is truly a college town – almost every business here caters to undergraduates or faculty – but it's also one of the prettiest villages in New England. Come here in summer when it's serene and free of boisterous college students, or the second weekend in February when Winter Carnival's skiing races, ice sculptures, and free-flowing beer bring everybody out of hibernation. For information, call the Hanover Chamber of Commerce (tel: 603/643-3115) or Dartmouth College (tel: 603/646-1110) for Winter Carnival details.

## For Kids

The Portland Sea Dogs are an affiliate of the Florida Marlins, and play their home games in Hadlock Field, an old-style ballpark with more seats than you'd expect for a minor-league team. Players are young and raw, with names you've never heard of, but the games are usually competitive, the stands are close to the field, and the emphasis is on family fun. The season runs from mid-April through the first weekend in September. Tickets are hard to come by, so call ahead (tel: 800/936-DOGS or 207/879-9500; web: www.portlandseadogs.com).

the center of the state where you can cool your toes on hot summer days. The biggest, and consequently the most popular, is Lake Winnipesaukee, just north of Laconia. Several communities around the lake have access to the water, but most people opt to stay around Weirs Beach because of its sandy shores, its boardwalk, its child-friendly amusements, and its proximity to I-93 and the towns of Meredith and Laconia. Those in search of a quieter lakeside stay should head over to Wolfeboro, on the eastern shore of the lake.

**Lakes Region Association**
🟥 205 D3 ✉ P.O. Box 430, New Hampton, NH 03256 ☎ (603) 744-8664; web: www.lakesregion.org

**Greater Laconia Weirs Beach Chamber of Commerce**
🟥 205 D3 ✉ 11 Veteran's Square, Laconia, NH 03246 ☎ (603) 524-5531; web: www.laconia-weirs.org

### 🔟 Canterbury Shaker Village

If you missed the Hancock Shaker Village (➤ 104–105) or want to

Shaker craftsmanship is still practiced at Canterbury Shaker Village

learn more about the lives of the Shakers, then visit this outpost a half hour north of Concord. More than two dozen original buildings remain from the days when this was a working 19th-century Shaker village. To get a real feel for how the community lived, come at lunch or dinner time and have a meal at the Creamery Restaurant. Seating is at long communal tables, where you'll be treated to a four-course dinner made from fresh local ingredients. Afterward, you can take the candlelight tour of the village (weather permitting).

🟥 205 D2 ✉ 288 Shaker Road, Canterbury, NH 03224 ☎ (800) 982-9511 or (603) 783-9511; web: www.shakers.org 🕐 Daily 10–5, May–Oct.; Sat.–Sun. 10–5, Apr. and Nov.–Dec. Tours leave on the hour and last 60–90 minutes 🎟 Moderate. Reductions for children aged 6–15

# Where to... Stay

## Prices

Expect to pay for two people sharing a double room, excluding taxes

**$** under $150  **$$** $150–250  **$$$** over $250

PORTSMOUTH

### ◆◆ Martin Hill Inn $

This elegant 19th-century inn, decorated with antique mahogany furniture and oriental porcelain, captures the essence of Portsmouth, one of New England's oldest communities. Bedrooms are themed, from formal colonial to country Victorian; all have queen-size beds and air-conditioning. Strawbery Banke and downtown are a 10-minute stroll away.

✠ 205 E2 ✉ 404 Islington Street, Portsmouth, NH 03801 ☎ (603) 436-2287; web: www.portsmouthnh.com/martinhillinn

KENNEBUNKPORT

### ◆◆◆ Captain Lord Mansion $$–$$$

The popular inn (with conference facilities and 20 bedrooms) would be unrecognizable to its first owner, shipbuilder and merchant Nathaniel Lord. Some elements of Lord's 19th-century home remain, including the impressive four-story staircase. There are four quiet rooms in a separate house behind the main inn.

✠ 205 E2 ✉ 6 Pleasant Street, Kennebunkport, ME 04046 ☎ (207) 967-3141 or (800) 522-3141; fax: (207) 967-3172; web: www.captainlord.com

### ◆◆◆ White Barn Inn $$$

This luxury inn may be housed in a converted barn, but there is nothing rustic about the setting: galleries of antiques, a piano bar and plain, polished wood floors. By contrast, some of the bedrooms are quite plain, though the six suites are as luxurious as any in North America. The inn's restaurant is renowned for its excellent cuisine.

✠ 205 E2 ✉ 37 Beach Street, Kennebunkport, ME 04046 ☎ (207) 967-2321; fax: (207) 967-1100; web: www.whitebarninn.com

BAR HARBOR

### ◆◆ Ledgelawn Inn $–$$

The grandiose Ledgelawn is more luxury hotel than inn. The three-story mansion has a plush interior and a hushed atmosphere of Edwardian formality. The armchairs, however, are squashy and relaxing, the dress code casual and the 33 sumptuous bedrooms beautifully furnished, and with central

heating and air-conditioning.

✠ 203 E2 ✉ 66 Mount Desert Street, Bar Harbor, ME 04609 ☎ (207) 288-4596 or (800) 274-5334; web: www.barharborvacations.com

### ◆◆ Manor House Inn $

Hidden behind tall hedges and set back from the street, Manor House is typically Victorian, with deep gables and wraparound porch. Its interior is equally authentic, with oriental rugs, polished wood floors and antique desks. Even the beds in the 14 rooms exude character, with tall, carved head- and footboards.

✠ 205 D3 ✉ 106 West Street, Bar Harbor, ME 04609 ☎ (207) 288-3759 or (800) 437-0088; fax: (207) 288-2974; web: www.acadia.net/manorhouse

### ◆◆ Mira Monte Inn and Suites $

The owners of this 19th century inn scoured local barn sales for old, rather than antique, furniture to create a family atmosphere. The library, furnished with large overstuffed chairs, is a favorite room. The simply furnished bedrooms have spectacular views: Mira Monte means "look at the mountains." Acadia National Park and Cadillac Mountain fill the windows.

**✚ 205 D3** **⊠ 69 Mount Desert Street, Bar Harbor, ME 04609** **☎ (207) 288-4263 or (800) 553-5109; fax: (207) 288-3115; web: www. miramonte.com**

## WHITE MOUNTAINS

### ◆◆◆ Darby Field Inn $-$$

The inn stands high above the frenzied shopping of North Conway. Expect peaceful gardens and lovely views. Odd spaces in the building are filled with antiques. Several rooms have whirlpool tubs and one is all Victorian, with an enthusiastic ficus plant. Evening meals are like a dinner party.

**✚ 205 D3** **⊠ 185 Chase Hill Road, Conway, NH 03818** **☎ (603) 447-2181 or (800) 426-4147; fax: (603) 447-5726; web: www.darbyfield.com**

### ◆◆◆ ◆ Inn at Thorn Hill $$$

This handsome 19th-century inn is close to Mount Washington and the stores in North Conway. In winter, skiers flock to local downhill slopes and cross-country trails. Bedrooms are Victorian-style in the main inn, but more rustic in the carriage house. A cheerful pub and fine restaurant complete the picture.

**✚ 205 D4** **⊠ Thorn Hill Road, Jackson, NH 03846** **☎ (603) 383-4242 or (800) 289-8990; fax: (603) 383-8062; web: www.innatthornhill.com**

## LAKE WINNIPESAUKEE

### ◆◆◆ Red Hill Inn $-$$

This 100-year-old inn is a relaxed place, where children are welcome. There are collectibles everywhere, from old license plates and signs to antique cameras and maps. Bedrooms are comfortable, and the restaurant has a growing reputation.

**✚ 205 D3** **⊠ Route25B, Center Harbor, NH 03226** **☎ (603) 279-7001 or (800) 573-3445**

# Where to... Eat and Drink

## Prices

Expect to pay per person for a three-course meal, excluding drinks and service

**$** under $15 **$$** $15–30 **$$$** over $30

## PORTSMOUTH

### ◆◆◆ Lindbergh's Crossing $$$

Close to the river and with an atmosphere like a small French country bistro, Lindbergh's Crossing is a busy place. If you want to eat downstairs, rather than in the upstairs wine bar, reservations are a must. Dishes in both areas of the restaurant range from tenderloin au poivre to seared tuna with mushroom risotto. Popular desserts include a "medium rare" chocolate cake, crème brûlée and peach crisp. French and California wines can be bought by the glass.

**✚ 205 E2** **⊠ 29 Ceres Street, Portsmouth, NH** **☎ (603) 431-0887** **Ⓣ Daily 5.30–9.30 (also Sat.–Sun. 9.30–10 p.m.) Wine bar from 4 p.m.**

## KENNEBUNKPORT

### Nunan's Lobster Hut $

For a no-frills lobster feast, head north from Kennebunkport to this Cape Porpoise institution. Sit at picnic tables, order a No. 2 lobster dinner (two one-pounders, potato chips, rolls, pickles and melted butter), put on your paper bib and dig in. Geary's or Shipyard ale is the best accompaniment. Leave room for the famous blueberry or apple pie. They do not take reservations or credit cards.

➕ 205 E2 ⊠ Route 9, Cape Porpoise, ME ☎ (207) 967-4362 ⊙ Daily 5–9, late-Mar to mid-Oct.; closed Mon.–Wed. early in season

## Windows on the Water $–$$

With linen tablecloths and napkins, this is more formal than many of Maine's seafood spots. The food has gained a reputation for excellence, picking up awards for specialties such as lobster ravioli and crème brûlée. The dish most in demand, at both lunch and dinner, is the hearty lobster-stuffed potato. Don't be misled by the restaurant's name, by the way: A new building now blocks part of the once-excellent view of the Kennebunk River.

➕ 205 E2 ⊠ Chase Hill Road, at junction of routes 9 and 3, Kennebunkport, ME ☎ (207) 967-3313 ⊙ Daily 11:45–2:30, 5:30–8:30

## BAR HARBOR

### Lompoc Café and Brew Pub $$

This is the sort of informal spot you need in a coastal town. Eat at tables inside or sit outside and watch the action on the boccie court. From the brewery, which is out of town, they serve seasonal ales, including an unusual blueberry brew. Expect bistro food, such as mushrooms stuffed with seafood and chicken baked with garlicky cheese.

➕ 203 E2 ⊠ 32 Rodick Street, Bar Harbor, ME ☎ (207) 288-9392 ⊙ Daily 11:30–9:30, mid-May through Oct.

### ◆ The Reading Room $$

The Reading Room (part of the Bar Harbor Inn) is a meeting point for locals and visitors alike. All the seats in the restaurant have views of Frenchman's Bay, and in summer lunch is served at the open-air Terrace Grill. Although steak and pasta are on the menu, order the classic lobster bake, which includes

clam chowder, steamed mussels and clams, a lobster and blueberry pie.

➕ 203 E2 ⊠ Bar Harbor Inn, Newport Drive, ME ☎ (207) 288-3351 ⊙ Daily 5:30–9, Apr.–Nov.

## WHITE MOUNTAINS

### ◆◆ 1785 Inn $$$

Beams, an old brick oven and a stone fireplace in the dining room are testimony to the inn's long history. The menu mixes tradition with invention. Although entrées such as rack of lamb are always popular, appetizers can be unusual, like blackened scallops or smoked salmon ravioli. Desserts are calorific. How about coffee mousse in a crunchy walnut pastry shell?

➕ 205 D3 ⊠ Route 16, North Conway, NH ☎ (603) 356-9025 or (800) 421-1785 ⊙ Daily 5–9

### ◆◆ The Wentworth Inn $$$

This is one of the finest, and most formal, restaurants in the state. The seasonal menus use the best New Hampshire produce. Summer sees vegetables and fruits with beef, lamb and fish. In fall, salmon is poached in cider, with crab apples. With apple Betty and pumpkin pie for dessert, tradition is never far away.

➕ 205 D4 ⊠ Route 16A, Jackson, NH ☎ (603) 383-9700 or (800) 637-0013 ⊙ Daily 6–9 p.m. (also Sat.–Sun. 9–10 p.m.)

## LAKE WINNIPESAUKEE

### ◆◆ The Corner House Inn $$

This converted farmhouse, dating back to 1840, has the relaxed atmosphere of the New England countryside. The informal first-floor restaurant is decorated with hurricane lamps and has blue-checkered napkins on the tables. Seafood is prepared with a sure touch: the lobster and mushroom bisque is a signature dish.

➕ 205 D3 ⊠ 22 Main Street, Center Sandwich, NH ☎ (603) 284-6219 ⊙ Daily 11:30–2:30, 5:30–9; Tue.–Sun., Nov.–May

# Where to...
## Shop

### MAINE

Shopping is changing Maine's image. The state known for its rugged outdoors is transforming its post-industrial towns into retail outlets, thanks to its imaginative craftspeople who are producing "tomorrow's antiques" and its bargain-priced factory outlet stores.

**Outlet Stores** Every year over 6.5 million shoppers flock to **Kittery Outlets**, about 90 minutes north of Boston, with its 120 brand-name factory outlets in 13 malls (exit 3 off I-95, tel: 888-KITTERY; web: www.thekitteryoutlets.com). Farther north (about 2½ hours from Boston) is **Freeport**, best known as the home of L.L. Bean (▶ 24–25).

But the attractive town has expanded, with 125 stores and designer outlets attracting 4 million visitors a year (tel: 800/865-1994; web: www.freeportusa.com).

**Crafts** At the other end of the shopping spectrum are the collectibles created by the potters and painters, jewelers and quilters who continue the craft traditions of old. See their work in specialty shops and galleries at the **Old Port** historic district of Portland, or out at **Deer Isle Village** and **Stonington.** Contact the **United Maine Craftsmen** (tel: 207/621-2818) for the latest listings about the regular arts and crafts shows held statewide throughout the year. To find out what is for sale, from old prints to furniture, pick up a copy of the monthly *Maine Antiques Digest*.

### NEW HAMPSHIRE

Shopping in New Hampshire is boosted by its lack of sales tax.

**Outlet Stores** Only 90 minutes north of Boston, there are about 50 name-brand and designer stores conveniently assembled under one roof at the **Lakes Region Factory Stores** in Tilton. Up in North Conway, the **Tanger Outlet Centers** boast all the top names, including Liz Claiborne, L.L. Bean and Calvin Klein. This is also home to the **Chuck Roast Mountainwear** outlet (Route 16, tel: 603/356-5589), famous for its lifetime guarantees on rugged jackets, hats, mitts and vests.

**Antiques and Crafts** For more down-to-earth deals, such as locally made blankets and throws, visit the **Woolen Mill** store, part of the still-working mill in Guild, near Sunapee Lake. Over in Keene, former mills have been converted into the **Colony Mill Marketplace** (tel: 603/357-1240), a complex with 35 specialty stores and the added bonus of an antiques market that has up to 240 dealers. The **League of New Hampshire**

**Craftsmen** (64 Center Street, Wolfeboro Falls, tel: 603/569-3309) has half a dozen stores across the state, including North Conway, Center Sandwich, Meredith, Hanover and Concord. Pieces are juried, and you can buy smaller articles such as fragrant soaps, candles and brightly colored quilts, even if the large pieces of furniture won't fit into the car. Some 75 years ago, **Sandwich Home Industries** of Center Sandwich (junction of routes 109/113, tel: 603/284-6831) were the inspiration for the League of New Hampshire Craftsmen when local women started up a co-op, making attractive souvenirs and household items using local materials. Watch artisans working on pewter at the artists at **Gibson Pewter** (18 East Washington Road, tel: 603/464-3410) make bowls and tankards from lead-free material for everyday use. Unusually, they have attractive contemporary as well as traditional designs.

# Where to...
## Be Entertained

## MAINE

**Hiking and Bicycling** The **Maine Bureau of Parks and Lands** (tel: 207/287-3821) provides hiking maps for the vast state parks.

Cyclists can meander along quiet back roads or go mountain biking at ski resorts such as **Sugarloaf/USA** (tel: 207/237-2000) and **Sunday River** (tel: 207/824-5093). For details, contact **Maine Bicycle Coalition** (tel: 207/288-3000).

**Water Sports** Whether you want to go canoeing, river rafting, sailing or sea kayaking, outfitters abound.

For a taste of the Maine of yesteryear, take a three- or six-day cruise aboard a windjammer (a traditional sailing ship). Contact the **Maine Windjammer**

**Association** (tel: 800/807-WIND) for details. In Kennebunkport **Chick's Marina** (tel: 207/967-2782) offers boat charters with licensed captains for fishing trips or a day's exploring. Former Coast Guard captain Rich Woodman organizes cruises aboard the schooner **Lazyjack** (tel: 207/ 967-8809). Gil Gilpatrick leads **Allagash Canoe Vacations** (tel: 207/453-6959) out of Skowhegan, near Waterville.

**Spectator Sports** There is an avid following for the **Portland Sea Dogs** (Hadlock Field, 71 Park Avenue, Portland, tel: 207/874-9300 or 800/936-3647) during the summer months. They may be a minor-league baseball club, but this Double-A team is low on ticket prices and high on atmosphere.

## NEW HAMPSHIRE

New Hampshire has a well-organized network of trails and campgrounds, outfitters and marinas. For details contact **general park information** (tel: 603/271-3556).

**Fishing** Nonresidents require a license: contact **New Hampshire Fish and Game Department** (tel: 603/271-3421). Fishing is hugely popular on Lake Winnipesaukee, where there are many lakes and streams. Every small town has an agent who sells fishing licenses. Agents, in turn, know the nearest outfitter.

**Water Sports** The **Science Center of New Hampshire** (tel: 603/968-7194), at Holderness, on Lake Winnipesaukee, organizes nature cruises to see the loons on Squam Lake (Golden Pond) between July and October. For canoe rental and instruction, **Wild Meadow Canoes and Kayaks** near Centre Harbor

are open year round (tel: 603/253-7536 or 800/427-7536). For more information, contact the **Greater Laconia/Weirs Beach Tourist Information** (tel: 603/524-5531 or 800/531-2347).

**Bicycling** Mountain biking is a fast-growing sport, with ski resorts such as Loon Mountain running summer centers. Experienced riders can put their bikes aboard the Mountain Skyride Gondola and do the scary ride back to the valley floor.

**Skiing** New Hampshire was the cradle of American skiing, with a club dating back to 1872. The first trails were cut at Cannon Mountain in 1930. In winter, just two hours from Boston, both cross-country and downhill skiing are varied and well priced at the resorts of **Ski 93**, the catchall for the five areas strung along i-93: Tenney Mountain, Waterville Valley, Loon Mountain, Cannon and Bretton Woods (tel: 603/745-8101).

# Walks & Tours

1 Boston's Beacon Hill and Back
  Bay 174 – 177
2 Old King's Highway 178 – 180
3 Southern Vermont 181 – 183
4 Newport's Cliff Walk 184 – 186

# 1

# BOSTON'S BEACON HILL AND BACK BAY

*Walk*

Boston is relatively compact and you can easily stroll from one end of the city to the other. In fact, there are times when this is the fastest way around town. The historical Beacon Hill neighborhood is where the upper echelons of Boston society once lived, and many still do today, though you'll also see plenty of ordinary folks out walking their dogs or bringing home groceries to their red-brick town houses.

Until the 1830s, the Back Bay was under water. A massive landfill project lasting nearly

*Victoriana rules in Back Bay*

**DISTANCE** 1.7 miles (one way) **TIME** 1½ hours or all day if you linger
**T STOP** Red Line to Charles/MGH or Blue Line to Bowdoin
**START POINT** Harrison Gray Otis House, Beacon Hill ✚ 198 C3
**END POINT** the Back Bay ✚ 201 F3

50 years turned it into Boston's most easily navigable neighborhood. The streets lie perpendicular to each other, unlike the meandering streets in other parts of the city, and the cross streets even go in alphabetical order. Home to Boston's premier shopping street, Newbury Street (▶ 71), the Back Bay is crowded on sunny summer Sundays, with what seems like the entire city looking for an outdoor table where they can park their bags and refuel.

## 1–2

Start your tour in Beacon Hill at the **Harrison Gray Otis House**. Colonial architect Charles Bulfinch built the home in 1796 for his friend Otis, an aspiring young lawyer who later became a member of Congress and later still the mayor of Boston.

Cross Cambridge Street and walk downhill one block to Joy Street, turn left and walk one block to the **Boston African American National Historic Site**. From here, you can take free guided the narrow alley to the left, and follow it as it bends right and deposits you on Russell Street. You've just retraced a part of the route that fugitive slaves took in the 19th century on the Underground Railroad (the network of safe houses that provided shelter for escapees).

Turn left onto Russell Street, and then right on Myrtle Street. Go three blocks to Anderson Street and turn left. Then take the first right onto Pinckney and follow it downhill one block to **Louisburg Square**, home to some of the finest old Beacon Hill homes. Most of these town houses have been lovingly restored, making this one of the priciest addresses in Boston. The park is private and you need a key to get in, so is more for looking at than for doing.

## 3–4

Continue across Mount Vernon Street, then take the first right onto **Acorn Street.** The street appears in many photographs of Beacon Hill, perhaps not so much because it is the most picturesque, but because thick cobblestones prevent all but the most intrepid from driving down the narrow passageway. Free

**The cobblestoned Acorn Street looks today as it did in the 18th century**

*Boston Common*

STREET

Washington Monument

ARLES STREET

*Public Garden*

LINGTON STREET

**(5)**

0    250 yards

0    250 metres

COMMONWEALTH    AVENUE

BERKELEY    STREET

BACK    BAY

CLARENDON    STREET

The Tortoise & the Hare

DARTMOUTH    ST

Trinity Church

COPLEY SQUARE

John Hancock Tower

**(8)**    ST

NEWBURY    ST

BOYLSTON    STREET

**(7)**

Boston Public Library

EXETER    STREET

**(6)**

HUNTINGTON AVE

tours of the **Black Heritage Trail** or do a self-guiding tour of the 13 sites. The best is the **African Meeting House,** a half block away from the visitor center. Once known as "the Black Faneuil Hall," this 1805 building is the oldest black church in the United States still in existence. In 1832, William Lloyd Garrison founded the New England Anti-Slavery Society at this historic spot.

## 2–3

As you exit the building, turn left and follow Smith Court to the end. Then proceed along from cars, you could almost imagine you'd been transported back to 1776.

Turn left at West Cedar Street and right at Chestnut. Cross busy Charles Street (or stop and wander through the interesting collection of shops), turn left onto Brimmer Street and follow it until it dead-ends at Beacon Street. At the corner you'll see the **Bull and Finch Pub,** better known as the bar from the popular TV show "Cheers." The exterior is the one seen at the opening of every episode, but walk inside and you won't recognize the furnishings (the show's interior scenes were shot on a sound-stage in Hollywood and do not look at all alike). These days, the "gang at Cheers" is made up mostly of visitors to the city rather than Bostonians, but the food is pretty good, as is the selection of beers.

## 4–5

Cross Beacon Street and walk a half block left to the entrance to the **Public Garden** (▲ 58). If you're in town at the right time of year and in the mood for a ride on one of the **swan boats,** go clockwise around the lagoon. Otherwise, stroll counterclockwise toward the Washington Monument. Exit the Public Garden at Arlington Street and walk a block left to exclusive **Newbury Street** (▲ 71).

## 5–6

Chanel, Armani, Versace, Ann Taylor and Burberry's are just some of the tenants in the high-rent blocks closest to the Public Garden, but equally intriguing and less familiar retailers line both sides of this popular shopping boulevard. If it's a sunny day, there's nothing better than lunch at one of the excellent restaurants or myriad outdoor cafés. Shop your way as far as Exeter Street (or farther, if you like, and then double back; the quirkier shops are farthest from the Public Garden) and turn left. Continue one block to Boylston Street and then turn left again.

## 6–7

Boylston between Exeter and Dartmouth is home to the old and new buildings of the **Boston Public Library.** The old, a 1895 Renaissance Revival by architects McKim, Mead and White, has been widely imitated throughout the United States. It boasts relief panels on its façade by Saint-Gaudens, bronze doors sculpted by Daniel Chester French, and interior murals by John Singer Sargent and Edwin Abbey. The new, a stark 1972 creation by Philip Johnson, is constructed from the same color granite as the original, but that is about all that the two buildings have in

common. The old building has the added benefit of facing **Copley Square** and its pleasant open lawn.

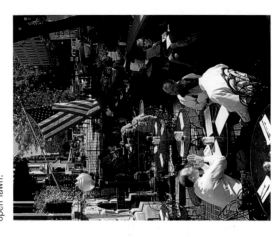

Exclusive **Newbury Street,** *the* place to stop for lunch

## Taking a Break

### Harrison Gray Otis House
198 C3  Cambridge Street at Hancock Street  (617) 227-3956  Tours Wed.–Sun. on the hour between 11 and 4  Inexpensive

### Boston African American National Historic Site
198 C3  46 Joy Street  (617) 725-0022  Daily 10–4, Jun.–Sep.; Tue.–Sat. 10–4, Oct.–May  Inexpensive

### African Meeting House
198 C3  8 Smith Court  (617) 742-5415  Daily 10–4, Jun.–Sep.; Tue.–Sat. 10–4, Oct.–May  Inexpensive

### Boston Public Library
201 F3  700 Boylston Street  (617) 536-5400  Mon.–Thu. 9–9, Fri.–Sat. 9–5, Sun. 1–5; closed Sun., May–Sep.  Inexpensive

### Trinity Church
201 F3  Clarendon and Providence streets  (617) 536-0944  Daily 8–6

### John Hancock Tower
201 F3  200 Clarendon Street  (617) 572-6429  Mon.–Sat. 9 a.m.–11 p.m., Sun. 10 a.m.–11 p.m.

## 7–8

Cross Dartmouth Street (be careful of the traffic) and walk across the lawn to **Trinity Church**, built in 1877 by Henry H. Richardson, the dean of American architecture. This granite and sandstone building introduced the popular style that became known as Richardson Romanesque. On Fridays, there is an organ recital here at 12:15 p.m.

As you face the church, to your left are two low bronze statues likely bearing at least one or two small children. This is **The Tortoise and the Hare at Copley Square**, a Nancy Schon sculpture that pays tribute to the thousands of runners each year who complete the Boston Marathon (the finish line is actually a block away on Boylston Street between Exeter and Dartmouth streets). The statues were unveiled in 1996 in honor of the 100th anniversary of the event.

**The 19th-century Trinity Church mirrored in the 20th-century John Hancock Tower**

Towering above Copley Square, and reflecting Trinity Church's glory to the rest of Boston, is the glass-sheathed **John Hancock Tower**. From some angles, the building's unusual shape and mirrored exterior make it look no wider than a flagpole. The 60th-floor **Observatory** provides a view of the city that nearly rivals that from the Prudential Center Skywalk (▶ 58). Visitors can also enjoy the multimedia exhibits and good historical presentation recounting the events leading up to the Revolutionary War.

# 2 OLD KING'S HIGHWAY
*Tour*

**DISTANCE** 40 miles **TIME** 1½ hours, longer if you stop en route
**START POINT** Sagamore Bridge ✚ 206 D2
**END POINT** Cape Cod National Seashore Salt Pond Visitor Center ✚ 206 E2

Though today's Route 6A linked the colonial towns of Provincetown and Plymouth in the 17th century (hence the name, the Old King's Highway), there was a trail here used by Native Americans long before European settlers arrived. It may no longer be the fastest way to get from one end of the Cape to the other – what scenic route is? – but it is the prettiest. Along the way, keep your eyes open for tree-lined avenues, picturesque New England towns and 18th-century houses.

**1–2**
Start your trip just as you cross the Sagamore Bridge onto Cape Cod. Take exit 1 and turn right at the traffic light onto Route 6A. Follow it about a mile to the town of Sandwich and turn right onto Route 130 south into the center of town. After about 2 miles, you'll see the turnoff for **Heritage Plantation** (▶ 86). This is an unusual hodge-podge of a museum – antique cars, military

memorabilia, fine art and luxurious gardens – but each collection is top-notch.

### 2-3

Double back to 6A and turn right to resume the route east. This is the beginning of what is known as "Antique Alley," which continues as far as Eastham. There are more antiques shops than even the most inveterate bargain-seeker can possibly visit in one day (be assured that many have tried and failed). A map/guide to the shops in the area produced by the dealers is available, though not all the shops are listed. If you're looking for something specific, you may just have to hunt until you've exhausted all the possibilities.

Just past the 11-mile mark (you'll see green mile-marker signs on the right-hand side of the road), the road splits. Stay left on 6A; don't take Route 132.

### 3-4

At about the 14-mile mark, you'll pass through the town of **Barnstable**, which has a great concentration of antiques shops and other interesting stores. Drive on for 3 miles until you come to **Yarmouth.** The town is also known as Yarmouth Port, to distinguish it from the tacky strip of tourist shops in the adjacent town of

South Yarmouth. Blink twice and you could miss this charming collection of shops, restaurants and antiques dealers. You might stop here for a visit to Design Works, which sells candles, linens, soaps and towels in a historic 19th-century dry-goods mercantile, or Hallet's drugstore, with its old-fashioned soda fountain, lunch counter and lone wooden booth.

### 4-5

From Yarmouth, continue to the **Antiques Center of Cape Cod** (just before the 21-mile marker). With more than 265 dealers in several buildings on a giant campus, this is somewhere that a serious antiques-hound could easily spend all day.

Theater enthusiasts should stop at the Cape Playhouse in the nearby town of **Dennis.** Producer Raymond Moore desperately wanted to get into the theater business, so in 1927 he moved a 19th-century Unitarian meeting house to this location and attracted big-name stars of stage and screen to perform. Basil Rathbone starred in the opening-night production, and since then the theater claims "almost every well-known star of stage, screen and TV has walked the stage of the Cape Playhouse" – Helen Hayes, Humphrey Bogart, Gregory Peck, Lana Turner and a young acting student named Jane Fonda, to name just a few. The theater is still going strong, and the original pews, now with cushions, still serve as seats. The adjacent Cape Cinema, which is also housed in a replica of a church, shows first-run movies. Continue on toward Brewster.

**An antiques hound at Yarmouth**

## 5–6

Just before the 27-mile mark, you'll find the **Cape Cod Museum of Natural History**. Its displays on the local flora and fauna will recharge restless kids, and adults will enjoy the walking trails out to the beach. On weekday mornings, a resident archeologist gives talks on the archeological dig going on near the beach, which has unearthed evidence of a Native American community that lived here approximately 9,000 years ago.

Just before the 31-mile mark, you'll pass Cobie's, an old-fashioned clam shack and ice-cream stand. It's the very essence of Cape Cod. If a small bite here fills you with energy, look for signs a few hundred yards ahead on the right for the **Cape Cod Rail Trail** (▶ 88). This is about the midpoint of the Dennis–Wellfleet

route, and you can rent bicycles right here at the Idle Times hut (tel: 508/896-9242) and go whichever way you like.

A half mile farther on the right is **Nickerson State Park**, also ideal for biking, as well as many other outdoor activities including hiking, fishing and horseback riding. Call far in advance if you want a campsite, however.

Finally, Route 6A peters out in the town of **Orleans**, where the more commercial and less scenic Route 6 joins it.

### Taking a Break

**Antiques Center of Cape Cod**
✛ 206 E2 ⊠ 243 Route 6A, Dennis
☎ (508) 385-5133; web: www.antiquescenterofcapecod.com
⊙ Mon.–Sat. 10–5, Sun. 11–5

**Cape Playhouse**
✛ 206 E2 ⊠ 820 Route 6A, Dennis, MA 02638 ☎ (508) 385-3911

**Nickerson State Park**
✛ 206 E2 ⊠ 3488 Main Street, Route 6A, Brewster, MA 02631 ☎ (508) 896-3491 ⊙ Day use: daily 8–8. Camping permitted

## 6–7

It is worth continuing from Orleans on Route 6/6A to Eastham, home of **Cape Cod National Seashore Salt Pond Visitor Center** (▶ 78–80). You can learn all about this beautiful seashore, or simply park your car and spend the rest of the day lazing about on the beach.

**The Cape Playhouse (▶ 179) is a must for theater buffs**

# 3 SOUTHERN VERMONT

*Tour*

This drive takes you past the rolling hills, leafy forests, meandering streams and peaceful farms of southern Vermont. It begins in Manchester, ranges north to Woodstock, and then completes a loop back to Manchester.

Come in October during the foliage season to see the countryside at its best, but be prepared for the road to be crowded and the drive slow.

**DISTANCE** 134 miles **TIME** 3½ hours, longer if you stop en route
**START/END POINT** Manchester Center ✚ 204 A2

## 1–2

Begin the tour in Manchester Center, where routes 11, 30 and 7 all intersect. Drive east on Route 11 toward Londonderry. In about 6 miles, you'll see a turnoff on the left-hand side leading to the **Long Trail** (▶ 121–122), the hiking path that stretches across the spine of the Green Mountain range from Massachusetts to Canada. It's a nice place to stop for a hike.

## 2–3

Continue along Route 11 east to Londonderry. Turn left onto Route 100 north. Route 100 may be the prettiest road in all of Vermont. It passes most every major ski area in the state, including Mount Snow, Killington and Stowe, but few towns extend more than a block or two. The first such town on this tour is **Weston,** around 5 miles north of Londonderry. Stop at

**Spectacular fall foliage near the town of Weston**

**Vermont prides itself on maintaining age-old traditions**

the Weston Village Store (on the left), a particularly good example of an old-fashioned general store that is still making a go of it today. It features all things Vermont, from the original wooden floorboards to the homemade cheese

and fudge behind the counter. Pick up a picnic lunch here and eat it on the town green, or else save it for an even more secluded area farther along the drive.

## 3–4

From Weston, Route 100 twists and turns, but every turn is marked, so you won't get lost. Stay on Route 100 for 21 miles to Route 100A, which forks to the right. Follow 100A about a mile to the **President Calvin Coolidge State Historic Site**, in the tiny town of Plymouth. When America's 30th President died, Dorothy Parker asked, "How could they tell?" and the attractions here reflect Silent Cal's unassuming personality. But the scenic grounds (with picnic tables) are a lovely spot for stretching your legs or eating that picnic lunch you bought in Weston.

## 4–5

Continue northeast along Route 100A for 5.8 miles to Route 4, turn right and follow it 8.8 miles to the center of **Woodstock**. This is the halfway point of the trip. But don't turn around quite yet; stop and spend some time here even if you're not staying the night. Woodstock has lovely

shops, good restaurants and several attractions of its own.

## 5–6

To begin the second half of the trip, loop around the town green to get to Route 106 south. Turn right and follow it 22.8 miles to Route 10 west. Turn right onto Route 10 west and stay on it for 4.3 miles until it reaches Gassetts.

**The Old Tavern at Grafton is the centerpiece of the beautifully restored 18th-century town**

## 6–7

Make a left to Route 103 south and follow it 4.6 miles to Chester. Take Route 35 south from here by bearing right at the fork, then at the next intersection take the soft left (not the hard left). Take Route 35 about 7.3 miles to Route 121 and turn right into the village of **Grafton** (▲ 122). The entire place, which fell on hard times in the 20th century, has been lovingly restored to its 18th-century majesty

by the private Windham Foundation (it owns more than 50 buildings spread over 2,000 acres). There's an inn here (The Old Tavern), as well as a cheese cooperative down the road.

## 7–8
Stay on Route 121 west from Grafton; the road soon turns to dirt. During rainy or snowy weather, it floods, but on clear summer or fall days, it may be the most beautiful part of the whole trip. (If the weather is inclement, take Route 35 north back to Chester, then turn left onto Route 11, continuing west back to Manchester.) About a mile after Grafton, you will pass a Christmas tree farm on your left. Stay on Route 121 as it turns from dirt to pavement to dirt again, for a total of 9.8 miles until it ends at Route 11.

Turn left onto Route 11 west and take it 4 miles to Londonderry.

## 8–9
Turn left onto Route 100 south for 7 miles to Bondville. At Bondville, turn right onto Route 30 north. After about 3 miles, you'll see the access road to **Stratton Mountain** on your left. In winter, this is one of Vermont's most popular downhill ski areas. In summer, it offers a wealth of activities, including hiking and biking (you can take a chairlift to the top, then hike or bike your way down).

From the Stratton access road, it's another 9 miles on Route 30 north and the intersection with Route 11 west. The two roads overlap for the last 6.5 miles back to Manchester.

## Taking a Break

### President Calvin Coolidge State Historic Site
✚ 204 B3
⊠ Route 100A, Plymouth Notch, VT 05056
📞 (802) 672-3773 🕒 Daily 9:30–5:30, late May to mid-Oct.
🅿 Parking: free

# 4 NEWPORT'S CLIFF WALK

**DISTANCE** short walk 1 mile, full walk 6 miles **TIME** about 3 hours for the full walk
**START/END POINT** Narragansett Avenue ✚ 206 D2

Newport's Cliff Walk, a path bordered by the Atlantic on one side and the majestic mansions of Bellevue Avenue on the other, is a lovely way to see the best of what Newport has to offer. It was developed by the owners of some of these estates between 1880 and 1920, and has survived efforts by subsequent owners to destroy it: when landowners tried to barricade their stretches of the walk, Newporters simply ripped up the obstacles and hurled them into the ocean. The walk was restored in 1976 and designated a National Historic Walking Trail.

The entire Cliff Walk is 3.5 miles long, but you can do as little or as much of it as you like. There aren't any restaurants or even refreshment stands along the way, and though on hot summer days some enterprising youngsters may set up a lemonade stand on the route, you

The Cliff Walk passes some of Newport's finest mansions

should take plenty of water. The last 2 miles of the route are the least traveled (and also the most difficult), but they are also filled with idyllic spots for an alfresco lunch.

**1–2**

Begin your walk at the Narragansett Avenue entrance, where there is limited free street parking. Below you, you'll see the **40 Steps,** which lead from the path almost down into the water. Each of the steps was donated by a Newport resident. Turn right onto the path, where you'll pass **Ochre Point,** an 1882 Queen Anne mansion. Depending on the season, you may have a hard time seeing it behind the high hedges.

can relax on the lush green grass and pretend you're a 19th-century estate owner surveying your kingdom. The next two buildings, one a gorgeous brownstone with a red-tile roof, the other an ugly, modern beige brick building, are also part of Salve Regina's campus.

**2–3**

A bit farther along is **Ochre Court,** the first of Richard Morris Hunt's Beaux Arts estates. It is now a part of the campus of Salve Regina University. Unlike the fenced-in topiary gardens separating the private estates from the Cliff Walk, the large, open lawns around the university are open to the public, so you

**3–4**

The last building before Ruggles Avenue is the highlight of the walk: Cornelius Vanderbilt II's 1895 **The Breakers** (▶136–137). It's the biggest, the most opulent and the most extravagant of all the mansions in Newport. The massive lawns fronting the ocean (as well as the 70 rooms inside the house) are open only to those paying for the house tour. But the view that the Vanderbilts enjoyed each summer is absolutely free. There are even some benches here overlooking the ocean.

**4–5**

After Ruggles Avenue, the trail turns to dirt and then to rocks. Those with mobility problems should turn right onto Ruggles Avenue, then right again onto Ochre Point Avenue and stroll through one of Newport's loveliest neighborhoods (and to see several of the same mansions from the front). Turn right again on Narragansett to get back to your car.

There are fine views of Newport from the Cliff Walk

The energetic, however, should continue, as several of the most interesting mansions lie ahead. Just before Marine Avenue is a small public beach in front of a simple wooden home. It is a lovely place to stop, but this is no secret, so you may have to share the sand.

## 5–6

From Marine Avenue, it's another 2 miles to the end of the walk, over similarly rocky terrain. If you continue this far, you'll be rewarded with glimpses of (in order) **Rosecliff**, the **Astors' Beechwood** (▶ 139–140) and **Marble House** (▶ 142). Rosecliff, a white terra-cotta edifice, is shielded from the Cliff Walk by an imposing balustrade at the end of the lawn. Astors' Beechwood, a pale white stucco building with stone dog statues standing sentry over the lawn, was the home of Mrs. Caroline Astor (*the* Mrs. Astor). Marble House was the estate of Mrs. William K. Vanderbilt, who commissioned the rather jarring Chinese Tea House that overlooks the ocean.

The four major mansions on this trail are all open to visitors (▶ 137), so if you want to see inside, pop in at any one that piques your interest. Or just wander leafy Bellevue Avenue back to Narragansett Avenue and your car.

## 6–7

The remainder of the Cliff Walk is rocky. Don't attempt it in foul weather, or without good walking shoes. If you do proceed, the next mansion you'll pass is **Rough Point**, a red

sandstone building that was the summer home of heiress Doris Duke, once the richest woman in America. Clamber across more rocks to **Land's End**, a yellow stucco home with a gray cedar-shingle roof, that once belonged to author Edith Wharton. Around the next bend is **The Waves**, a 1927 half-timbered Tudor building with a crazy-quilt roof line.

From here, the end is in sight: **Bailey's Beach**, a private enclave with luxurious cabanas. Don't worry about the exclusivity: There is a section of the beach called **Reject's Beach** (no fooling!) where the general public is allowed. There are no lifeguards or facilities here, but you can swim or picnic, and enjoy same view as folks at Bailey's Beach without having to pay for the privilege. From the beach, you can walk back along the Cliff Walk, or take a more leisurely 3-mile stroll beneath the copper beech trees on Bellevue Avenue to Narragansett Avenue and your car.

**The paved path of the Cliff Walk (below) turns to dirt and then to rocks beyond Ruggles Avenue (left)**

## GETTING ADVANCE INFORMATION

**Websites**

- Massachusetts Office of Travel and Tourism:
  www.mass-vacation.com
- Boston Visitors Bureau
  www.bostonusa.com
- Connecticut Office of Travel & Tourism:
  www.tourism.state.ct.us
- Maine Office of Tourism:
  www.visitmaine.com

**In the U.S.A**

Greater Boston Convention & Visitors Bureau
2 Copley Place, Suite 105
Boston, MA 02116-6501
☎ 1-888-SEE BOSTON

---

# BEFORE YOU GO

## WHAT YOU NEED

- ● Required
- ○ Suggested
- ▲ Not required
- △ Not applicable

| | U.K. | Germany | U.S.A. | Canada | Australia | Ireland | Netherlands | Spain |
|---|---|---|---|---|---|---|---|---|
| Passport/National Identity Card | ● | ● | ▲ | ▲ | ● | ● | ● | ● |
| Visa (waiver form to be completed) | ▲ | ▲ | ▲ | ▲ | ▲ | ▲ | ▲ | ▲ |
| Onward or Return Ticket | ● | ● | ▲ | ● | ● | ● | ● | ● |
| Health Inoculations (tetanus and polio) | ▲ | ▲ | ▲ | ▲ | ▲ | ▲ | ▲ | ▲ |
| Health Documentation (► 192, Health) | ▲ | ▲ | ▲ | ▲ | ▲ | ▲ | ▲ | ▲ |
| Travel Insurance | ○ | ○ | ○ | ○ | ○ | ○ | ○ | ○ |
| Driving License (national) | ● | ● | ● | ● | ● | ● | ● | ● |
| Car Insurance Certificate | △ | △ | ● | ● | △ | △ | △ | △ |
| Car Registration Document | △ | △ | ● | ● | △ | △ | △ | △ |

## WHEN TO GO

**Boston & New England**

High season  Low season

| JAN | FEB | MAR | APR | MAY | JUN | JUL | AUG | SEP | OCT | NOV | DEC |
|---|---|---|---|---|---|---|---|---|---|---|---|
| 36°F | 38°F | 46°F | 56°F | 67°F | 76°F | 82°F | 80°F | 73°F | 63°F | 52°F | 40°F |

☀ Sun  ☁ Cloud  🌧 Wet  ⛅ Sun/Showers  ❄ Snow

The temperatures listed above are the **average daily maximum** for each month. New England has many different climates. It is often said that if you don't like the weather in New England, just wait half an hour.

**Summer** (June–August) is the preferred time to visit, as many of the outdoor activities are in full swing. September is not as reliably warm as summer, but there are frequent beach days, and it's seldom too cool for a hike, a bike ride or a picnic. October is **fall foliage season**, when all the leaves turn from green to red, orange and yellow. **Skiing season** begins as early as October (but usually November) and ends sometime in mid-April. Late March and early April are known as mud season in the northern states, during which it rains a lot.

## GETTING THERE

**From the U.K.** Flying time from London to Boston is approximately 7.5 hours. British Airways, United Airlines and American Airlines offer services from Heathrow, while Virgin Atlantic and Continental fly out of Gatwick.

**From Ireland** Aer LIngus has one daily non-stop flight from Dublin to Boston, and a second flight on Mondays, Tuesdays, Thursdays and Saturdays.

**From Australia and New Zealand** Qantas, Air New Zealand, American and United Airlines fly to Boston from both Sydney and Auckland, with a change of planes either in Los Angeles or San Francisco. Flying time to the West Coast of the U.S. is 12 hours from Auckland and 14 hours from Sydney. The length of the layover can vary from 2 to 4 hours; the flight between the West Coast and Boston is about 5 hours.

**From Canada** Flying time to Boston is about an hour from Montreal, an hour and a half from Toronto and 5 hours from Vancouver.

**From the U.S.** All the major U.S. carriers serve Boston's Logan International Airport. US Airways and Delta Airlines both operate a shuttle service between New York's La Guardia Airport and Boston; flights leave each city every hour from 6 a.m. to 10 p.m.

**Ticket prices** The most popular times to visit are usually when airfares are highest and seats scarcest, so make your flight arrangements as soon as you know your travel dates. Travel mid-week for the lowest rate, but stay over at least one Saturday night before you return. Stick to one airline, as using two different companies will cost more.

**By Rail or Bus** Intercity **Amtrak** trains from major U.S. cities arrive at Boston's South Station. For more information call Amtrak at 1-800-872-7245, or look on the Web at www.amtrak.com. **Greyhound** (tel: 1-800-231-222 or www.greyhound.com) provides nationwide bus service and has information on services throughout New England.

## TIME

All of New England is on **Eastern Standard Time**, five hours behind Greenwich Mean Time (GMT– 5). Between the first Sunday in April and the last Sunday in October, clocks are set ahead 1 hour for **Daylight Saving**.

## CURRENCY AND FOREIGN EXCHANGE

**Currency** The monetary unit of the United States is the dollar ($), divided into 100 cents (¢). **Coins** come in 1 cent (penny), 5 cents (nickel), 10 cents (dime), 25 cents (quarter), and the very rare 50-cent pieces (half dollars) and one-dollar coins. **Bills** come in denominations of $1, $5, $10, $20, $50, $100 and seldom-seen denominations higher than 100.

**Exchange** The Airport, banks and most large city hotels have facilities for changing foreign currencies and travelers' checks. **Cash withdrawals** can be made at automatic teller machines throughout New England, but check with your bank for details of where your card is accepted and to find out if your personal identification number (PIN) is internationally valid. **Debit cards** may be accepted at retail outlets that are validated for international access. **Credit cards** are widely accepted – the most commonly accepted credit cards are MasterCard, Visa and American Express. Less common, but accepted by many establishments, are Discover, Diners Club and Carte Blanche.

| GMT | Boston | USA New York | Germany | Spain | Australia |
|---|---|---|---|---|---|
| 12 noon | ← 7 a.m. | ← 7 a.m. | → 1 p.m. | → 1 p.m. | → 10 p.m. |

## WHEN YOU ARE THERE

### CLOTHING SIZES

| U.K. | Rest of Europe | U.S.A. | | |
|---|---|---|---|---|
| 36 | 46 | 36 | | Suits |
| 38 | 48 | 38 | | |
| 40 | 50 | 40 | | |
| 42 | 52 | 42 | | |
| 44 | 54 | 44 | | |
| 46 | 56 | 46 | | |
| 7 | 41 | 8 | | Shoes |
| 7.5 | 42 | 8.5 | | |
| 8.5 | 43 | 9.5 | | |
| 9.5 | 44 | 10.5 | | |
| 10.5 | 45 | 11.5 | | |
| 11 | 46 | 12 | | |
| 14.5 | 37 | 14.5 | | Shirts |
| 15 | 38 | 15 | | |
| 15.5 | 39/40 | 15.5 | | |
| 16 | 41 | 16 | | |
| 16.5 | 42 | 16.5 | | |
| 17 | 43 | 17 | | |
| 8 | 34 | 6 | | Dresses |
| 10 | 36 | 8 | | |
| 12 | 38 | 10 | | |
| 14 | 40 | 12 | | |
| 16 | 42 | 14 | | |
| 18 | 44 | 16 | | |
| 4.5 | 38 | 6 | | Shoes |
| 5 | 38 | 6.5 | | |
| 5.5 | 39 | 7 | | |
| 6 | 39 | 7.5 | | |
| 6.5 | 40 | 8 | | |
| 7 | 41 | 8.5 | | |

### NATIONAL HOLIDAYS

| Jan. 1 | New Year's Day |
|---|---|
| Third Mon. Jan. | Martin Luther King Day |
| Third Mon. Feb. | George Washington's Birthday |
| Mar./Apr. | Easter |
| Last Mon. May | Memorial Day |
| Jul. 4 | Independence Day |
| First Mon. Sep. | Labor Day |
| Second Mon. Oct. | Columbus Day |
| Nov. 11 | Veterans' Day |
| Fourth Thu. Nov. | Thanksgiving |
| Dec. 25 | Christmas Day |

Massachusetts also celebrates Patriots' Day on the third Monday in April. Banks, post offices and state offices are closed by law on national holidays.

### OPENING HOURS

○ Stores     ● Post Offices
● Offices    ● Museums/Monuments
● Banks      ● Pharmacies

8 a.m. 9 a.m. 10 a.m.  noon  1 p.m. 2 p.m.  4 p.m. 5 p.m. 7 p.m.

☐ Day     ■ Midday     ☐ Evening

**Stores** Generally open between 9 and 6, Monday through Saturday (later on Thursday); some open Sunday afternoons. In Massachusetts and Connecticut, liquor stores are closed on Sunday.
**Banks** Most are open weekdays from 9 to 5, though many close as early as 3 p.m. Some banks open Saturday mornings as well.
**Post Offices** are open at least from 9 to 5, Monday through Saturday, and sometimes later.
**Museums** Hours vary. Most are closed on Monday.

**POLICE 911**

**FIRE 911**

**AMBULANCE 911**

## PERSONAL SAFETY

Take the standard precautions regarding personal safety. Outside of Boston, you are unlikely to encounter much danger and petty crime is infrequent.

- Hitchhiking is not as prevalent in the U.S. as it is in other countries. It is not recommended, and is illegal in many places.
- Women should avoid walking alone at night and should guard their purses when on uncrowded buses or trains.
- Always hike with a trail map; take plenty of water.
- Wear a cycle helmet – it's the law in many states.

**Police assistance:**
 **911** from any phone

## TELEPHONES

cards for long-distance calls come in denominations of $5, $10 and $20. To call long-distance, dial 1, the area code, and then the number. To call other countries, dial 011, the country code, then the city code, and the phone number. Dial 0 for operator assistance, but you'll pay a premium for an operator-assisted call.

Pay phones are ubiquitous in Boston, but harder to find elsewhere. They require exact change (35¢ for a local call) or a telephone calling card. Pre-paid calling

**International Dialling Codes**
**Dial 011 followed by**

| | |
|---|---|
| **U.K.:** | 44 |
| **Ireland:** | 353 |
| **Australia:** | 61 |
| **Germany:** | 49 |
| **Netherlands:** | 31 |
| **Spain:** | 34 |

## POST

Post offices usually open Mon.–Fri. 9–5, though some larger branches are open longer. Vending machines sell stamps but at a 25 percent premium. You can buy postcard stamps at many hotels, or at local post offices.

## ELECTRICITY

The power supply is 110/120 volts AC, 60 cycles. Most sockets take two-pronged or three pronged plugs. Visitors from Europe, or anywhere that uses 220/240 volt power, will need to bring a converter and a plug adaptor.

## TIPS/GRATUITIES

Tipping is expected for all services. As a general guide:
Yes ✓   No ✗

| | | |
|---|---|---|
| Restaurants (service not included) | ✓ | 15–20% |
| Bar service | ✓ | $1–2 |
| Tour guides | ✓ | discretion |
| Hairdressers | ✓ | 15% |
| Taxis | ✓ | 15% |
| Chambermaids | ✓ | $1–2 per day |
| Porters | ✓ | $1 per bag |

## CONSULATES

**U.K.**
(617) 248-9555

**Ireland**
(617) 267-9330

**Canada**
(617) 262-3760

**Australia**
(617) 542-8655

**New Zealand**
(202) 328-4848

## HEALTH

 **Insurance** The U.S. lacks comprehensive medical or dental coverage; medical services must be paid at the time rendered, either with cash or through insurance. It is strongly recommended that you take out a travel insurance policy that covers medical and dental treatment.

 **Dental Services** As with medical treatment, dental treatment in the U.S. is extremely costly. Travelers are advised to make sure that their medical insurance policy also includes an adequate dental cover.

 **Weather** New England winters can bring subfreezing temperatures, so bring plenty of warm clothing. In summer, you can get a serious sunburn; wear sunscreen and cover up.

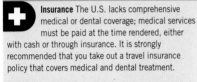 **Drugs** Nonprescription medicines are available in supermarkets, drugstores, and some convenience stores. Prescription drugs are available only from pharmacies. If you take prescribed medications, bring them with you, plus a copy of your prescription as well, in case you need to refill it while in the U.S.

 **Safe Water** It is safe to drink the water everywhere in the U.S. Bottled water is available in most supermarkets, drugstores and convenience stores, as well as in upscale restaurants.

## CONCESSIONS

**Students/children** Hostels are not as common in the U.S. as they are in Europe, but there are some. Youths should join the **International Youth Hostel Federation** before leaving home. Most attractions offer discounts on admission for students (with current identification card) and for children under 12.

**Senior Citizens** Many attractions and some hotels offer senior discounts, some for travelers as young as 50. American travelers over the age of 50 should join the **American Association of Retired Persons** (AARP), which entitles you to various discounts on hotel rooms, car rentals and some airfares. Call (202) 434-2277.

## TRAVELING WITH A DISABILITY

The major car-rental companies have vehicles adapted for travelers with disabilities. Most Boston hotels are thoroughly wheelchair-accessible and many lodgings have made strides to accept travelers with disabilities. If in doubt, call in advance. Mobility International USA (tel: 541/343-1284) publishes a 658-page book of resources.

## CHILDREN

Restaurants are usually child-friendly, and family-style restaurants offer children's menus. Small inns sometimes prohibit children under 12. Baby-changing facilities are available in most large public restrooms.

## RESTROOMS

Free public toilets are a rarity in the U.S. Department stores, hotels and fast-food restaurants have public restrooms which can be used, especially if you make a small purchase.

## LOST PROPERTY

Contact the nearest police station, however, you are not likely to get lost property back. Dial 555-1212 for a non-emergency number for the police; do not call 911.

Acadia National
  Park 150, 158–
  160
  Bar Harbor 159
  Cadillac
    Mountain 27,
    159, 160
  Mount Desert
    Island 159, 160
  Somes Sound 159
accommodations
  35
see also individual
  areas
admission charges
  34
African Meeting
  House 175, 177
airports and air
  services 32, 189
Alcott, Louisa May
  29, 30, 61
Allagash
  Wilderness
  Waterway 166
American Museum
  of Fly-Fishing
  116, 117
American
  Revolution 8–9
antiques 26–27, 37,
  123, 179
Appalachian Trail
  100–101, 122
Aquinnah, cliffs
  88–89
Astors' Beechwood
  139–140, 184,
  186

baby-changing
  facilities 192
Back Bay 174–177
banks 190
Bar Harbor 159
Barnstable 179
Baxter State Park
  165–166
Beacon Hill 60,
  174-177
Beartown State
  Forest 100, 101
The Berkshires
  95–108
  accommodations
    106
  Appalachian Trail
    100–101
  Beartown State
    Forest 100, 101
  Chesterwood 105
  eating out 107
  entertainment
    108
  Great Barrington
    105
  Hancock Shaker
    Village 104–105
  Jacob's Pillow
    Dance Festival
    102

John Drummond
  Kennedy Park
  101
  Lee 105
  Lenox 105
  The Mount 103
  Naumkeag 105
  Norman
    Rockwell
    Museum 103
  October
    Mountain State
    Forest 100,
    101
  shopping 108
  Stockbridge 103,
    105
  Tanglewood
    98–99
  two-day itinerary
    97
  Williamstown
    105
bike rental 26, 88,
  94, 108, 130, 172
Billings Farm and
  Museum
  118–119, 120
Boston 39–72
  accommodations
    65–66
  Acorn Street
    175–176
  African American
    National
    Historic Site
    174, 177
  African Meeting
    House 175, 177
  Back Bay 71,
    174–177
  Beacon Hill 60,
    174–177
  Black Heritage
    Trail 175
  Boston Common
    44, 58
  Boston Public
    Library 176–177
  Boston Tea Party
    Ship and
    Museum 57
  Bull and Finch
    Pub 176
  Bunker Hill
    Monument 46,
    47
  Children's
    Museum 57
  Copp's Hill
    Burying Ground
    46
  eating out 67–70
  entertainment 72
  Faneuil Hall 44,
    45–46
  Fenway Park
    60
  Freedom Trail 6,
    44–47
  Granary Burying
    Ground 45, 47

Harrison Gray
  Otis House
  174–175, 177
  Harvard 54–56
  Isabella Stewart
    Gardner
    Museum
    59–60
  John F. Kennedy
    Library and
    Museum 57
  John Hancock
    Tower 9, 177
  King's Chapel
    and Burying
    Ground 45
  Louisburg Square
    175
  Museum of Fine
    Arts 48–51
  Museum of
    Science 52–53
  New State House
    44, 47
  Newbury Street
    60, 71, 176
  North End 60
  Old Corner Book
    Store 45
  Old North
    Church 46, 47
  Old South
    Meeting House
    45
  Old State House
    45, 47
  Park Street
    Church 44–45,
    47
  Paul Revere
    House 46, 47
  Prudential Center
    58–59
  Public Garden
    58, 176
  public transport
    32, 33
  Quincy Market
    46
  shopping 71
  South End 60
  three-day
    itinerary 42–43
  Trinity Church
    177
  USS Constitution
    46, 47
  walking tours 72
Boston Red Sox
  14–17, 27
Boston Tea Party
  Ship and
  Museum 57
Botanical Museum
  55, 56
The Breakers
  136–137, 185
Brenton Point State
  Park 138
Brook Farm 28
Brown University
  144

Bunker Hill
  Monument 46,
  47
Busch-Reisinger
  Museum 55
buses 32

Cadillac Mountain
  27, 159, 160
Calvin Coolidge
  State Historic Site
  182
Cambridge see
  Harvard
Canterbury Shaker
  Village 167
Cape Cod and the
  Islands 73–94
  accommodations
    90–91
  Cape Cod
    Museum of
    Natural History
    87, 89, 180
  Cape Cod Rail
    Trail 88, 180
  Chatham 74, 86
  dune tours 82
  eating out 92–93
  entertainment 94
  four-day itinerary
    76-77
  Heritage
    Plantation 86,
    178–179
  Martha's
    Vineyard 74–75,
    88–89
  Monomoy
    National
    Wildlife Refuge
    87
  Nantucket 75,
    83–85
  National Marine
    Fisheries Service
    Aquarium 89
  Provincetown 74,
    81–82
  shopping 94
  whale-watching
    cruises 87
Cape Cod National
  Seashore 78–80,
  180
  Coast Guard
    Beach 79
  Eastham 78
  Head of the
    Meadow Beach
    79
  Herring Cove 80
  Marconi Beach 79
  Marconi Wireless
    Station Site 79
  Nauset Beach 78
  Nauset Light
    Beach 78–79
  Race Point 80
  Truro 79
  Wellfleet 79

Cape Playhouse 179, 180
car rental 34
Chateau-sur-Mer 142
Chatham 74, 86
Chepstow 143
Chesterwood 105
children 192, 59, 89, 142, 167, 192
Children's Museum 57
climate and seasons 10–13, 188, 192
clothing sizes 190
Coastal Maine to the White Mountains 149–172
Acadia National Park 150, 158–160
accommodations 168–169
Allagash Wilderness Waterway 166
Baxter State Park 165–166
Canterbury Shaker Village 167
eating out 169–170
entertainment 172
Franconia Notch State Park 163–164
Hanover 166
Kancamagus Highway 162–163
Kennebunk 155–157
Kennebunkport 155–157
Lake Winnipesaukee 166–167
L.L. Bean 24–25, 165
Maine Maritime Museum 165
Mount Washington 161–162
Ogunquit 157
Portland 150
Portland Head Light and Museum 165
Portsmouth 154
shopping 171
six-day itinerary 152–153
White Mountains 150, 161–164
concessions 192
Connecticut see Rhode Island and Southeastern Connecticut

Concord 8, 9, 61
Orchard House 30, 61
consulates 192
Conway Scenic Railroad 164
Copp's Hill Burying Ground 46
credit and debit cards 189
currency 189

Dennis 179
dental services 192
disabilities, travelers with 192
drinking water 192
driving 33, 34, 188

Eastham 78, 179
eating out 36
see also individual areas
Edgartown 88
electricity 191
The Elms 141
Emerald Lake State Park 121
emergency phone numbers 191
Emerson, Ralph Waldo 28, 29, 45
entertainment 38
see also individual areas
Faneuil Hall 44, 45–46
Fenway Park 60
festivals and events 10, 12, 38
Flume 163
Fogg Art Museum 55
food and drink 36
clam chowder 18
ice cream 26
lobster 18–20, 26, 36
maple syrup 124
see also eating out
foreign exchange 189
Fort Adams State Park 138, 143
Foxwoods casino 145
Franconia Notch State Park 163–164
Flume 163
Frost Place 163–164
Old Man of the Mountains 163
Freeport 25, 27, 165
Frost Place 163–164

Gloucester 63
Rocky Neck Art Colony 63
Wingaersheek Beach 63
Grafton 122, 182–183
Great Barrington 105
Great Point 84
Green Animals Topiary Garden 142

Hancock Shaker Village 104–105
Hanover 166
Harrison Gray Otis House 174–175, 177
Harvard 54–56
Botanical Museum 55, 56
Busch-Reisinger Museum 55
Carpenter Center for the Visual Arts 55
Fogg Art Museum 55
Harvard Square 56
Massachusetts Hall 54
Statue of Three Lies 54
Tercentenary Theater 55
Widener Memorial Library 55
Hawthorne, Nathaniel 30, 62, 99
health 188, 192
Heritage Plantation 86, 178–179
Herring Cove 80
Hildene 114–115
history 6–9
hitchhiking 191
hotels 35 see also accommodations
House of the Seven Gables 62

inns 21–23, 35
insurance 188, 192
International Tennis Hall of Fame 141
Isabella Stewart Gardner Museum 59–60

Jackson 164
Jacob's Pillow Dance Festival 102

John Brown House 144
John Drummond Kennedy Park 101
John F. Kennedy Library and Museum 57
John Hancock Tower 9, 177

Kancamagus Highway 162–163
Kennebunk 155–157
Gooch's Beach 156
Mother's Beach 156
Kennebunkport 155–157
Colony Beach 157
Goose Rocks Beach 156
Seashore Trolley Museum 156–157
King's Chapel and Burying Ground 45

Lake Winnipesaukee 166–167
Land's End 186
leaf-peeping 11, 26, 108
Lee 105
Lenox 105
Lexington 8, 61
L.L. Bean 24–25, 27, 165
Long Trail 121–122, 181
lost property 192

Maddaket 27, 84
Maine 10, 150
see also Coastal Maine to the White Mountains
Maine Maritime Museum 165
Manchester 110, 116–117, 181
American Museum of Fly-Fishing 116, 117
Orvis 116, 117
Marble House 142–143, 186
Marblehead 62–63
Marconi Wireless Station Site 79

Marsh-Billings-
  Rockefeller
  National
  Historic Park
  118–120
Billings Farm and
  Museum
  118–119, 120
Marsh-Billings-
  Rockefeller
  Mansion
  119–120
Mount Tom
  Forest 118
Woodstock Ski
  Touring Center
  120
Martha's Vineyard
  74–75, 88–89
Aquinnah, cliffs
  88–89
Edgartown 88
Oak Bluffs 88
Vineyard Haven
  88
Massachusetts Hall
  54
Massachusetts State
  House 44, 47
*Mayflower II* 64
Melville, Herman
  30
Minute Man
  National Historic
  Park 61
Mohegan Sun
  casino 145
money 189
Monomoy National
  Wildlife Refuge
  87
The Mount 103
Mount Desert
  Island 159, 160
Mount Tom Forest
  118
Mount Washington
  161–162
Mount Washington
  Auto Road 162
Mount Washington
  Cog Railway 162
Museum of Fine
  Arts 48–51
museum opening
  hours 190
Museum of Science
  52–53
Museum of
  Yachting 143
Mystic 145
Mystic Aquarium
  145
Mystic Seaport
  145

Nantucket 75,
  83–85
Great Point 84
Maddaket 84
Nantucket 84

Sanford Farm 85
Siasconset 84
national holidays
  190
National Marine
  Fisheries Service
  Aquarium 89
Naumkeag 105
New Hampshire *see*
  Coastal Maine to
  the White
  Mountains
New State House
  44, 47
Newport 132,
  136–144,
  184–186
Astors'
  Beechwood
  139–140, 184,
  186
Bailey's Beach
  186
The Breakers
  136–137, 185
Brenton Point
  State Park 138
Chateau-sur-Mer
  142
Chepstow 143
Cliff Walk
  184–186
Easton's Beach
  138
The Elms 141
Fort Adams State
  Park 138, 143
Green Animals
  Topiary Garden
  142
International
  Tennis Hall of
  Fame 141
Land's End 186
Marble House
  142–143, 186
Museum of
  Yachting 143
Ochre Court
  185
Ochre Point 185
Reject's Beach
  186
Rosecliff 186
Rough Point 186
Sachuest Beach
  138
Third Beach 138
Touro Synagogue
  141
The Waves 186
Newport and
  Southeastern
  Connecticut
  131–148
accommodations
  146
casinos 145
eating out 147
entertainment
  148
map 132–133

Mystic 145
shopping 148
three-day
  itinerary
  134–135
Nickerson State
  Park 180
Norman Rockwell
  Museum 103
North Conway 164

Oak Bluffs 88
Ochre Court 185
Ochre Point 185
October Mountain
  State Forest 100,
  101
Ogunquit 157
Old King's Highway
  178–180
Old Man of the
  Mountains 163
Old North Church
  46, 47
Old South Meeting
  House 45
Old State House 45,
  47
opening hours 37,
  190
Orchard House 30,
  61
Orleans 180
Orvis 116, 117

Park Street Church
  44–45, 47
passports and visas
  188
Paul Revere House
  46, 47
Peabody Essex
  Museum 62
personal safety 191
Pilgrim Monument
  and Province-
  town Museum 82
Pilgrims 6–7, 64
Plimoth Plantation
  64
Plymouth 64
*Mayflower II* 64
Plimoth
  Plantation 64
Plymouth Rock
  64
police 191
Portland 150
Portland Head
  Light and
  Museum 165
Portsmouth 154
Strawbery Banke
  154
postal services 190,
  191
Providence 144
Arcade 144
Brown University
  144

John Brown
  House 144
Rhode Island
  School of Design
  144
Rhode Island
  State House 144
Provincetown 74,
  81–82
art galleries
  82–83
dune tours 82
Herring Cove 80
Pilgrim
  Monument and
  Provincetown
  Museum 82
Race Point 80
whale-watching
  cruises 87
Prudential Center
  58–59

Quechee Gorge 123
Quincy Market 46

Race Point 11, 80
restaurants *see*
  eating out
restrooms 192
Revere, Paul 8, 45,
  46
Rhode Island 132
Newport 132,
  136–143,
  184–186
Providence 144
Rhode Island
  School of Design
  144
Rhode Island State
  House 144
Rocky Neck Art
  Colony 63
Rosecliff 186
Rough Point 186

Sabbaday Falls
  162–163
Salem 7, 62
Cry Innocent 62
House of the
  Seven Gables 62
Peabody Essex
  Museum 62
Salem Witch
  Museum 62
Sanford Farm 85
Seashore Trolley
  Museum
  156–157
senior citizens 192
Sheffield 26–27
Shelburne Museum
  123–124
shopping 37, 190
  *see also*
  individual areas
Siasconset 84

skiing 13, 115, 120, 164, 183
Skyline Drive 121
Somerset Reservoir 117
Somes Sound 159
Sterling and Francine Clark Art Institute 105
Stockbridge 103, 105
Stratton Mountain 183
Strawbery Banke 154
students and young travelers 192
sun protection 192

Tanglewood 98–99
taxis 33
telephones 191
Third Beach 138
Thoreau, Henry David 28, 29–30, 61
*Ticonderoga* 124
time differences 189, 190
tipping 36, 191
toilets 192
tourist information 188–189

Touro Synagogue 141
trains 32
Transcendentalist movement 9, 28–30, 61
travel documents 188
Trinity Church 177
Truro 79

USS *Constitution* 46, 47

Vermont 109–130
accommodations 125–127
Calvin Coolidge State Historic Site 182
eating out 127–128
Emerald Lake State Park 121
entertainment 130
four-day itinerary 112–113
Grafton 122, 182–183
Hildene 114–115

Long Trail 121–122, 181
Manchester 110, 116–117, 181
Marsh-Billings-Rockefeller National Historic Park 118–120
Quechee Gorge 123
Shelburne Museum 123–124
shopping 129
Skyline Drive 121
Somerset Reservoir 117
Stratton Mountain 183
Vermont Raptor Center 122, 123
West Barnet 110
Weston 181–182
Woodstock 110, 182
Vineyard Haven 88

Walden Pond 11, 30, 61
The Waves 186
Wellfleet 79
West Barnet 110

Weston 181–182
whale-watching cruises 87
Wharton, Edith 103, 186
White Mountains 150, 161–164
Conway Scenic Railroad 164
Franconia Notch State Park 163–164
Jackson 164
Kancamagus Highway 162–163
Mount Washington 161–162
North Conway 164
Sabbaday Falls 162–163
Widener Memorial Library 55
Williamstown 105
Williamstown Theatre Festival 105
Woodstock 110, 182

Yarmouth 179

## Picture credits

Abbreviations for terms appearing below: (t) top; (b) bottom; (l) left; (r) right; (c) centre

Front and back cover (t) AA Photo Library/Chris Coe, (ct) AA Photo Library/Clive Sawyer; (cb) AA Photo Library/Clive Sawyer; (b) AA Photo Library/Robert Holmes.
The Automobile Association wishes to thank the following photographers and libraries with their assistance in the preparation of this book.
ALLSPORT UK LTD 14 (D Strohmeyer), 16t (J Daniel), 16/7 (J Daniel); ART DIRECTORS AND TRIP PHOTO LIBRARY 98t (J Greenberg); THE ASTOR'S BEECHWOOD MANSION 140b (Sheli Beck); L . L BEAN INC. 24t, 24c, 24b, 25t; THE BRIDGEMAN ART LIBRARY, LONDON 49 The Market at Pontoise, 1887 by Camille Pissarro (1831-1903), Museum of Fine Arts, Boston, Massachussetts, MA, USA; 50 Dance at Bougival, 1882-3 by Pierre Auguste Renoir (1841-1919), Museum of Fine Arts, Boston, Massachusetts, MA, USA; BRUCE COLEMAN COLLECTION 87, 122; CORBIS UK LTD 17 (Bettmann), 26cr (Richard T. Nowitz), 97t (Jonathan Blair); JAMES DAVIS TRAVEL PHOTOGRAPHY 76b, 77t, 78, 82b, 85; MARY EVANS PICTURE LIBRARY 8cl, 28t, 28b, 29bl, 29br, 30t, 30b, 136c; EYE UBIQUITOUS 2(i), 5; FRIENDS OF HILDENE, INC. 112t, 114b, 115; GETTYONE/STONE 2(vi), 3(iii), 10, 13t, 15t, 15b, 55, 109, 110t, 159t, 166, 173; ROBERT HARDING PICTURE LIBRARY 79t, 81t, 152, 155, 156t; JEREMY HOARE 23t, 180r, 187; CATHERINE KARNOW 18, 21, 22t, 23b, 26b, 74, 77b, 79b, 83, 84t, 144, 179; KEDRON VALLEY INN 22b; KELLY/MOONEY PHOTOGRAPHY 11t, 29t, 84b, 89, 104b, 132t, 135t, 135bl, 137, 140t, 142, 143t, 143b, 186l, 186r; TOM MACKIE 2(v), 3(i), 12t, 44l, 64b, 73, 110b, 138 b/g, 149, 151b, 153t, 153c, 159b, 160; PETER NEWARK'S PICTURES 6cl, 6cr, 7cr, 7b, 8cr, 8/9; PERFORMING ARTS LIBRARY/CLIVE BARDA 98b, 99l, 99r, 102; PICTURES COLOUR LIBRARY 76t, 81b; POWERSTOCK/ZEFA 6t, 12b, 120, 154, 158, 161, 162/3; THEARTARCHIVE 48l
The remaining photographs are held in the Association's own photo library (AA PHOTO LIBRARY) and were taken by Chris Coe with the exception of the following:
Richard Elliott 191t, Robert Holmes 9cl, 11c, 26cl, 27br, 45c, 48r, 52bl, 57, 59l, 88, 151c, 162, 177; John Lynch 9t, 61; Molly Lynch 13b, 20, 25b, 56, 58l, 75, 80, 100t, 111r, 116, 119b, 123b, 133t, 133c, 145c, 151t, 153b, 157t, 157b, 165, 167, 180l, 182; Tom Lynch 113b, 123t; Clive Sawyer 2(ii), 3(iv), 9cr, 31, 43t, 43b, 44c, 45l, 45r, 46l, 52/3, 52br, 59r, 62, 64t, 174, 176.

## Author's acknowledgment

The author would like to thank his wife, Lisa Renaud, and Cheryl Leas and Jeannette Foster for their help during the research of this book.

# Atlas

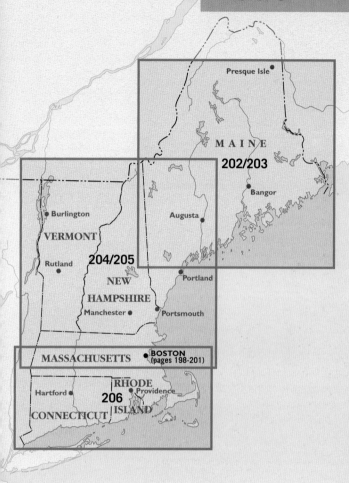

Presque Isle

MAINE

202/203

Bangor

Augusta

Burlington

VERMONT

204/205

Rutland

NEW

HAMPSHIRE

Manchester

Portland

Portsmouth

MASSACHUSETTS • BOSTON
(pages 198-201)

RHODE

Hartford • 206 • Providence

CONNECTICUT ISLAND

## Regional Maps

| | | | |
|---|---|---|---|
| —·—·— | International boundary | □ | City |
| —··—··— | State boundary | ▫ | Major town |
| 95 | Interstate highway | o o | Other town |
| 3 | Federal highway | ▪ | Place of interest |
| 10 | Other highway | ✈ | Airport |
| ············ | Trail | | |
| | Park, Forest | | **City Plan** |
| | Built-up area | • | Rapid Transit stop (T) |
| | | ▣ | Featured place of interest |

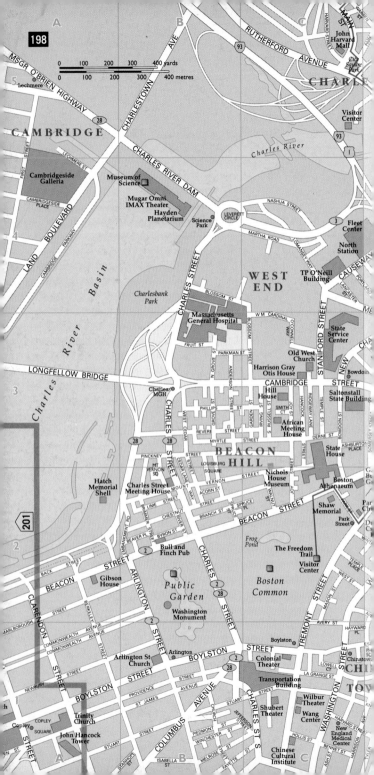

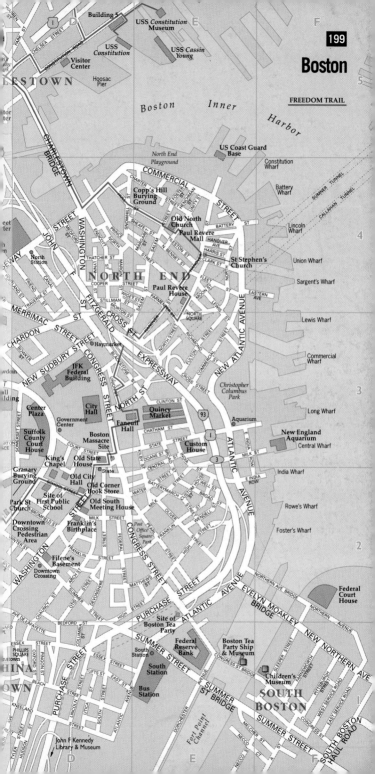

FREEDOM TRAIL

Building 5

USS *Constitution* Museum

USS *Constitution*

USS *Cassin Young*

Visitor Center

Hoosac Pier

LESTOWN

CHARLESTOWN BRIDGE

*Boston* *Inner*

*Harbor*

North End Playground

US Coast Guard Base

Constitution Wharf

Battery Wharf

SUMNER TUNNEL

CALLAHAN TUNNEL

COMMERCIAL

STREET

Copp's Hill Burying Ground

Old North Church

Paul Revere Mall

St Stephen's Church

Lincoln Wharf

Union Wharf

Sargent's Wharf

WASHINGTON

JOHN

STREET

North Station

Paul Revere House

FITZGERALD

CROSS ST

**N O R T H   E N D**

Lewis Wharf

Commercial Wharf

MERRIMAC

STREET

CHARDON

NEW SUDBURY STREET

Haymarket

JFK Federal Building

CONGRESS

EXPRESSWAY

NORTH ST

NEW ATLANTIC AVENUE

Christopher Columbus Park

Long Wharf

93

City Hall

Government Center

Quincy Market

Clinton St

Aquarium

Center Plaza

Suffolk County Court House

Faneuil Hall

Boston Massacre Site

ATLANTIC AVENUE

New England Aquarium

Central Wharf

King's Chapel

Old State House

Custom House

State

India Wharf

Granary Burying Ground

Old City Hall

Old Corner Book Store

Park St Church

Site of First Public School

Old South Meeting House

Rowe's Wharf

Foster's Wharf

Downtown Crossing Pedestrian Area

Franklin's Birthplace

CONGRESS STREET

Post Office Square Park

Filene's Basement

Downtown Crossing

WASHINGTON

Federal Court House

PURCHASE

ATLANTIC AVENUE

EVELYN MOAKLEY BRIDGE

NEW NORTHERN AVE

NORTHERN AVE BRIDGE

CHINA TOWN

PHILLIPS SQUARE

ESSEX STREET

SUMMER STREET

Site of Boston Tea Party

Federal Reserve Bank

South Station

Boston Tea Party Ship & Museum

Children's Museum

**SOUTH BOSTON**

Bus Station

SUMMER ST BRIDGE

SUMMER STREET

SOUTH BOSTON HAUL ROAD

PURCHASE STREET

Fort Point Channel

John F Kennedy Library & Museum

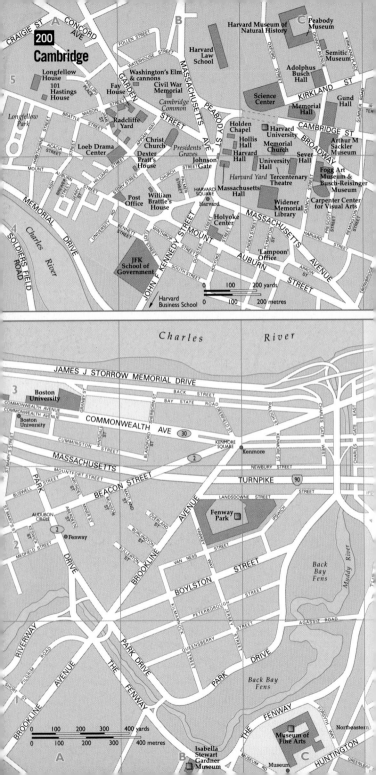

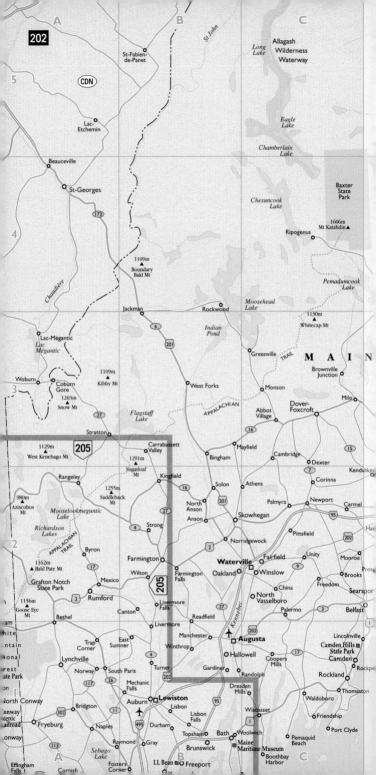

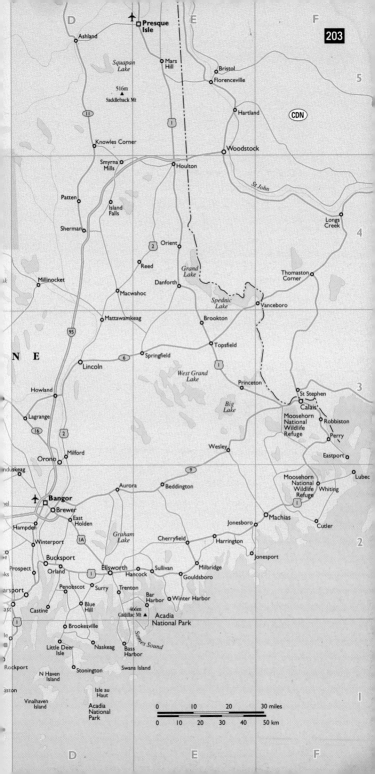

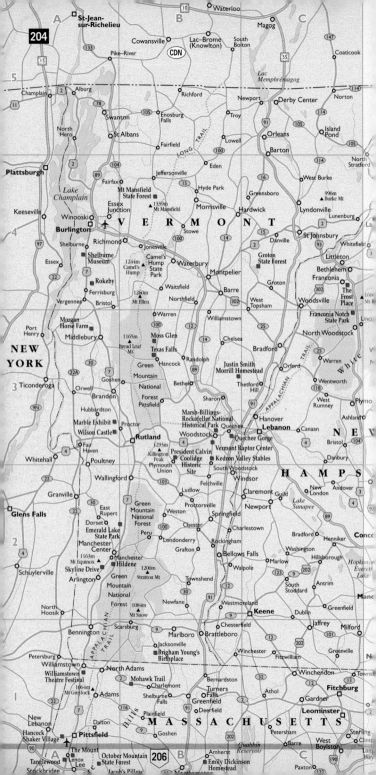

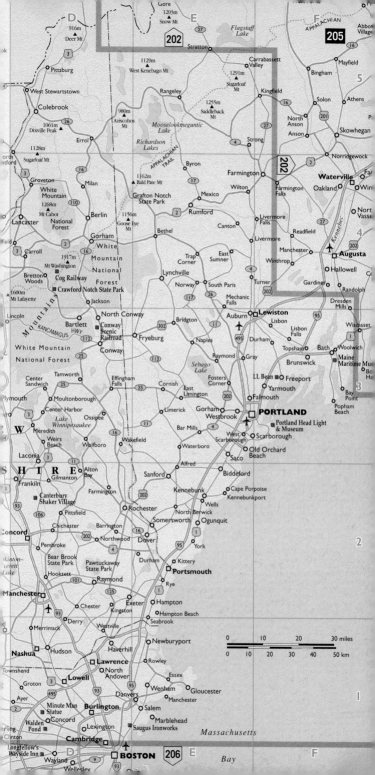

# SPIRAL GUIDES

# Questionnaire

## Dear Traveler

**Your comments, opinions and recommendations are very important to us. So please help us to improve our travel guides by taking a few minutes to complete this simple questionnaire.**

*Send to:* Spiral Guides, MailStop 66, 1000 AAA Drive, Heathrow, FL 32746–5063

## Your recommendations...

We always encourage readers' recommendations for restaurants, nightlife or shopping – if your recommendation is added to the next edition of the guide, we will send you a FREE AAA Spiral Guide of your choice. Please state below the establishment name, location and your reasons for recommending it.

_____

_____

_____

_____

_____

**Please send me AAA Spiral** _____

(see list of titles inside the back cover)

## About this guide...

**Which title did you buy?**

_____ **AAA Spiral**

**Where did you buy it?** _____

**When?** m m / y y

**Why did you choose a AAA Spiral Guide?** _____

_____

_____

_____

_____

**Did this guide meet your expectations?**

Exceeded ☐   Met all ☐   Met most ☐   Fell below ☐

**Please give your reasons** _____

_____

_____

_____

_____

continued on next page...

Were there any aspects of this guide that you particularly liked?

______________________________

______________________________

______________________________

______________________________

______________________________

Is there anything we could have done better?

______________________________

______________________________

______________________________

______________________________

______________________________

## About you...

Name (Mr/Mrs/Ms) ______________________________

Address ______________________________

______________________________

______________________________ Zip ______________

Daytime tel nos. ______________________________

Which age group are you in?

Under 25 ☐ 25–34 ☐ 35–44 ☐ 45–54 ☐ 55–64 ☐ 65+ ☐

How many trips do you make a year?

Less than one ☐ One ☐ Two ☐ Three or more ☐

Are you a AAA member? Yes ☐ No ☐

Name of AAA club ______________________________

About your trip...

When did you book? m m/ y y When did you travel? m m/ y y

How long did you stay? ______________________________

Was it for business or leisure? ______________________________

Did you buy any other travel guides for your trip? ☐ Yes ☐ No

If yes, which ones? ______________________________

______________________________

Thank you for taking the time to complete this questionnaire.

All information is for AAA internal use only and will NOT be distributed outside the organization to any third parties.